# POETS AND CRITICS READ VERGIL

# POETS AND CRITICS READ VERGIL

Edited by

## SARAH SPENCE

Yale University Press/New Haven & London

Designed by Mary Valencia.
Set in Quadraat type by Binghamton Valley Composition.
Printed in the United States of America by Sheridan Books, Chelsea, Michigan.

Library of Congress Cataloging-in-Publication Data

Poets and critics read Vergil / edited by Sarah Spence.
    p.    cm.
    Includes bibliographical references.
    ISBN 0-300-08376-9 (alk. paper)
    1. Virgil—Criticism and interpretation.  2. Epic poetry, Latin—History and criticism.
3. Aeneas (Legendary character) in literature.  4. Rome—In literature.  5. Virgil.
Aeneis.  I. Spence, Sarah, 1954–

PA6825 .P545 2001
871'.01—dc21  00-033445

A catalogue record for this book is available from the British Library.

The paper in this book meets the guidelines for permanence and durability of the Committee
on Production Guidelines for Book Longevity of the Council on Library Resources.

10  9  8  7  6  5  4  3  2  1

FOR when one writes verse, one's most immediate audience is not one's own contemporaries, let alone posterity, but one's predecessors. Those who gave one a language, those who gave one forms. Frankly, you know that far better than I. Who wrote those asclepiadics, sapphics, hexameters, and alcaics, and who were their addressees? Caesar? Maecenas? . . . Fat lot they knew about or cared for trochees and dactyls! And you were not aiming at me, either. No, you were appealing to Asclepiades, to Alcaeus and Sappho, to Homer himself. You wanted to be appreciated by them, first of all. For where is Caesar? Obviously in his palace or smiting the Scythians. And Maecenas is in his villa . . . Whereas your beloved Greeks are right here, in your head, or should I say in your heart, for you no doubt knew them by heart. They were your best audience, since you could summon them at any moment. It's they you were trying to impress most of all. Never mind the foreign language. In fact, it's easier to impress them in Latin: in Greek you wouldn't have the mother tongue's latitude. And they were talking back to you. . . .

So if you could do this to them, why can't I do that to you?

—JOSEPH BRODSKY, "Letter to Horace"

# CONTENTS

# Note on Text and Translations

Text of Vergil's works: *Opera*, ed. R. A. B. Mynors (Oxford, 1972).
The translations of Greek and Latin works are by the individual authors unless otherwise noted. The bibliography for published translations is as follows:

Virgil, *The Georgics*, trans. L. P. Wilkinson (Harmondsworth, 1982)
——, *The Aeneid*, trans. Robert Fitzgerald (New York, 1983)
——, *The Eclogues*, trans. M. C. J. Putnam, *Virgil's Pastoral Art* (Princeton, 1970)
Dante, *Purgatory*, trans. Allen Mandelbaum (Berkeley, 1982)
Homer, *The Iliad*, trans. Robert Fitzgerald (New York, 1970)
——, *The Odyssey*, trans. Robert Fitzgerald (New York, 1963)

# ACKNOWLEDGMENTS

The editor gratefully acknowledges the support of the Office of the Vice President for Research, the Office of the Vice President for Academic Affairs, the Center for Humanities and Arts, and the department of classics at the University of Georgia. Heartfelt thanks are also extended to Matthew Payne, Jennifer Cunningham, and Brandon Wester, graduate assistants, and Mary Ricks and Karen Coker, production specialists in the department of classics, and Harry Haskell, editor at Yale University Press.

Excerpts from "On Grief and Reason" are taken from *On Grief and Reason: Essays*, by Joseph Brodsky (copyright 1996 by Joseph Brodsky, reprinted by permission of Farrar, Straus and Giroux, LLC, Sheil Land Associates, and Penguin Books, Ltd.). Excerpts from "Letter to Horace" are taken from the 1995 typescript, printed by permission of the author. Lines from "Vespers" are from *W. H. Auden: Collected Poems by W. H. Auden*, edited by Edward Mendelson (copyright 1955 by W. H. Auden, reprinted by permission of Random House, Inc.). The six lines from "A Walk after Dark" are from *W. H. Auden: Collected Poems by W. H. Auden*, edited by Edward Mendelson (copyright 1966 by W. H. Auden, reprinted by permission of Random House, Inc.).

The twelve figures in Chapter 9 are from the Junius Spencer Morgan Collection of Vergil, Department of Rare Books and Special Collections, Princeton University Library.

# INTRODUCTION
## After Grief and Reason

SARAH SPENCE

When Aeneas fails to embrace his father Anchises in the underworld at the center of the *Aeneid*, his inability to grasp more than empty air is emblematic of both the poem as a whole and our relation to it:

> 'da iungere dextram,
>     da, genitor, teque amplexu ne subtrahe nostro.'
> sic memorans largo fletu simul ora rigabat.
> ter conatus ibi collo dare bracchia circum;
> ter frustra comprensa manus effugit imago,
> par levibus ventis volucrique simillima somno.
>             (*Aen*. VI.697–702)

> ("But let me have your hand, let me embrace you,
>     Do not draw back."
> At this his tears brimmed over
> And down his cheeks. And there he tried three times
> To throw his arms around his father's neck,
> Three times the shade untouched slipped through his hands,
> Weightless as wind and fugitive as dream.)
>             (Fitzgerald, VI.936–42)

Reading the classics is often just such a process as we grasp at figures that we can never fully embrace. The fact that Anchises is standing in a beautiful, pastoral, lush landscape only increases the melancholy of our efforts: the poem remains pristine and remote; try as we might we can never quite inhabit its world. The readings that provide the core of this volume derive originally from a conference that took place at the University of Georgia in March 1995, *After Grief and Reason: Poets and Critics Read Vergil*. The conference aimed to come to terms, in a small way, with what is involved when we read the classics from such a distance. Six speakers were invited to talk about their approaches to reading Vergil: three poets, Joseph Brodsky, Mark Strand, Rosanna Warren, and three classicists, Michael Putnam, Helen Bacon, and Christine Perkell. Our goal was to create a conversation between two groups who, to paraphrase W. H. Auden, transform the dead in the guts of the living: literary critics of Vergil's works and poets who have drawn on Vergil in their poetry. Initially the poets and scholars were paired off, each pair offering readings of the same passage in Vergil. The shape of the final talks took on a more globally cohesive form as the same themes surfaced again and again—themes of embrace, echo, and loss—as all the speakers addressed not only their reading of the texts but also their relationship to them.

It is these themes that I hoped to invoke by using Joseph Brodsky's words for the title of both the conference and this essay, "after grief and reason." I take this in two ways when applied to Vergil. Certainly there is the way in which Brodsky meant it: Vergil goes after, in the sense of "pursues," grief and reason, which, Brodsky says, "while poison to each other are language's most efficient fuel . . . poetry's indelible ink." But the poem of the *Aeneid* is also a monument to these themes, something that occurs in their wake, something that is written after grief and reason have both fallen away.

This book, while retaining the spirit of the conference, expands the topic somewhat as it aims to address the broader question of "how?"—how do we approach the work of a poet dead two thousand years? Part 1 consists of the opening chapter, by W. R. Johnson, which in its exploration of the lack of homogeneity of every audience of Vergil's epic, from the first to the last, introduces questions of historicism, reception, and translation that then permeate the book. Johnson suggests that the problem of how Vergil is to be read and understood is unsolvable because the diffuse mission of founding, of defining "Rome" is inscribed in the epic itself, a question posed by its very plot and reenacted by every subsequent audience.

Part 2 begins with selections from Joseph Brodsky's essay, "On Grief and Reason," which first appeared in the *New Yorker* in 1994, a meditation on the pastoral in Robert Frost and Vergil through a consideration of "Home Burial" and the *Eclogues*. In Chapter 3, Christine Perkell responds to Brodsky through an analysis that presents Vergilian pastoral as constructing a moral condition that makes humane action possible. This chapter focuses on the first and last of Vergil's earliest poems, the *Eclogues*, and on the last of his middle, didactic works, the *Georgics*, in which, in the story of Orpheus and Aristaeus, "power is ironized as pitiless and pity as useless." The poet, she concludes, is impotent in the world of power unless readers are moved to enact a poem's values. In Chapter 4, Gian

Biagio Conte reinterprets the same Aristaeus epyllion by placing it in the system of ideas that structures the *Georgics* overall. He interprets the story as weighing the cost of elegy and lamenting the bitter price of Vergil's choice of the didactic mission. Where Perkell sees Vergil as fearing that readers will separate the world of art and the world of power, Conte asserts that one must approach a poetic work by seeing "history flash like lightning in it."

The subject of the first two chapters on Vergil's final work, the *Aeneid*, by Mark Strand and Helen Bacon, is the embrace of parent and child. In Chapter 5, Strand's reading looks at the lyric in the epic by comparing the embrace of father and son in Book VI of the *Aeneid* to its precursors in Homer, its later use by Dante, and its immediate echo in Book II, that of Aeneas failing to embrace his first wife Creusa after she dies in Troy. In Chapter 6, Bacon compares the scene of the failed embrace in the underworld to a similar embrace between Aeneas and his mother, the goddess Venus, later in the work, an embrace that succeeds. From this contrast the author offers a discussion of the poem as a whole in terms of its double message and double gifts to its hero from his mortal father and immortal mother. In this Bacon concurs with Strand's melancholic reading of *Aeneid* VI, glossing it, however, with the more optimistic reading of Book VIII, and suggesting, in conclusion, that one of the glories of the poem and its hero is its irresolvable complexity.

In Chapters 7 and 8, Michael Putnam and Rosanna Warren each analyze the last lines of the epic in which Aeneas kills his rival Turnus. Putnam's approach is a word-by-word analysis in which he aims to show how finished, polished, and yet problematical the end of the poem is. Warren's broader interpretation centers on Turnus' death as a sacrifice needed for the founding of Rome. In treating the final climactic scene of the epic, which deals with many themes central to Vergil's purpose, these two chapters serve admirably as the final ones in Part 2 of this volume.

Putnam's and Warren's readings bring to the fore Vergil's awareness of his place in history, both imperial and literary. In Part 3, the book closes with four chapters that aim to set both the epic poem and its interpretation in a historical and theoretical context. In Chapter 9, Craig Kallendorf draws on Charles Martindale's reception study of the *Aeneid*, demonstrating how the changing values and interests of audiences affect the ways in which they illustrate (and thus interpret) the *Aeneid*. Kallendorf makes a case for the scholar's stance: times change, interpretations change, values change, and, as a result, the original purpose and even meaning of the poem may become unavailable or at least obfuscated; subjectivity, he points out, is "difficult to banish." Stephen Foley's Chapter 10, on translation, draws out the other side of the historicist argument made implicitly in the preceding readings of Vergil's poems: despite changing times, values, languages, something remains of a great poem such as the *Aeneid* that is accessible to every reader. These two chapters work together to highlight questions central to this study that arise in the readings in Part 2: How is the poem available to us; how do we reach it? How does history interact and intersect with translation?

The book concludes with two chapters that expand the scope of these questions. In Chapter 11, an interview with Robert Fagles, Vergil is approached as a reader and translator of Homer who, in Fagles' words, wants to "bring his individual voice into harmony with the enormous, global dilemmas he wants to narrate." Through this glimpse of Vergil's complex self-positioning at the intersection of art and politics, we are offered yet another perspective on the place and role of art in time. The final chapter, Chapter 12, is a compilation of vignettes from noted poets and critics on Vergil's significance to them. This conversation further illustrates the complex interaction of poetry and history, offering glimpses of how Vergil's poetry is read and used by a wide range of poets and critics.

The difference between the poets and critics—and between approaches to the poems apparent in these chapters—surfaced gradually during the conference. During the final roundtable discussion, the speakers were asked a key question by conference participant and Boccaccio scholar James McGregor: Why is it that the classicists seem to fear mauling Vergil while the poets feel free to savage (and so reinvigorate) him? A portion of that debate follows:

STRAND: Why can't someone in fiction behave irrationally? . . . Why can't [Aeneas] behave uncharacteristically? Why can't he do a terrible thing? Why does it have to be resolved? Of course this isn't life, this is art, but art should account for irrationality. . . . Poets naturally read all poetry as contemporaneous with themselves. . . .

BACON: [This is true of Vergil as well.] The way Vergil deals with Homer you can never trust him to do with a Homeric model what Homer did. In fact, he rather enjoys transforming it. Sometimes Aeneas plays the role of Paris, sometimes he's Achilles, and sometimes he seems to be Hector. You just can't trust him and that's part of his playfulness and joy with another poet. . . . We terribly need poets to act as though Vergil were their contemporary because no scholar can. We're not part of that fellowship of art that the poets immediately feel and assume as soon as they read another poet. And so the message we get from the poets is not one we're qualified to deliver. . . . We need you.

WARREN: The violence that Vergil does to Homer, the violence that Joseph may do to Horace and Vergil, the violence that Pound does to Homer, etc., is a sort of sacrificial communion that involves death and dismemberment. There are complex and dark energies released in this dismemberment which is also a communion and a participatory rite. . . . What we're trying to do [here] is conjure an ancient poetic energy to come among us.

STRAND: Poets do feel that *poetry* is the important thing. If poetry continues, that's fine. . . . You bear the burden of the past, you want to extend it into the future. In the process you erase yourself. You're your own sacrificial lamb. As a poet your survival depends upon what you can provide for the next generations. But in the process of providing you give over. You yourself are lost . . . you write with a sense of doom [but also with a sense that] you have participated in something larger than us and that will be around a long time.

PUTNAM: In Dante, *Purg.* XXX, Vergil is made to disappear by Dante; it is also the canto in which there are more Vergilian allusions than in any other moment in the poem. In one way he's gotten rid of, in another he's immortalized even further. . . .

BRODSKY: But this is not dismemberment or violence. . . . If Vergil had anybody in his mind for the audience he obviously had above all Homer, the figure that dominates that work. [His] eye [is] constantly kept on Homer, not so much on his contemporaries.

WARREN: To clarify—this sacrifice is a ritual of communion in which a former poet, a most beloved poet, as Homer for Vergil, is taken in and reconstituted in the very cell structure of the living poet and I see it as a constant kind of transaction between the living and the dead among the poets and it's that transaction that continues the life of literature. If that ever were to stop, writing, a certain kind of thinking, of feeling, would stop.

BACON: That kind of life [exists as well] between text, reader, and poet . . . there is this context of people actively engaged—and they can be readers, too. Frost had a wonderful way of talking about this: the art of *taking* a figure of speech is as great as the art of *making* a figure of speech. . . . We are readers, not poets.

PERKELL: To go back to the question of poets mangling the poem. [Poets] are willing to make a negative judgment about an effect that you think is deficient whereas I'm thinking it's a thing that I should interpret and understand because it never crosses my mind that Vergil is deficient, or that he would fail to observe an effect that I might.

STRAND: Your presumption is that this is a masterpiece, a *fait accompli*. A poet will acknowledge that publicly—otherwise he'd be thought a fool—on the other hand, in our deepest selves we're willing to test what we read . . . as readers we're more aggressive—it may seem like cruelty. . . .

BACON: Vergil is one of those poets who robs, sponges, performs an assimilation of a tradition, and a transformation. . . . That happens with modern poetry too.

The poets made it clear that they approach the works of Vergil as they approach their own, in terms of process more than product. The critics, rather, asserted that Vergil's works are finished products that beg for interpretation. The poets were more pragmatic, perhaps, the critics more reverential. Yet throughout the day, as throughout this volume, each group found a way to celebrate the poems Vergil produced, whether it was Mark Strand's evocation of the elegiac melancholy of the Elysian fields or Michael Putnam's clear admiration of Vergil's artistry in the last thirty lines of the *Aeneid*.

Ever since James Joyce's *Ulysses*, if not John Milton's *Paradise Lost*, the importance of classical epic to modern poetry has been evident. Joyce mined the *Odyssey* for metaphor and plot, even as Derek Walcott later used the *Iliad* to focus his Caribbean epic. While the classics, then, are a thriving source for the poet, as they have been for as long as they have been considered ancient, the versions that surface in these poems differ radically from the originals. So much is perhaps obvious, but the questions of why and how are vast. What is the *Iliad* to Walcott, the *Odyssey* to Joyce? How do they read these poems?

These questions are thrown into relief in the answers proffered by those who read the classics as a business, classical scholars who have made these epics their life projects. They—we—are in the business of answering precisely this question of how to read these poems. Whether they see them as artifacts of the age that can be dug up and deciphered or as well-wrought monuments whose beauty is to be appreciated formally, they approach the ancient epic as an object to be revered. Yet such reverence sometimes backfires: pure admiration can deprive a work of art of its voices, its purpose in the world out of which it was created. No doubt the *Iliad* outlined by Richmond Lattimore would be recognizable to Robert Fagles, while the one that appears in *Omeros* might not be. Yet the very straitness of the outline may keep the poem from truly being a poem.

The question becomes further complicated when the scholars approached are ones who have worked to draw out the poetry of the poem. Putnam's now-canonical 1966 work, *The Poetry of the Aeneid*, taught succeeding generations to see the epic more as a complex work of poetry than as simple propaganda. His attention to the metaphoric resonance and echo within Vergil's oeuvre has brought new issues to bear on the work. Yet there is little doubt that readings like this set themselves the task of unlocking the secrets of the poem; using the distance between work and critic, literary analysis of the *Aeneid* remains a sort of dissection of the discrete body that is the poem.

But the distance, as well, provides a context in which the work becomes, per force, a mirror. As much as the critic tries to see the ancient work objectively— ← and tries to instruct the audience that reading such a poem is an effort requiring knowledge of the time in which it was composed—the work invariably reflects the concerns of its readers. While as scholars we insist on setting the poem in the purest, truest light, we do not always take into consideration the fact that our angle, our perspective, is always partial and culturally determined. Poems are not purveyors of objective truth, nor are they meant to be. As important as it is to read the poem the poet wrote, we cannot ever do this. We will also always see something of ourselves as well.

Poets such as Brodsky or Strand, Karl Kirchwey, or J. D. McClatchy are not only aware of the reflective qualities of these ancient works but approach them with this very much in mind. In Brodsky's "Letter to Horace" he writes:

"All the literati keep / An imaginary friend," says Auden. Why should I be an exception?

At the very least I can sit myself down in front of my mirror and talk to it. That would be fairly close, although I don't believe that you [Horace] looked like me. But when it comes to the human appearance, nature, in the final analysis, doesn't have that many options. What are they? A pair of eyes, a mouth, a nose, an oval. For all their diversity, in two thousand years nature is bound to repeat itself. Even a God will. So I could easily claim that that face in the mirror is ultimately yours, that you are me. Who is there to check, and in what way? As conjuring tricks go, this might do. But I am afraid I am going too far: I'll never write myself a letter. Even if I were truly your look-alike. So stay faceless, Flaccus, stay unconjured. This way you may last for two thousand millennia more. Otherwise, each time I mount a woman she might think that she deals with Horace. Well, in a sense she does. . . . Nowhere does time collapse as easily as in one's mind. That's why we so much like thinking about history, don't we? If I am right about nature's options, history's like surrounding oneself with mirrors, like living in a bordello.

Strand's summation of the *Aeneid* in his prose poem "A Poet's Alphabet" as "lamenting the loss of something we never possessed" talks both about the plot ← of the poem and also about our position as readers from any century. We do not possess these poems. We may observe them; we will see ourselves reflected in them; if we are lucky we will hear them sing to us. But we will never own them.

The closest we can come is Warren's image of making them a part of our cell structure, but the form, then, will be ours, not theirs.

How do we read the ancient poem? The answer would seem to be dual: we must try to see the poem from a distance while we acknowledge the fact that there is no distance at all, that once read the *Aeneid* becomes a part of us, affecting our judgment, our morals, our values even as it is affected by our judgment, morals, and values. It is a new food, providing sustenance, or, in Brodsky's metaphor in his letter to Horace, a new lover, providing excitement, helping us in the constant remaking of ourselves. If we acknowledge the distance first, it would seem, we are reading as scholars; if we acknowledge the poem's ability to have an effect on us, we are reading as poets. Both are different, both are necessary.

When Turnus is killed by Aeneas in the final moments of the *Aeneid* the work abounds with echoes: of the crowd as it groans when Turnus falls; of Turnus himself as he groans on being slain; of Vergil's own words, as Turnus' dying line is an exact quotation of the dying line of an earlier heroine, Camilla; of scenes from the *Iliad* and, some would argue, the *Odyssey*. Echoing, the poem both ends and fails to close. It both destroys the pastoral dream and reevokes the pastoral voice. If we cannot embrace the past, and capture it, perhaps we can make it ours through echoing, reflecting ourselves in it. We see ourselves in the poem, the embrace of a dream from which we will awaken, yet in that echo we find the pastoral mode reasserted with all its beauty and promise. There is a difference—this is not the pastoral, after all, but the epic, and epic requires sacrifice. But beneath the epic rawness of the poem, and our own undoing of the past, lies the pastoral potential that runs, like the river Arethusa, under the surface of the poem. As long as we can lament the loss of the past, we have not fully lost it. We will never possess it, perhaps, and our embrace will always be empty, but we will gain a sense of beauty that remains unparalleled.

Part 1

# THE FRAME

Chapter 1

# IMAGINARY ROMANS
## Vergil and the Illusion of National Identity

### W. R. JOHNSON

Mantua dives avis, sed non genus omnibus unum:
gens illi triplex, populi sub gente quaterni,
ipsa caput populis, Tusco de sanguine vires.

(*Aen.* X.201–3)

(O Mantua,
so rich in ancestors, and yet not all
of one race; for you are the capital
of peoples rising from three races, each
the rulers of four towns; but you yourself
have drawn your chief strength from your Tuscan blood.)

### CARTOGRAPHIES

On a sunny day in July, riding on the train from Rome to Naples, looking out on
the farmscape, it is hard to suppress an archaic notion that bubbled up from its
dimnesses: "These lands are worth fighting for, always have been, always will
be." The violence and pleasure of that fragmented "thought" gradually gave way
to, and hid under, the memories of three maps that an embarrassed mind fished
up and collaged. I wanted (apparently) my (momentary) acquiescence in the
bloody struggles, the endless killing and dying for Campania, to be blotted out,
I wanted both the carnage and my complicity in it (meshed perhaps with the sort
of *jouissance* that one finds in Pessoa's "Ode Maritima") to be expunged by Reason
(history, cartography, the law and order that maps and chaps confer). Instinctively
(the constructed instinct of a bookman when exposed to "too much reality"), as
self-help, I pieced together some mental representations of three representations,
three different kinds of maps, of the struggle for Campania.

The first one (not extant), on view in the Porticus Vipsania, created from the

3

sketches for it by Agrippa, was a representation of the Augustan world empire (Pliny, *Natural History* III.17). The next one, doubtless influenced by Agrippa's map, is Florus' diachronically synchronic representation (*Epitome* I.3.6) of the domination/pacification/unification of the Italian peninsula:

> liber iam hinc populus Romanus prima adversus exteros arma pro libertate corripuit, mox pro finibus, deinde pro sociis, tum gloria et imperio, lacessentibus adsidue usquequaque finitimis; quippe cum patrii soli glaeba nulla, sed statim hostile pomerium, mediusque inter Latium atque Etruscos quasi in quodam bivio conlocatus omnibus portis in hostem incurreret; donec quasi contagio quodam per singulos itum est et proximis quibusque correptis totam Italiam sub se redegerunt.

> (The Roman people, henceforward free, took up arms against other nations, first to secure their liberty, then to extend their bounds, afterward in defense of their allies, and finally to win glory and empire; for they were continually harassed by their neighbors on every side, since they possessed not a clod of soil of their own, but the land immediately outside their walls belonged to enemies, and, being placed as it were at the meeting-place of two roads between Latium and Etruria, they met the enemy outside all their gates. Finally, spreading just as a fever spreads, they attacked their enemies one by one and, by continually fastening on the nearest of them, brought the whole of Italy under their sway.)[1]

The last map (actually a series of maps), placed by Mussolini on a wall near the Colosseum, represents the evolution of the ancient Roman Empire from its minuscule origins to its full flowering (and the first stirrings of its rebirth in modern times).[2]

Agrippa's map was visual (spectacular), synchronic, teleological. It revealed the result of Rome's progress toward its destiny; it gestured to Augustus as the (divine) engineer who had effected the purposes of universal history. Florus, as he proceeds with his paraphrase and compression of Livy, will offer various verbal maps which, fueled by the dialectics of Fortuna and Virtus, will end by refiguring the map of Agrippa and reinscribing it.[3] But here, at this early turning point in his tale, Florus is concerned with emphasizing the difficulties that beset the Romans' initial intimations of empire and with justifying (rationalizing) its motives as its will to expansion increased. *Quasi contagio quodam* deconstructs itself. The simile stands tradition ("all our wars were just," "we were always the victim," "the Romans stumbled into empire") on its head. The ferocity of this simile, the fever (or plague) of Roman expansion, dissolves the traditional Roman alibis (about how the North and South and East were won) by forcing us to rethink them in the light of the perspective that the disruptive picture (plague devouring Italia) pins us inside. Nevertheless, it hints (it insists) that what worked in the subjugation of Italy will work in the subjugation of the world. That was doubtless the prime message of Mussolini's diachronic maps (moving from the pinpoint marking a little town on the Tiber through the huge, final triumphs, modern and antique, of its manifest destiny). While the *contagium* simile works its deconstructive magic on my memory, I can forget my frisson at the conquest of Campania, and can forget as well whatever uneasiness with the ideology of (Roman, Latin, my Latin) empire my maps could not manage to sweeten. What I don't remember noticing (as the maps fused to make their dreamwork function) was how the maps of Agrippa and Mussolini obscured what Florus showcases: all the trouble there was in making Italy Roman, in making the contingencies of geography mirror the contingencies of history, or, more precisely, those of local, communal cultural memories (and illusions).

If we think of Roman history, if we "remember" the Roman history we learned at school, the process of turning Italy into Rome seems to be inevitable, "natural," "ordained": *imperium sine fine dedi*. There were, of course, problems in achieving this end: *per singulos itum est*. But through the centuries, bit by bit, people by people, town by town, Italy was finally and completely made Roman. So, in II.6.1 Florus can insist that the war that completes this process, the Social War, is misnamed:

> sociale bellum vocetur licet, ut extenuemus invidiam, si verum tamen volumus, illud civile bellum fuit. quippe cum populus Romanus Etruscos, Latinos Sabinosque sibi miscuerit et unum ex omnibus sanguinem ducat, corpus fecit ex membris et ex omnibus unus est; nec minore flagitio socii intra Italiam quam intra urbem cives rebellabant.

> (Though we call this war a war against allies, in order to lessen the odium of it, yet, if we are to tell the truth, it was a war against citizens. For since the Roman people united in itself the Etruscans, the Latins and the Sabines, and traces the same descent from all alike, it has formed a body made up of various members and is a single people composed of all these elements; and the allies, therefore, in raising a rebellion within the bounds of Italy, committed as great a crime as citizens who rebel within a city.)

But Florus' strategy of rechristening the war hardly solves all the difficulties involved in trying to characterize it and to name it, and in fact to call the war a civil war erases (or tries to erase) those difficulties. Here is Syme's condensation of the events in question:

> The Marsi provided the first impulsion to the insurrection, a great general, Q. Poppaedius Silo, and the earliest official title of the War, Bellum Marsicum. The name Bellum Italicum is more comprehensive and no less revealing: it was a holy alliance, a coniuratio of eight peoples against Rome, in the name of Italy. Italia they stamped as a legend on their coins, and Italia was the new state which they established with its capital at Corfinium. This was secession. The proposal to extend the Roman franchise to the allies was first made by agrarian reformers at Rome, with interested motives. A cause of dissension in Roman politics, the agitation spread and involved the allies. Reminded of other grievances and seeing no redress from Rome . . . the Italians took up arms. It was not to extort a privilege but to destroy Rome. They nearly succeeded. Not until they had been baffled and shattered in war did the fierce Italici begin to give up hope. An amnesty in the form of an offer of the citizenship to any who lay down their arms within sixty days may have weakened the insurgents by encouraging desertion, but it did not arrest hostilities everywhere. Samnium remained recalcitrant.[4]

Syme speaks of "insurrection" and "secession" and thus emphasizes that the Italians are not (yet) Romans; they have been subjugated by them, they are (taken as a fictive entity) a subject people. What Florus' prolepsis does is to squeeze several hundred years of inconclusive wars and quashed "rebellions" into totam Italiam sub se redegerunt, to elide ferocious, perennial struggles between Romans and various non-Romans neatly (and prematurely) into civile bellum and ex omnibus unus est.

The maps of Agrippa and Mussolini, in their different ways, take the unification of Italy by Rome for granted; for them, in them, Italy was always already Roman. In his narrative, in its snapshots of the process of Romanization, Florus will concur with this vision of the end as being in the beginning, of the inevitability of Italy's becoming/being Rome. But his contagium gainsays that belief in a natural evolution that works toward this destiny. The image of the plague that devours what is other than itself comes from a post-colonial perspective. Florus, the North African who is also Roman, has probably no (conscious) qualms about the empire or about being Roman, but that doesn't mean that there don't remain in or under his consciousness fragments of another set of feelings, memories of other values, other convictions, other attitudes to Roman power. The dialectics of hybridity function variously. Some immigrants become wholly assimilated (the massive purity of the recent convert), but some remain, in some degree, émigrés. What we need is a history of Roman literature that searches for traces of such conflictedness, such indeterminate feelings, in all the Roman writers who are émigrés (which means, most of them).⁵

## ROMANIZING ITALY/ITALIANIZING ROME

'hic tibi (fabor enim, quando haec te cura remordet,
longius, et volvens fatorum arcana movebo)
bellum ingens geret Italia populosque ferocis
contundet moresque viris et moenia ponet'
(Aen. I.261–64)

("Your son [I now speak out—I know this anxiousness
is gnawing at you; I unroll the secret
scroll of the Fates, awake its distant pages]
shall wage tremendous war in Italy
and crush ferocious nations and establish
a way of life and walls for his own people")

Since Venus is gripped with such anxiety, her father decides to reveal to her in detail the nature of her son's mission and its huge and fated success. The zeugma of *ponet* effects an elegant allegory: Aeneas will build the walls for men (who are both Trojan conquerors and "Italian" conquered, so merging them), while Augustus (the new Aeneas and his Julian heir) will restore morality to men (Romans and newly Romanized "Italians") who had lost it over the long decades of brutalizing civil war that had decimated both the city and "its" peninsula. But the range of meaning for "the great war he will wage in Italy" and "the ferocious peoples he will crush" is not exhausted even by that ambiguous, allegorical polysemy (Aeneas and his war and his establishment of order = Augustus and his wars and his restorations of order): many hearers/readers of the passage when it was just made public will also have thought when they heard/read the words *bellum ingens geret Italia populosque ferocis / contundet* of the Social War of the Italian Wars. In this reading, "he" is the Roman people or the various generals they (that is, the anxious senators) sent forth to meet the various challenges that Italica kept presenting them with. But the "he" of *contundet* and of *ponet* probably evokes Sulla and the *coup de main* he gave to the Italian Wars in 83 BCE. How would those readers feel about that complex "he" and that new element in the polysemic mix?

Those readers ("the original audience") were not, of course, a unified, homogeneous entity. They will have consisted of an intricate spectrum of origins, perspectives, sympathies, desires, values. I'm not concerned here with impossibilities (what percentage of them, say, were pro-/anti-Augustan, pro-/anti-imperial) but rather with what I consider both possible and probable: that not a few of these readers had some share in a post-colonial mentality, that is, that they or their families had recently become naturalized Romans; that they had some memory of their Italian (that is, non-Roman) heritage; that many of these people felt, to some degree, conflict between their new and their old "communal" identities. I don't mean that they hated Augustus or hated the Roman empire. I mean that they were the site, at some level of their being, in some corner of their consciousness, of a struggle between an old and a new sign-system, and that that struggle determined, in large measure, who they were and therefore how they read what they read, how, in particular, they read the verses in question. Some will not have noticed that *bellum ingens geret Italia* could connote the Italian Wars of recent memory (as well as Aeneas' and Augustus' wars); some will have noticed the possibility of that connotation and then decided to ignore it (because that war and ancestral memories of it no longer had much meaning for them). But some will have been bothered by that connotation; may have tried to shake it from their minds and not have been able to. These readers, at least some of them, will have started to read a different poem from the poem that (most) native Romans and other naturalized Romans will have been reading. For them the poem's (notorious) polysemy will have begun to work steadily, powerfully. The poem these people were reading was about Aeneas and the founding of Rome and was also about Augustus and the refounding of Rome; but it was also about what Allecto says to Juno when she reports back to her mistress that she has more than successfully carried out the orders she had been given:

> 'en, perfecta tibi bello discordia tristi;
>   dic in amicitiam coeant et foedera iungant.
>   quandoquidem Ausonio respersi sanguine Teucros.'
> (Aen. VII.545–47)

> ("See the discord I made ripe
>   for you in bitter war. Just let them try
>   to join in peace and friendship, now that I
>   have splashed the Trojans with Ausonian blood!")

And the poem was also about the despairing question that Vergil asks Jupiter just as Aeneas' war with Turnus is about to reach its slap-in-the-face closure: *tanton placuit concurrere motu, / Iuppiter, aeterna gentis in pace futuras?* (Aen. XII.503–4: O Jupiter, was it / your will that nations destined to eternal / peace should have clashed in such tremendous turmoil?). The question is emphatic by virtue of placement of its aporia (*quis mihi nunc tot acerba deus . . . expediat,* Aen. XII.500–503: What god can now unfold for me in song?), just as the momentum toward denouement gathers force, and emphatic too by virtue of the ring composition that links it with the bitter question that concludes the poem's invocation (*tantaene animis caelestibus irae,* Aen. I.11: Can such resentment hold the minds of gods?).[6] But it is emphatic also by virtue of its cruel irony: *aeterna gentis in pace futuras* connotes, at the level of Aeneas' story, the "Italians" against whom Aeneas wars in this poem. After Aeneas' death *and* after a few more centuries of inconclusive struggle, there will indeed be a lasting peace in Latium, and, at the level of the Augustan story, by prophetic prolepsis, there may well be lasting peace in Rome, in Italy, and in the world. But at the level of the Italian Wars, which were begun only two decades before Vergil was born and which were ended scarcely a decade before his birth, the phrase takes on a flavor of angry irony. So many wars had been fought with the non-Romans in Italy, so many treaties had been signed, so many promises had been broken; was that *pax aeterna* or *concordia?*

One of the readers for whom an Italian (other than Roman) perspective may have been in sharp focus was Propertius (*Umbria Romani patria Callimachi,* Elegies IV.1A.64), the closure of whose first volume resonates with a powerful post-colonial *ressentiment* that has hardly been extinguished by the time he writes the ironic palinode that opens his final volume (Book IV). In this verse he pretends to express his having come to terms not only with Augustus and the sign systems that have begun to cluster about him but also with the "disappearance" of his native land and with his complex feeling of becoming both Roman and not Roman, of becoming both himself and not himself (in the immortal words of Rimbaud, poised on the edge of a similar abyss, *je est un autre*).[7] According to Propertius, *nil patrium nisi nomen habet Romanus alumnus: / sanguinis altricem non putet esse lupam* (IV.1A.37–38: The Roman of today has nothing from his ancestor but his name: he would not believe that a she-wolf nurtured the blood from which he sprang).[8] Propertius and his contemporaries (whom, in this volume, he offers to escort through the city and its histories) are Romans in name only because they have become, caught between two sign systems, the monkey in the middle. The small rustic village that was the seed of the huge metropolis they live in, now the hub of a world empire's wheel, is so remote from them in time, is, in the paucity of its physical remains, so hidden from them, that they cannot "connect with" their founding myths. Therefore, they need the help of a Roman Callimachus to reveal to them Rome's *aitia* (its causes) by expounding the significance of the extant monuments that they see about them every day as they go about their business in the old/new city. (One would never know from this poet's brazen offer that a great epic poet had perhaps literally worked himself to death trying to write a poem that would reincarnate the myth on which all the other Roman myths depended.)[9] But who is an Umbrian to explain to Romans the truth of their city? It is he, after all, who stands as *alumnus*, the naturalized citizen, in this equation between those who know that their mother's milk was from the famous wolf and those who don't believe in that myth.

Is the poet blind to this indecorum? Not really. The irony of the palinode and of the poet's duplicitous offer to escort born Romans (back) to their beginnings hinges on the fact that Roman identity, in addition to being trapped in a collision of sign systems, being pinned between the primal virtues of archaic forebears in their tiny village and the prosperous, cosmopolitan sophistication of "we moderns," has become defabricated. Italians have become Roman (and, moreover, many of the best Romans have died in the process of the Romanizing of non-Romans, of "Italians"); furthermore, the progeny of the Romans who lived and died during that (most recent) struggle (to keep Italians from becoming Romans, to force them into becoming Romans) now live in a city (but it is no longer a city-state, it is a world, the world, metropolis) that is as much Italian (and is indeed much more polyglot even than that) as it is, remains, Roman.[10] In short, the Romans too are *alumni*; they, too, have been, are becoming, naturalized as citizens of a new city that is not merely (or more precisely, is no longer) Roman but also Italian and Multinational and Universal. The old myths, the old virtues, the old monuments are no longer central to this new space-time. (Does anyone dare say that they no longer really matter to it—except as school texts, as iconic decoration, as mise-en-scène? Propertius says it in the rest of this volume, and Ovid will continue saying it after Propertius vanishes.) But in concluding IV.1, the poet claims he can banish these troublesome paradoxes (Roman/non-Roman; bad yet good old/good yet bad new) and restore the pristine simplicities (55–58):

> optima nutricum nostris, lupa Martia, rebus,
> > qualia creverunt moenia lacte tuo!
> moenia namque pio coner dispondere versu:
> > ei mihi, quod nostrost parvus in ore sonus.

(She-wolf of Mars, best of nurses for our fortunes, what walls have
sprung up from your milk! For I would fain lay out those walls in dute-
ous verse: ah me, that a voice so feeble sits upon my lips!)

The fabulous den mother, earlier dismissed as implausible, here returns in triumph, her credibility fulsomely restored to her. Her guarantor, typically, confesses that he feels not quite up to the task he sets himself (he is perhaps thinking
of Horace's playful homage to Vergil in Satires: ingenium cui sit, cui mens divinior atque
os | magna sonaturum, des nominis huius honorem (I.4.43–44: Give the supreme title
of poet to any one who has a gift born with his bones that mere teaching cannot
better, who has an unusual vein of spirituality, whose lips are destined to celebrate
true greatness). Nevertheless, he will shoulder his new duties and plod manfully
on.

It is inside the perspective of this conflicted hybridity (Roman/Umbrian; epic
grandeur/Callimachean irony) that we can discover traces of the level of the Aeneid
where Vergil comes to grips with the aftermath of the Italian Wars (all of them,
but most particularly those last Italian Wars that were fought just before he was
born). It is one of the thoughts/feelings that issues from that perspective that we
hear in Propertius II.34.59–66:

> mi lubet hesternis posito languere corollis,
>     quem tetigit iactu certus ad ossa deus;
> Actia Vergilio custodis litora Phoebi,
>     Caesaris et fortis dicere posse rates,
> qui nunc Aeneae Troiani suscitat arma
>     iactaque Lavinis moenia litoribus.
> cedite Romani scriptores, cedite o Grai!
>     nescio quid maius nascitur Iliade.

(My pleasure is to loll amid the garlands of yesteryear, for the god [Eros]
of unerring aim has pierced me to the bone: that of Virgil is to be able to
sing the Actian shores o'er which Apollo watches, and the brave fleet of
Caesar; even now he is stirring to life the arms of Trojan Aeneas and the
walls he founded on Lavine shores. Make way, ye Roman writers, make
way, ye Greeks! Something greater than the Iliad is coming to birth!)

This affectionate, friendly mockery dates from the time when Propertius was still
content to enact the decadent dandy unashamedly, to wallow unrepentant in

idleness and in lust. He had not yet thought of the amusing insincerity that will provide closure for his career (the pose of being reborn as pure, red-blooded Roman), but he already knows enough of the epic that is taking shape (very possibly he has heard Vergil reading at various times from the work in progress) to realize that one thing the poem will attempt is the imagination of Roman unity, the construction of a new Roman subjectivity into which non-Roman Italians will have been blended. He kids Vergil with the sort of bantering hyperbole that friends (in this case, good acquaintances) are wont to indulge in (he has his fun, I have mine, his is epical, mine is not; Homer had better look to his laurels, and Ennius too, because this guy is a heavy hitter); but he suspects that genuine greatness is in the offing (*os magna sonaturum*). That pleases him (he may feel a little professional envy, but he also likes Vergil and, in general, he likes it when any poet makes it big). Moreover, as a Roman who likes being a Roman and who admires Augustus for having made it possible for Romans (old and new) to continue being Romans (instead of being swept into the dustbins of barbarism and oblivion), he is not unhappy at the prospect that soon there will be a great poem that will incarnate the (new) national identity.

So, alien to his tastes and his temperament though the coming epic may be, foreign though its myths and its grandeurs will be to his style of seeing and doing, Propertius can welcome it, with a touch of irony: Roman writers? who might they be, since you hardly need the fingers of one hand to count Rome's writers who were actually from Rome, who were not from one of the other, non-Roman communities? And the irony of *o Romani scriptores* triggers a deeper irony, one that "remembers" what is always already the fundamental disunity in national unification ("a thing inseparate" that "divides more wider than the sky and earth"). The Umbrian Roman or Roman Umbrian knows (already) that the gist of Allecto's savage joke and the passion of Vergil's last, wild question to the God of History are as true as (or truer than) Jupiter's bland promises to make *ex pluribus unus*. And he knows, too, that even as Vergil's complex, conflicted image of a united (and new) Roman identity is coming into being, the people of Rome, both the old and the new, are Romans now in name only. They are all hybrids now. It is the empire not the city that matters, and the empire's center (this is the heart of the tales of Tacitus) is now beginning to be ubiquitous.

## TOTA ITALIA: THE FUTURE OF AN ILLUSION

'sermonem Ausonii patrium moresque tenebunt,
utque est nomen erit; commixti corpore tantum
subsident Teucri. morem ritusque sacrorum

adiciam faciamque omnis uno ore Latinos.
hinc genus Ausonio mixtum quod sanguine surget,
supra homines, supra ire deos pietate videbis,
nec gens ulla tuos aeque celebrabit honores.'

(Aen. XII.834–40)

("the Ausonians will keep
their homeland's words and ways; their name will stay;
the body of the Teucrians will merge
with Latins and their name will fall away.
But I shall add their rituals and customs
to the Ausonians', and make them all—
and with one language—Latins. You will see
a race arise from this that, mingled with
the blood of the Ausonians, will be
past men, even past gods, in piety;
no other nation will pay you such honor.")

Jupiter constructs the bribe he offers Juno with meticulous care, answering her specific demands with ironic gallantry and real guile. She had been worried (lines 819–28) that in marrying Lavinia, Aeneas would blot out Latium and "her" Latins. She is determined that for them, hybridity does not mean that they lose their name: "do not let the native-born Latins lose their ancient name, become Trojans, or be called Teucrians." She swallows her resentment, she plays her final card: *sit Romana potens Itala virtute propago* (Aen. XII.827: let the sons of Rome / be powerful in their Italian courage).

When this specious bartering is completed (it is specious because she has lost, has nothing left to bargain with), the *Romana propago* will be the product of the hybridization of Latins and Trojans, but in her view (and her view is perhaps not entirely incorrect, because what the Italian Wars were partly about was the dependence of Rome's empire on Italian manpower and military prowess), the essence of the new entity (Rome) will be its Italian manhood (guts, aggression, power). Whether this view is true or not, Jupiter, dazzling casuist that he is, affirms Italian dominance in the fated fusion by assuring Juno that the Trojans will sink like lees to the bottom of the mixture (*subsident*), mingled with the native stock in body only. Furthermore, the Trojans will start speaking Latin, which will manifest their complete unity with the natives. One in body, language, customs, soul.

Yes, eventually, centuries later, that will be the case. Juno had spoken of the

Latins and of Italy. To denote these, Jupiter uses the word "Ausonia." By synec-
doche the name can of course connote Italy, but this particular metonymic slide
involves a peculiar sleight-of-hand with space and time.[11] "Ausonia" properly
refers to central and southern Italy. Aeneas is not fighting against Ausonians in
this poem; Romans *will* be fighting with them off and on for centuries—until 83
BCE, when Sulla completes his ethnic cleansing in Samnium, or, better still, until
32 BCE, when Octavian, soon to be Augustus, stages the *coniuratio Italiae* (*tota
Italia*), which may be said to mark the final unification of Italy and Rome (*iuravit
in mea verba tota Italia sponte sua et me belli quo vici ad Actium ducem depoposcit, Res
Gestae Divi Augusti,* 25.2: All Italy freely swore its allegiance to me and made me
their general in the war I won at Actium; so, in the crucial image on the shield
of Aeneas, *hinc Augustus agens Italos in proelia Caesar, Aen.* VIII.678: Augustus Caesar
is leading the Italians into battle).

Before Octavian had succeeded in completing, symbolically and actually, the
long process that Jupiter foretells (and presents to Juno as imminent, as about
to occur in the *Aeneid's* "story-time"), there had been another moment when
Italy's unification seemed about to take place. This unification was not Italy's
with Rome but Italy's with itself. The Italians (i.e., non-Romans) who allied
themselves against Rome in 91 called the entity they were trying to construct
"Italica," and they established their capital in Corfinium in the country of the
Paeligni (near where Ovid was born). The Roman wolf was to be challenged by
the Italian bull; us against them, them against us.[12] But the "us" were disparate;
they were various nations, separated from one another geographically and linguistically. They were one by virtue of their grievances against Rome. But even
here, the peoples involved were unlike in their likeness. Many of the Italian
oligarchs were in fact satisfied with their arrangements with Rome, but some
wanted the franchise and the other liberties that went with it, and some, the
Samnites in particular, wanted absolute independence. Still, their differences do
not seem to have weakened them, and they came close to winning the war. But
had they won it, it is not at all clear they would have remained "together." It was
their common enemy that provided them with a temporary identity, whereas,
when they had got what they wanted from Rome (and in that sense won rather
than lost their war with Rome), a process of assimilation had begun that was
ready for consummation when Octavian presented non-Romans with new common enemies (Cleopatra and her Roman consort) whose defeat would symbolize
not just the triumph of Rome over the sinister Orient, not just the end of civil
war (Antony, supposedly the last of this kind of villain), not just the restoration
of peace and abundance, but also, finally, the hybridization of Italy and Rome,

which Jupiter's promise to Juno (dimly) announces. The time was ripe for complete hybridity, and the right man for the job had at last come along:

> Octavian could himself claim to be a symbol of Italo-Roman union. Roman by birth, and even ultra-Roman by instinct, he was, nevertheless, a son of rural Italy. His *patria* was Velitrae, where his family was of long standing and some substance. In 61 the family suddenly obtained prominence in Rome when Octavian's father became praetor. His mother Atia was also from a rural background. She was from a prominent family in Aricia, although she too had a close link with Rome. Her mother was Julia, the sister of Julius Caesar. Thus Octavian, a patrician by Caesar's fiat since 44 and a consular by his own insistence since 43, could not unfairly represent himself as an Italian, as well as a Roman.[13]

What might Vergil have thought and felt about the *coniuratio*? Probably relief or, better perhaps, something like joy. The powerful idealism that shapes, for example, the *laudes Italiae* in *Georgics* II more than balances the anxiety of nostalgia that pervades the *Eclogues* (and much of the *Georgics* itself). As for the *Aeneid*, the great set pieces of Books VI and VIII alone, those wonderfully baroque patriotic tableaux, testify to a desire for the hybridity to become a reality. Nevertheless, like many (most?) of his "naturalized" (ex-non-Roman, Italian) contemporaries, poets and non-poets alike, he may well have been deeply conflicted; may have hailed the fusion, and yet, so strong was the pull of birthplace and homeland, so bitter too were the memories of recent slaughter and oppression and humiliation, he may also have experienced confusion and grief, an ugly sense of a wrong ending, of annihilation of something dead and fragile and unrecoverable: his childhood, the memories of his (non-Roman) ancestors and the multinational homeland they shared: *Mantua dives avis, sed non genus omnibus unum: | gens illi triplex, populi sub gente quaterni.* Roman Italy was something both to be loved and hated. That—not Augustus or the empire he inherited from his Republican predecessors and bequeathed to his imperial successors—is where the pain is.[14]

Roman Italy was real, but it was also unreal. Just when Italy became Roman, Rome became Italian. Then, by the time Augustus died, long before Juvenal complained that "his" city had lost its Romanitas, both Rome and Roman Italy had entered another sign system, something more like that of a Hellenistic world monarchy than anything one might be willing to call Roman or Italian (something not unlike the sort of world Cleopatra and her forebears had had in mind). So, the Roman Italy, the becoming of Roman Italy, that haunts late Republican and

Augustan poetry in general and the *Aeneid* in particular was not (always) an illusion—yet, in most ways it was.

Among the more elegant of fortune's ironies was her decision to bury Leopardi and Vergil in what is essentially the same tomb (in the Parco Virgiliano in that least Roman and most Greek of cities, Naples)—two of Italy's greatest poets, one antique and one modern, both of them from the north, joined in the south, another grand hybrid. Entombed together, they incarnate humankind's frequent (maybe almost universal) yearning for national unification. Open the pages of *The Times Atlas of World History* and you see how and why it is that "natural," national (communal) identities shift and vanish and reemerge to rearticulate themselves as constantly as do the boundaries within which they attempt to find their reality and permanence (look at the pages that represent, in its various configurations through the centuries, the territory that not long ago we knew as Yugoslavia).

Vergil knew, no less well than his tomb-mate, what *inane* (empty) means. *Le illusioni per quanto sieno illanguidite e smascherate dalla ragione, tuttavia restano ancora nel mondo, e compongono la massima parte della nostra vita* (Leopardi, *Zibaldone di pensieri* I.213: No matter how often reason manages to enfeeble illusions and unmask them, nevertheless they persist in the world, and they make up the biggest part of our life). Among these—inevitably tragic if they flourish and tragic if they fail—are national identities.[15] The *Aeneid* is pure in its determination to snare the complexities of this illusion, to question it sternly, never to degenerate into the complacencies of a moral tract, never to succumb to the illusions' delicious alibis. That is one of the reasons the *Aeneid* abides whereas most political poems yellow and crumble even before the generations that spawned them have vanished.

Part 2

# THE CANVAS: READINGS OF VERGIL

Chapter 2

# ON GRIEF AND REASON

TWO SELECTIONS FROM THE ESSAY BY JOSEPH BRODSKY

[Robert Frost's] "Home Burial" is not a narrative; it is an eclogue. Or, more exactly, it is a pastoral—except that it is a very dark one. Insofar as it tells a story, it is, of course, a narrative; the means of that story's transportation, though, is dialogue, and it is the means of transportation that defines a genre. Invented by Theocritus in his idylls, refined by Virgil in the poems he called eclogues or bucolics, the pastoral is essentially an exchange between two or more characters in a rural setting, returning often to that perennial subject, love. Since the English and French word "pastoral" is overburdened with happy connotations, and since Frost is closer to Virgil than to Theocritus, and not only chronologically, let's follow Virgil and call this poem an eclogue. The rural setting is here, and so are the two characters: a farmer and his wife, who may qualify as a shepherd and a shepherdess, except that it is two thousand years later. So is their subject: love, two thousand years later.

To make a long story short, Frost is a very Virgilian poet. By that, I mean the Virgil of the *Bucolics* and the *Georgics*, not the Virgil of the *Aeneid*. To begin with, the young Frost did a considerable amount of farming—as well as a lot of writing. The posture of gentleman farmer wasn't all posture. As a matter of fact, until the end of his days he kept buying farms. By the time he died, he had owned, if I am not mistaken, four farms in Vermont and New Hampshire. He knew something about living off the land—not less, in any case, than Virgil, who must have been a disastrous farmer, to judge by the agricultural advice he dispenses in the *Georgics*.

With few exceptions, American poetry is essentially Virgilian, which is to say contemplative. That is, if you take four Roman poets of the Augustan period, Propertius, Ovid, Virgil, and Horace, as the standard representatives of the four known humors (Propertius' choleric intensity, Ovid's sanguine couplings, Virgil's phlegmatic musings, Horace's melancholic equipoise), then American poetry—indeed, poetry in English in general—strikes you as being by and large of Vir-

These excerpts are from Joseph Brodsky, "On Grief and Reason," *On Grief and Reason: Essays* (New York: Farrar Straus Giroux, 1995), pp. 234–36 and 260–66.

gilian or Horatian denomination. (Consider the bulk of Wallace Stevens' solilo-
quies, or the late, American Auden.) Yet Frost's affinity with Virgil is not so much
temperamental as technical. Apart from frequent recourse to disguise (or mask)
and the opportunity for distancing oneself that an invented character offers to
the poet, Frost and Virgil have in common a tendency to hide the real subject
matter of their dialogues under the monotonous, opaque sheen of their respective
pentameters and hexameters. A poet of extraordinary probing and anxiety, the
Virgil of the *Eclogues* and the *Georgics* is commonly taken for a bard of love and
country pleasures, just like the author of *North of Boston*.

To this it should be added that Virgil in Frost comes to you obscured by
Wordsworth and Browning. "Filtered" is perhaps a better word, and Browning's
dramatic monologue is quite a filter, engulfing the dramatic situation in solid
Victorian ambivalence and uncertainty. Frost's dark pastorals are dramatic also,
not only in the sense of the intensity of the characters' interplay but above all in
the sense that they are indeed theatrical. It is a kind of theater in which the author
plays all the roles, including those of stage designer, director, ballet master, etc.
It's he who turns the lights off, and sometimes he is the audience also.

That stands to reason. For Theocritus' idylls, like nearly all Augustan poetry,
in their own right are but a compression of Greek drama. In "Home Burial" we
have an arena reduced to a staircase, with its Hitchcockian banister. The opening
line tells you as much about the actors' positions as about their roles: those of
the hunter and his prey. Or, as you'll see later, of Pygmalion and Galatea, except
that in this case the sculptor turns his living model into stone. In the final analysis, "Home Burial" is a love poem, and if only on these grounds it qualifies as
a pastoral.

∾

So what was it that he was after in this, his very own poem? He was, I think,
after grief and reason, which, while poison to each other, are language's most
efficient fuel—or, if you will, poetry's indelible ink. Frost's reliance on them here
and elsewhere almost gives you the sense that his dipping into this ink pot had
to do with the hope of reducing the level of its contents; you detect a sort of
vested interest on his part. Yet the more one dips into it, the more it brims with
this black essence of existence, and the more one's mind, like one's fingers, gets
soiled by this liquid. For the more there is of grief, the more there is of reason.
As much as one may be tempted to take sides in "Home Burial," the presence of
the narrator here rules this out, for while the characters stand, respectively, for
reason and for grief, the narrator stands for their fusion. To put it differently,
while the characters' actual union disintegrates, the story, as it were, marries
grief to reason, since the bond of the narrative here supersedes the individual

dynamics—well, at least for the reader. Perhaps for the author as well. The poem, in other words, plays fate.

I suppose it is this sort of marriage that Frost was after, or perhaps the other way around. Many years ago, on a flight from New York to Detroit, I chanced upon an essay by the poet's daughter printed in the American Airlines in-flight magazine. In that essay Lesley Frost says that her father and her mother were co-valedictorians at the high school they both attended. While she doesn't recall the topic of her father's speech on that occasion, she remembers what she was told was her mother's. It was called something like "Conversation as a Force in Life" (or "The Living Force"). If, as I hope, someday you find a copy of North of Boston and read it, you'll realize that Elinor White's topic is, in a nutshell, the main structural device of that collection, for most of the poems in North of Boston are dialogues—are conversations. In this sense, we are dealing here—in "Home Burial," as elsewhere in North of Boston—with love poetry, or, if you will, with poetry of obsession: not that of a man with a woman so much as that of an argument with a counterargument—of a voice with a voice. That goes for mono-logues as well, actually, since a monologue is one's argument with oneself; take, for instance, "To be or not to be. . . ." That's why poets so often resort to writing plays. In the end, of course, it was not the dialogue that Robert Frost was after but the other way around, if only because by themselves two voices amount to little. Fused, they set in motion something that, for want of a better term, we may just as well call "life." This is why "Home Burial" ends with a dash, not with a period.

## "Home Burial"

He saw her from the bottom of the stairs
Before she saw him. She was starting down,
Looking back over her shoulder at some fear.
She took a doubtful step and then undid it
To raise herself and look again. He spoke
Advancing toward her: "What is it you see
From up there always?—for I want to know."
She turned and sank upon her skirts at that,
And her face changed from terrified to dull.
He said to gain time: "What is it you see?"
Mounting until she cowered under him.
"I will find out now—you must tell me, dear."
She, in her place, refused him any help,
With the least stiffening of her neck and silence.

She let him look, sure that he wouldn't see,
Blind creature; and awhile he didn't see,
But at last he murmured, "Oh," and again, "Oh."

"What is it—what?" she said.
                              "Just that I see."
"You don't," she challenged. "Tell me what it is."

"The wonder is I didn't see at once.
 I never noticed it from here before.
 I must be wonted to it—that's the reason.
 The little graveyard where my people are!
 So small the window frames the whole of it.
 Not so much larger than a bedroom, is it?
 There are three stones of slate and one of marble,
 Broad-shouldered little slabs there in the sunlight
 On the sidehill. We haven't to mind those.
 But I understand: it is not the stones,
 But the child's mound—"
                              "Don't, don't, don't,

    don't," she cried.

She withdrew, shrinking from beneath his arm
That rested on the banister, and slid downstairs;
And turned on him with such a daunting look,
He said twice over before he knew himself:
"Can't a man speak of his own child he's lost?"

"Not you!—Oh, where's my hat? Oh, I don't need it!
 I must get out of here. I must get air.—
 I don't know rightly whether any man can."

"Amy! Don't go to someone else this time.
 Listen to me. I won't come down the stairs."
He sat and fixed his chin between his fists.
"There's something I should like to ask you, dear."

"You don't know how to ask it."
                              "Help me, then."

Her fingers moved the latch for all reply.

"My words are nearly always an offense.
I don't know how to speak of anything
So as to please you. But I might be taught,
I should suppose. I can't say I see how.
A man must partly give up being a man
With womenfolk. We could have some arrangement
By which I'd bind myself to keep hands off
Anything special you're a-mind to name.
Though I don't like such things 'twixt those that love.
Two that don't love can't live together without them.
But two that do can't live together with them."
She moved the latch a little. "Don't—don't go.
Don't carry it to someone else this time.
Tell me about it if it's something human.
Let me into your grief. I'm not so much
Unlike other folks as your standing there
Apart would make me out. Give me my chance.
I do think, though, you overdo it a little.
What was it brought you up to think it the thing
To take your mother-loss of a first child
So inconsolably—in the face of love.
You'd think his memory might be satisfied—"

"There you go sneering now!"

                                    "I'm not, I'm not!
You make me angry. I'll come down to you.
God, what a woman! And it's come to this,
A man can't speak of his own child that's dead."

"You can't because you don't know how to speak.
If you had any feelings, you that dug
With your own hand—how could you?—his little grave;
I saw you from that very window there,
Making the gravel leap and leap in air,
Leap up, like that, like that, and land so lightly
And roll back down the mound beside the hole.

I thought, Who is that man? I didn't know you.
And I crept down the stairs and up the stairs
To look again, and still your spade kept lifting.
Then you came in. I heard your rumbling voice
Out in the kitchen, and I don't know why,
But I went near to see with my own eyes.
You could sit there with the stains on your shoes
Of fresh earth from your own baby's grave
And talk about your everyday concerns.
You had stood the spade up against the wall
Outside there in the entry, for I saw it."


"I shall laugh the worst laugh I ever laughed.
I'm cursed. God, if I don't believe I'm cursed."


"I can repeat the very words you were saying:
'Three foggy mornings and one rainy day
Will rot the best birch fence a man can build.'
Think of it, talk like that at such a time!
What had how long it takes a birch to rot
To do with what was in the darkened parlor?
You couldn't care! The nearest friends can go
With anyone to death, comes so far short
They might as well not try to go at all
No, from the time when one is sick to death,
One is alone, and he dies more alone.
Friends make pretense of following to the grave,
But before one is in it, their minds are turned
And making the best of their way back to life
And living people, and things they understand.
But the world's evil. I won't have grief so
If I can change it. Oh, I won't. I won't!"


"There, you have said it all and you feel better.
You won't go now. You're crying. Close the door.
The heart's gone out of it: why keep it up?
Amy! There's someone coming down the road!"

"You—oh, you think the talk is all. I must go—
    Somewhere out of this house. How can I make you—"


"If—you—do!" She was opening the door wider.
    "Where do you mean to go? First tell me that.
    I'll follow and bring you back by force. I *will!*—"

If this poem is dark, darker still is the mind of its maker, who plays all three roles: the man, the woman, and the narrator. Their equal reality, taken separately or together, is still inferior to that of the poem's author, since "Home Burial" is but one poem among many. The price of his autonomy is, of course, in its coloration, and perhaps what you ultimately get out of this poem is not its story but the vision of its ultimately autonomous maker. The characters and the narrator are, as it were, pushing the author out of any humanly palatable context: he stands outside, denied re-entry, perhaps not coveting it at all. This is the dialogue's—alias the Life Force's—doing. And this particular posture, this utter autonomy, strikes me as utterly American. Hence this poet's monotone, his pentametric drawl: a signal from a far-distant station. One may liken him to a spacecraft that, as the downward pull of gravity weakens, finds itself nonetheless in the grip of a different gravitational force: outward. The fuel, though, is still the same: grief and reason. The only thing that conspires against this metaphor of mine is that American spacecraft usually return.

# Chapter 3

# PASTORAL VALUE IN VERGIL

## Some Instances

### CHRISTINE PERKELL

In his essay entitled "On Grief and Reason" Joseph Brodsky proposed a close reading of Robert Frost's "Home Burial" as pastoral, albeit dark and modern pastoral, on the grounds that "the pastoral is essentially an exchange between two or more characters in a rural setting, returning often to that perennial subject, love."[1] This generous definition points to features of pastoral as genre and thus serves as a useful focus for a reading of Vergil's pastoral poetry. I propose as a limited goal here to consider how Vergil constructs moral value in *Eclogues* I and X, his first and last pastoral poems, with some briefer observations on how these same values find expression subsequently in the close of the *Georgics*. Such values as are constructed in Vergil's pastoral poems may be considered *Vergil's* pastoral values, no matter how one reads later pastoral, such as, perhaps, Frost's, that constructs its own revisionary models of Vergil's. The values of Frost's pastoral appear to be conceived in significant opposition to Vergil's, as I will suggest in reflecting on Brodsky's reading of "Home Burial" from the perspective of Vergilian pastoral. In closing I offer some thoughts on the relationship of the poet to his speakers—not only the question of whether they are his mouthpiece or his target (as Harry Berger puts it)[2]—but the degree to which the poet represents himself as implicated in the conflicts that engage his speakers. This last point is in response to Brodsky's vision of Frost as a poet so distanced from his speakers' troubles in "Home Burial" as to resemble a rocket ship on a trajectory out of the earth's orbit, never to reenter our atmosphere (see Chapter 2 of this volume). Here I suggest that, to the degree that the "textual voice" coheres from poem to poem and persuades, it does perhaps imply engagement of the poet.

## READING PASTORAL AND VERGIL'S *ECLOGUES*: INTRODUCTION

A common assumption about pastoral is that idyllicism determines its meaning, therefore that pastoral gives voice to an escapist, nostalgic ideal. The work of

Bruno Snell, for example, on Vergil falls into this category.[3] But, as others have pointed out, inherent in Golden Age idyllicism is the potential for putting into question the values of the great world, or the world of power, which, by comparison to the green world of pastoral, appears clearly in its corruption.[4] Michael Putnam and A. J. Boyle, for example, have seen this subversive dimension in Vergil's pastoral.[5] Certainly contemporary political crises and widespread social upheaval figure in the opening verses of Eclogue I. Servius (ad Ecl. I.70), our oldest extant commentator on Vergil (fourth century CE), understood that Vergil was in some sense not only criticizing Octavian as the source of turmoil in the countryside but also giving thanks to Octavian for saving his own farm. Putnam and Boyle have read the predominant meaning of the Eclogues as critique of the inimical effect of urban and imperial values on the country and its song. Berger labels both these types of pastoral—the pure nostalgic pastoral and the satiric pastoral—"weak."[6] On his reading, "strong" pastoral, by contrast, or "metapastoral," calls into question not only the great world but also the conventions of pastoral itself, undermining its model of idyllicism, even while bearing witness to the power of its attraction.[7] If "weak" pastoral ironizes the world of power, "strong" pastoral ironizes idyllicism as well.

To what extent it is in the *nature* of pastoral to deconstruct its own conventions—that is, is it necessary to coin such a term as "metapastoral" to accommodate this critical dimension of pastoral?—is the essential focus of disagreement between Paul Alpers and Berger; but for the purposes of reading Vergil, this particular distinction may be inconsequential.[8] More consequential is Berger's casual assertion (his article is about Theocritus) that Vergil's pastoral is "strong" pastoral, an assumption at variance with all the readings cited above, which read the poems' idyllicism without irony. The fundamental postulate of Berger's ironic reading of pastoral is that the locus of meaning in the poem is not in the individual speakers but rather in the voice that impersonates the speakers and represents their dilemmas to readers, which he calls the "zero degree voice" or the "textual voice" (e.g., p. 12). The creator of the whole poem, who "impersonates" the speakers, has a perspective larger than theirs and is therefore separated from them by ironic distance.[9] The speakers may be either reliable or unreliable; they may be either the poet's mouthpieces or his targets; and it is precisely the task of criticism to ascertain which. Readers come to recognize a speaker as unreliable, as the poet's "target," when "the text that positions them in the role of subject asks us [readers] to view them critically, and thus dissociates its perspective from theirs" (p. 9). While many scholars and critics have assumed they knew when a speaker in the Eclogues was a figure or "mouthpiece" for Vergil,[10] Berger's reading assumes that all speakers, including the first-person speaker, are impersonations by the poet and consequently cannot be wholly equated with him. When they sense discontinuity between speakers and their own sense of the position of the textual voice, readers perceive speakers as "limited." The degree to which a speaker's values are in harmony with the textual voice—rather than the grammatical person of the speaker—is the indicator of the degree to which the speaker may be understood to speak for the poet.

That Brodsky thinks of pastoral as dialogic provides a useful focus for reading Vergil, since his pastoral often has opposing speakers (Eclogues I, III, V, VII, IX) and, even when it does not offer two speakers, nevertheless is constructed around opposing values.[11] The relationship between the speakers is usually agonistic, in that they embody values in conflict, although without necessarily contesting formally. (Eclogues III and VII contain formal contests, V and VIII two separate speeches; I, IX, and X two speakers expounding contrasting positions.) Pastoral value in Vergil's poems emerges from the relation of these oppositions to the textual voice. The essentially agonistic character of pastoral may be seen in oppositions between speakers, between speakers and the textual voice, and between the textual voice and the ideology of the genre as the poet constructs it through revisionary filiation. These concepts from Berger's essay—of the textual voice's ironic perspective on individual speakers and of "strong" pastoral that targets not only the great world but also its revisionary model of conventional pastoral—have great usefulness for interpreting Vergil's Eclogues. On my reading, the Eclogues do present all the speakers to some degree ironically and do critique both the great world as well as pastoral idyllicism, while still nevertheless giving proof of the moral value and attraction of the latter.

In Vergil, what I term the "pastoral vision" is expressed in certain individual speakers' longed-for ideal. This vision is characterized by music, poetry, repose, a sustaining and responsive natural environment, a perceived community of man and nature in song. Thus it is a powerfully attractive picture of life without pain or danger, focused on aesthetic fulfillment. Within the eclogue as a whole, however, the pastoral vision is perceived as unreal or unrealizable, since it is represented by the speaker himself as out of his reach, as defining someone else's situation, or as contrary to fact. The most famous pieces of pastoralism in the Eclogues—verses of Meliboeus in Eclogue I, of Corydon in II,[12] and of Gallus in X—illustrate this observation, as we see below. The pastoral vision, then, is represented as an act of imagination; thus irony here is stronger than nostalgia. The pastoral vision is a constitutive feature of the overall "pastoral design" (this latter term I take from Leo Marx), in which the meaning of the poem inheres. Marx defines the pastoral design as "the larger structure of thought of which the ideal is a part" and continues: "In addition to the ideal, then, the pastoral design . . .

embraces some token of a larger, more complicated order of experience" (pp. 24–25). This "token of a larger, more complicated order of experience" Marx calls the "counterforce," the alien reality that obtrudes upon the imagined ideal and signals its imaginary status. In Marx's study of pastoral in the American tradition the counterforce most often appears as technology, a sign of unwelcome "progress," such as the steam engine, for example, clanging and brazen, that interrupts the poet's rural reverie. In Vergil, the further irony available to readers is that idyllicism itself and its sustaining conventions are also put into question. The creator of the pastoral design, the poet of the whole poem, who "impersonates" the various speakers, has an intelligence and vision that transcends theirs. The meaning of the poem, therefore, lies beyond the speeches of individual speakers, beyond even the oppositions that the speakers embody, and rather in whatever suspension, contradiction, reconciliation, or interpretation of these oppositions emerges for the reader from the implied perspective of the textual voice.

## Pastoral Value in *Eclogue* I

Many would say that *Eclogue* IV is the most famous pastoral poem in the Western tradition; but *Eclogue* I is the most important in terms of establishing conventional pastoral values for subsequent poets and readers.[13]

> Tityre, tu patulae recubans sub tegmine fagi
> silvestrem tenui Musam meditaris avena.
>                 (Ec. I.1–2)

> (Tityrus, you, reclining under the shade of a
> spreading beech, woo the woodland muse on
> slender pipe.)[14]

The notions of careless repose, leisure, music, and benign rural setting introduced here have defined pastoral. After an intervening verse, the speaker continues:

> tu, Tityre, lentus in umbra
> formosam resonare doces Amaryllida silvas. (4–5)

> (You, Tityrus, at ease in the shade, teach the woods
> to echo "beautiful Amaryllis.")

These verses add the notion of beauty, love, and responsiveness between man and nature, since the woods are perceived as echoing Tityrus' song and Amaryllis is beautiful.[15] It is important—for the character of each speaker is constructed with sustained care—to note that this idyllic pastoral vision is Meliboeus' (as we later discover his name to be) reading of Tityrus' circumstances; Tityrus himself does not describe his circumstances in this way. Meliboeus' description of his own circumstances, on the other hand, is the contrary of idyllic, since he is being driven into exile.

> nos patriae finis et dulcia linquimus arva.
> nos patriam fugimus; tu, Tityre, lentus in umbra. . . . (3–4)

> (We are leaving the bounds of our fatherland and our sweet
> fields. We are exiled from our fatherland. You, Tityrus. . . . )

The context of this first *Eclogue* is revealed to be the confiscations of the so-called second triumvirate, in which many farmers were dispossessed in order to reward the returning veterans of Antony and Octavian. Meliboeus, forced to abandon his farm, attributes to Tityrus, so strangely exempt from these troubles, an idyllic pastoral existence, which is thus the creation of his imagination and from his perspective. Thus the pastoral idyll is perceived from its inception as the reality of the other, not of the self. *Nos* ("we") in line 3 implicitly encompasses the reader: the idyll is for "you" (Tityrus), while exile is for "us" (whoever "we" are). What Alpers calls the most famous piece of pastoralism in the poem[16] is also spoken by Meliboeus and is his vision, again, not of his own future but of Tityrus':

> fortunate senex, hic inter flumina nota
> et fontis sacros frigus captabis opacum;
> hinc tibi, quae semper, vicino ab limite saepes
> Hyblaeis apibus florem depasta salicti
> saepe levi somnum suadebit inire susurro;
> hinc alta sub rupe canet frondator ad auras,
> nec tamen interea raucae, tua cura, palumbes
> nec gemere aëria cessabit turtur ab ulmo.
> (Ec. I.51–58)

> (Fortunate old man, here among streams you know and holy founts, you
> will find cooling shade. Here, as always, the hedge along your neighbor's

border, whose willow flowers are fed upon by bees of Hybla, will often induce you to sleep by its gentle buzzing. Here, under a lofty rock, the pruner will serenade the air. Nor then, too, will your pets, the cooing pigeons, and the turtle-doves cease to moan from the lofty elm.)

Note that the pastoral ideal is not expressly nostalgic, for it has no acknowledged reality in the past; rather it is an act of imagination. In my reading, the creation of the pastoral vision from the otherwise unpleasing circumstances of "naked rock and swamp with marshy reed" (*quamvis lapis omnia nudus / limosoque palus obducat pascua iunco*, 47–48: although naked rock / swamp with marshy reed cover all the pasture) constitutes the imaginative climax of the poem.

Servius, in a reading still accepted by many scholars, identified Vergil himself with Tityrus and understood the poem primarily as Vergil's thanks to Octavian— the young god in the city who responds to Tityrus' appeal—for exempting his farm from the confiscations. The degree of this identification has been questioned recently, however, for Tityrus' moral and artistic values appear (in the view of some current critics) to be put into question. He is seemingly indifferent to the suffering of others all around him, as Meliboeus describes it and as he himself does not deny: while others are despoiled of their property and go into exile, Tityrus plays his pipe. Further, a related insensitivity may be reflected in his self-satisfaction and tactless evocation of his own easy future as opposed to Meliboeus' grievous one.[17] Pragmatic and purposeful, Tityrus takes action to save himself by going to the city to supplicate the young god there. A suggestive feature of the poet's characterization of Tityrus is his worship of the new urban god because that god has benefited him. This choice stands in contrast to Meliboeus' traditional religious spirit and sentimentality toward the countryside. Such a contrast between the speakers allows the reader to infer that Meliboeus is both more sentimental in general than is Tityrus and also that, in particular, he has a greater love for the *patria* (country, fatherland) (lines 3–4) than does Tityrus.

The reader may then wonder what rationale of the urban god underlies both the dispensation of land to Tityrus and the exile of Meliboeus. Meliboeus says he is not jealous, just amazed (11); but, as Annabel Patterson points out, the justice of these circumstances is put into question precisely by Meliboeus' denial of envy. The urban god's implied injustice, along with Tityrus' perceived ethical deficiencies, have led Boyle and Putnam, for example, to propose a dark interpretation of the eclogue as a thorough condemnation of Octavian—responsible for the exile of Meliboeus and the end of his poetry. Yet if the text puts into question Tityrus' indifference by juxtaposing it to Meliboeus' caring—for people, trees, flock, and home—it perhaps also puts into question Meliboeus' failings of another sort. Meliboeus' traditionalism correlates with a certain impracticality and a conservative or even regressive poetic sensibility, since his haunting, beautiful verses focus on absence and loss. Meliboeus' poetry finds the beautiful in the tragic. His longest song, envisioning what he will never see and never do again, concludes with his conviction that he will sing no more songs (67–78). Meliboeus thus loves failure and loss, making of them the central subjects of his song. Boyle and Putnam read this figure, essentially, without irony, as the wholly endorsed voice of the poem, seeing no distance between Meliboeus and the textual voice. But there is likely some irony here, as the poem reveals Meliboeus' passivity with respect to the world of power and his grievously impractical nature.

Given Tityrus' implied limitations as a poet, it has surprised some commentators that it is he who speaks the poem's famous and beautiful close, in haunting lines that epitomize the pastoral sensibility.

> Hic tamen hanc mecum poteras requiescere noctem
> fronde super viridi: sunt nobis mitia poma,
> castaneae molles et pressi copia lactis,
> et iam summa procul villarum culmina fumant
> maioresque cadunt altis de montibus umbrae.
>
> (Ec. I.79–83)

(Here nevertheless you could rest this night with me upon green leaves. I have ripe apples, soft chestnuts, and a supply of cheese. And now in the distance the high roofs of the farm houses smoke, and deeper shadows fall from the lofty hills.)

Some critics have attempted to reconcile the poem's beautiful close with their negative appraisal of Tityrus by characterizing his invitation as inept or too late or insincere. Others have argued that the verses are merely a "pastoral tag" or, contrarily, a "breakthrough to the sublime for the whole poem," and, therefore, attributable not to Tityrus, but, as it were, to Vergil.[18]

I have argued, and I still think it plausible, that, since the dramatic characterizations of Tityrus and Meliboeus are carefully sustained throughout the Eclogue, with attention even to small details, Vergil would not lightly imperil this illusion in the closing. I have therefore suggested that we can see Tityrus' beautiful verses as making both ethical and dramatic sense if we read them as the result, finally, of responsiveness on his part to the pastoral visions and values of Meliboeus. Drawn out of his complacency by the poetry of Meliboeus, Tityrus responds ultimately, if tentatively, with poetry and generosity, albeit limited (his offer of sustenance is only for the night) of his own. Nevertheless, this position is morally superior to the one he holds in the poem's opening. Therefore I see the effect of Meliboeus' song on Tityrus as morally elevating.

In my reading, generosity is revealed as Vergil's pastoral ideal—not so much the idyllic harmony of an eternal green world, as voiced in Meliboeus' poetry, but, from the perspective of the textual voice, the moral condition that makes humane action possible. The poem has a resonantly contradictory close with respect to the value and viability of pastoral. On the one hand, the finer poet, Meliboeus, is exiled, never to sing again (at least so he says now); remaining in the country will be the impious soldier (70) and the pedestrian Tityrus—a melancholy picture of the impact of the new, urban god on the countryside and its music. On the other hand, Tityrus' sensitivity to another's suffering and the birth of his beautiful new tone constitute moral growth. Thus the power of the pastoral vision to change hearts and to influence belief and action is manifest in the closing verses of Tityrus, even as the primary poet of this pastoral vision is exiled. The text, then, countenances the possibility of new song in new circumstances. The pastoral vision is not without moral consequence, even in an unjust world. The future would, therefore, not be entirely without hope. The pastoral design as a whole encompasses these contradictions.

## ECLOGUE X

While the speakers in Eclogue I are imaginary, the central speakers of Eclogue X are the elegiac poet and soldier Gallus, friend of Vergil, and the Eclogue poet himself (by which I mean the first-person speaker).[19] Because this voice speaks as the composer of the poem, the temptation is strong to read this voice as Vergil's own; nevertheless, it must be kept in mind, if only as a difficult hypothesis, that this voice is an impersonation of the same nature as those of the other speakers.

Although much is obscure about this poem, the dramatic situation is that Gallus is represented as having a disabling passion for Lycoris, who has gone off—"through snows and rough camps"—with another man (Antony, according to the commentators). Apollo, Silvanus, Pan, and various rural figures (Menalcas, shepherd, swineherds) come to question Gallus about his passion. Laurels and tamarisks, Mt. Maenalus and frozen rocks lament for him. Gallus attempts to solace his pain by imagining a life of pastoral refuge and love with pastoral figures. He would seek solace for the pain of lost love in pastoral idyllicism and/ or in the writing of pastoral or perhaps of pastoral elegy. Although there is debate about what sort of poetry Gallus is deemed to be writing, it is perhaps adequate to say that Gallus is represented as experiencing a crisis, whether emotional or creative or both simultaneously. Gallus imagines a pastoral vision, an idyllic escape from pain—first as a future less vivid condition (present subjunctives in lines 33–34), then as outright contrary to fact (imperfect subjunctives in lines 35–43). His dream recedes into unreality as he speaks.

> o mihi tum quam molliter ossa quiescant,
> vestra meos olim si fistula dicat amores!
> atque utinam ex vobis unus vestrique fuissem
> aut custos gregis aut maturae vinitor uvae!
> certe sive mihi Phyllis sive esset Amyntas
> seu quicumque furor (quid tum, si fuscus Amyntas?
> et nigrae violae sunt et vaccinia nigra),
> mecum inter salices lenta sub vite iaceret;
> serta mihi Phyllis legeret, cantaret Amyntas.
> hic gelidi fontes, hic mollia prata, Lycori,
> hic nemus; hic ipso tecum consumerer aevo.
>                               (Ec. X.33–43)

(O, how gently my bones might then rest if one day your pipe were to sing of my loves. And would that I had been one of you, either a guardian of your flock or trimmer of the ripening grape. Surely whoever my love was, whether Phyllis or Amyntas (what then if Amyntas is swarthy? Violets are dark and dark are hyacinths too), would lie with me amidst willows under a pliant vine. Phyllis would pluck garlands for me, Amyntas would sing. Here are cool springs, Lycoris, here soft meadows, here a grove; here with you I would be consumed by time alone.)

Gallus does not complete even this first idealizing utterance without inserting the name of Lycoris, to be followed by an admission of yet another counterforce, this one from within Gallus himself.

> nunc insanus amor duri me Martis in armis
> tela inter media atque adversos detinet hostis. (44–45)

(Now a mad love of hard Mars holds me in arms, in the midst of weapons and hostile foes.)

This *Eclogue*, therefore, even more than *Eclogue* I, self-consciously presents the idyllic vision as unrealizable: Lycoris, having chosen another man, is absent; Gallus himself has martial passion that precludes pastoral retreats. Real love and real war are more powerful than pastoral visions or the poet's utterance of those visions. Gallus is made to acknowledge that passion is greater than pastoral or even than elegy and to urge an affirmative yielding to love:

omnia vincit Amor: et nos cedamus Amori. (69)

(Love conquers all: let us also yield to love.)

However, this negative utterance of Gallus concerning the power of pastoral (or perhaps of any poetry), dramatic and famous as it is, is perhaps too easily read as the meaning of the whole poem, which is then taken to be the failure of poetry. David Ross, for example, has written: "There is no theme more Virgilian than this."[20] I propose, however, that, as one speech of one speaker, it must be understood within the context of the whole. For readers of this poem, the challenge is to understand the meaning of the *textual* "defeat" of Gallus by his passion for Lycoris. What function do Gallus' pastoral vision and renunciation serve in the design of the whole?

The poem's frame, that is, the opening and closing spoken by the Eclogue poet, is also essential to the poem's meaning and suggests a context for reading Gallus. The opening verses establish the ethical dynamic of this poem: that is, the poet of the eclogue gives to another poet, Gallus, the gift of a poem (*quis neget carmina Gallo?* allows the inference that he asked for a poem), in particular the gift of a love poem on Gallus' behalf to Lycoris (*quae legat ipsa Lycoris*), and, finally, the gift of speaking in this poem. This giving to Gallus of the power to sing in Vergil's own poem is a generous action on the part of the Eclogue poet—a generosity which is even more sustained if the verses in question are not only an interpretation of Gallus' style, but, as Servius indicates, precise phrases and subjects from Gallus' poems.[21] In an inversion of the characteristic pastoral amoebaean song, in which the singers try progressively to top each other (as in *Eclogues* III and VII), the Eclogue poet grants freely to another poet the gift of singing in his poem. Thus, in this last *Eclogue*, the giving of the gift precedes and supplants the contest, in a gesture ideally expressive of pastoral love and community.

Since the poem is explicitly described as a poem for Lycoris herself to read, she, along with Gallus, must be construed as its target reader. Therefore *Eclogue* X must be read as a love poem—to be precise, as a poem of seduction from Vergil on Gallus' behalf to Lycoris.[22] The Eclogue poet's love for Gallus

> Gallo, cuius amor tantum mihi crescit in horas
> quantum vere novo viridis se subicit alnus. (73–74)

> (Gallus, for whom my love grows hour by hour as
> much as a green alder shoots up in the spring.)

is so generous, so enabling, so pastoral, let us say, that it empowers him to write a love poem that will enhance Gallus' pursuit of another love. Most simply, the Eclogue poet shows Gallus' love for Lycoris when he represents Gallus as languishing for her. The well-recognized allusion to Theocritus intensifies the impact of this affirmation of love. From the perspective of this larger context, we may return to the question of what Gallus' "defeat" by passion for Lycoris and the "failure" of pastoral poetry may signify in the overall design of this poem.

As noted above, Gallus' situation in this eclogue alludes to Theocritus' *Idyll* I, where the shepherd poet Thyrsis sings of the death of Daphnis. Although the circumstances remain obscure, Daphnis is wasting away even to death, because he refuses to yield to Aphrodite. Priapus, Hermes, and Aphrodite arrive to question Daphnis about his passion. Pan, invoked, arrives to receive the syrinx from Daphnis' dying hand as Daphnis says, "For now defeated by Eros, I go down to the stream [of Hades]." Although Daphnis is the founder of pastoral, he is not the speaker of conventional pastoral poetry in this poem; rather, he is represented as a proud, uncompromising figure, insolent to Aphrodite, who chooses to die rather than to give in to passion. He becomes a heroic figure of sorts, as all of nature grieves responsively at his death.

In *Eclogue* X Gallus is in a parallel position: gods and various rural figures sense his suffering, surround and question him about his unhappy circumstance, counsel and exhort him. Commentators therefore tend commonly to refer to Gallus as the "dying Gallus," as if he were wholly parallel to the dying Daphnis. Yet this equation is not precise and likely obscures the main point of the allusion. For there is a crucial difference between Daphnis and Gallus that commentators do not discuss: the fates of Daphnis and of Gallus are not parallel, but rather precisely *opposed*, since, unlike Daphnis, Gallus does *not* die, but chooses instead to yield to love and hence to *live*.

omnia vincit amor: et nos cedamus amori. (69)

(Love conquers all: let us also yield to love.)

The language of defeat in which this affirmation is expressed has led some read-ers to understand the poem as a song of defeat, expressing the impotence of poetry.[23] Nevertheless, its meaning in context appears quite the opposite, since, through this allusion to Theocritus, Gallus in fact expresses his passion for Ly-coris and thus continues to court her. Because Gallus' passion for Lycoris is so compelling, he prefers it even to such glory as Daphnis' immortal death could confer upon him. For love of Lycoris—as she would surely note—Gallus is made to reject the very heroic paradigm which otherwise he pursues in his military career and even to give up immortal death. (Of course, ironically, in *Eclogue X* Gallus becomes famous or "glorious" precisely for saying *omnia vincit amor: et nos cedamus amori.*) In this reading, *Eclogue* X is not, as it might appear, a pessimistic yielding to defeat by passion, but an ironic use of the language of defeat for the seduction of Lycoris by Gallus, who, of course, owes his utterance of these subtle verses to the generosity of his friend, the Eclogue poet.

There are also other levels of seduction in this poem, namely the seduction of Gallus by the Eclogue poet and of readers by Vergil. In these latter cases, the seduction is a product of and consequent upon the generosity of the Eclogue poet's gift of the poem to Gallus. Gallus is likely moved by the Eclogue poet's expressions of generosity to him in this poem and therefore in some sense is seduced himself. And there is the seduction of readers, who, attracted by Vergil's pastoral representations, are still to be found reading this poem. *Eclogue* X is different from *Eclogue* I in that the moral force of generosity is not, as it is in *Eclogue* I, demonstrated in the text; how Lycoris and Gallus read this poem is not represented. Thus the more profound pastoral vision in this poem is expressed not in the speech of Gallus, but in the Eclogue poet's gift to Gallus. The moral power of the poem and its meaning are enacted only at the point of reception, if we readers are moved by its visions and values.

This last eclogue then, like *Eclogue* I, is characterized by the tension of unre-solved oppositions. On the one hand, the Gallus figure expresses explicitly the sentiment that pastoral is impotent when confronted by passion. The Eclogue poet himself is forsaking the genre of pastoral, as he indicates at the poem's start that this is the last of the collection (*extremum laborem*). Nevertheless, even as the Eclogue poet is leaving pastoral behind, he gives proof of the vitality of its values by means of this very poem, which demonstrates generosity, esteem, and love, as manifest in the Eclogue poet's gift to Gallus. Apparent oppositions between the two poets—of disabling elegiac love versus enabling pastoral love, of urban sophistication and worldly engagement versus pastoral retreat—are partially transcended by their simultaneous departures from the pastoral world and by the community of sentiment effected by the gift. In my reading, these contradictory messages about pastoral and the viability of its values are in some tension with the stability of the poem's conventional closural motifs (evening shadows, satiety, and homeward journey):

> nocent et frugibus umbrae.
> ite domum saturae, venit Hesperos, ite capellae. (76–77)

> (Shade indeed harms crops. Homeward, goats, filled from browsing, homeward. Evening has come.)

## THE ARISTAEUS EPYLLION

In the Aristaeus epyllion of *Georgics* IV.315–558, Aristaeus and Orpheus, like Tityrus and Meliboeus or Gallus and the Eclogue poet, embody opposing values.[24] I have argued elsewhere that the farmer, the normative figure in a georgic poem, is associated in Vergil's *Georgics* with technological progress, material value, usefulness, and pitilessness; his agricultural technology is most often, if not without exception, characterized as violent. The Georgic poet (the first-person speaker, analogous to the Eclogue poet), on the other hand, is represented as materially useless; he idealizes the Golden Age past, is inclined to pity, and sees himself as impotent in the world of power. These oppositions between the farmer and the Georgic poet, constructed throughout the first three books of the *Georgics*, are finely developed in the opposing pair of Aristaeus and Orpheus, who are linked in narrative here for, as far as we know, the first time. Further, only here is Aristaeus, familiar in myth and ritual as a culture hero, said to have instituted the fantastical *bougonia* (a procedure for creating a swarm of bees from the carcass of a dead calf), which forms the climactic conclusion to the poem. Orpheus, on the other hand, is the paradigmatic poet whose beautiful music animates even rocks, trees, and souls of the dead in the Underworld.[25]

In Vergil's unique version of their story, Aristaeus attempts to rape Eurydice, Orpheus' wife, who, as she flees, is bitten by a snake and dies. Subsequently Aristaeus' bees die. Having no insight into this disaster, Aristaeus descends into the depths of Ocean to consult his mother, Cyrene. She sends him on to Proteus, who interprets the death of his bees as a punishment from Orpheus for Aristaeus' violence against Eurydice. Cyrene then expounds to Aristaeus the expiatory ritual (modus orandi) of bougonia necessary to reacquire bees (534–47). This technique, termed an ars (315), is described twice in the poem (295–314, 538–47), with some significant variations between the versions. Both, however, require the sacrifice of a calf, whose body and spirit then serve to animate new bees. Bougonia has traditionally been described as "rebirth" and read as an image of resurrection, thus as an image of Vergil's faith in the renewal of Rome under Octavian.[26] The narrative, however, indicates without ambiguity that the generation of new bees requires the calf's death, which is rendered in brutal detail. Bougonia therefore likely figures, not resurrection, but rather the costly exchange of one life for another life. Aristaeus follows Cyrene's prescriptions, acquires new bees, and achieves the divinity promised by his mother. Orpheus, on the other hand, in retrieving Eurydice from Hades, pursues a true resurrection, for he would restore a once-dead figure to life. Descending to the Underworld, he so charms its inhabitants that he is granted permission to bring back Eurydice—not a new Eurydice, not a substitute for or presumed equivalent of Eurydice, but Eurydice herself—to the upper world, on the sole condition that he not look back at her during their journey. At the very point of success, however, Orpheus does look back—and loses Eurydice a second time and forever (485–502). After a period of inconsolable despair at her loss, Orpheus' death ensues. Music, then, would be a nonviolent and truly miraculous "technology," able to restore the dead to life, if not for the backward turn, the regressive passion of the poet, which renders useless his gift of compelling song.

The success in the world of power of the unmusical and pitiless Aristaeus, along with the failure in the world of power of the poet Orpheus, recalls the oppositions of Eclogue I between Tityrus and Meliboeus. On the one hand, Aristaeus, who succeeds in the world of power, has a negative ethical valence, epitomized by his pitiless technology. On the other, Orpheus, who makes the tragic beautiful, looks not forward but back. In the Iron Age world, it appears, success belongs to the pragmatic and pitiless, while the beautiful music of the poet perishes through his own inwardness. While, then, power is ironized in the poem as pitiless, pity is ironized as useless. Readers may be moved to reflect on their own implication in the success of force and the weakness of pity in the world of power, but such moral growth is not—as it is in Eclogue I—represented in the text.

## "Home Burial"

Let us now consider Frost's "Home Burial" from the perspective of Vergilian pastoral. "Home Burial" takes place in an isolated rural setting; it has two speakers, a man and his wife, and a narrator, who, with some spare suggestions, sets the scene. The speakers are at odds with each other; they have lost a child—her first, maybe his also. Their different responses to this loss have resulted in estrangement. (Or perhaps they were estranged even previously.) Brodsky summarizes their opposing positions in his title "On Grief and Reason," for he reads the wife as embodying Grief and the husband Reason.

In my reading, "Home Burial," understood as pastoral, appears a virtual inversion of Vergil's. In this poem we find impotence of power in the world of feeling rather than impotence of feeling in the world of power. Here, the male is the primary speaker and is associated, familiarly enough, with farm work and building, with progress, with pragmatism not to be slowed by sentiment.[27] Having just returned from burying his child, he is already reflecting on the next building project. His is the forward, linear movement of victors described by David Quint as the characteristic, teleological trajectory of imperialistic epic, of those who have a history.[28] As such, it functions in opposition to the back-and-forth or circular movement of the romance plot, the plot of the losers (again, Quint). In the case of the male in "Home Burial," as with Aristaeus, his forward movement correlates also with a certain violence or potential for violence. Of this, the narrator gives a hint near the poem's beginning when the man mounts the stairs and advances toward his wife, who cowers under him ("Mounting until she cowered under him"). The threat of the man's violence does not become explicit, however, until the end of the poem, when he says he will use force to return his wife to his house ("I'll follow and bring you back by force. I will !—"). Apparent to readers is the inadequacy of the man's building skills and of his violence to resolve emotional difference. In Vergil, poets have no power in the world; here, the powerful male finds his power useless in the world of emotion. He pursues his wife without success. Possessing her in the house, closing off other conversation, as he desires, have failed to make her love and approve of him. The irrelevance of his skills and threatened force is represented variously: not only by his inability to win over his wife, but also by the mold that "will rot the best birch fence a man can build" in four damp days; and, finally, by the unexpected approach into his restricted world of some other, of unknown potential ("Amy! There's someone coming down the road!"), just before the close of the poem.

If the text asks us to read the male as limited by his reliance on force and his deficient sensibility, it also asks us to read the female as limited by her lack of poetry and insight. If she were a figure in a poem of Vergil's, standing in opposition to a figure of her husband's ethical valence, she would be a poet. Yet this dimension is emphatically lacking. She has given birth to a child, but its death has disabled her. Her back and forth movement, to and from the window, suggests the romance plot, the trajectory of the losers. But in her case, the tragic does not correspond with the beautiful. She has no creativity or insight to show for her grief, no moral message, however impotent in the world of power. The narrator, who is the closest to a poet-figure in this poem, leaves the poem at just about the mid-point. Thus there is no interpretation, no intelligibility, no resolution implicitly offered to readers.

Brodsky, surprisingly to my view, reads the oppositions between the speakers as Grief and Reason. The male, "Reason," he reads as the focus of greater sympathy, but, he says, no final comparative judgment between the two speakers is invited, because the poet shares in both speakers and has left them still indissolubly married, as it were, in the poem. Brodsky's reading does not accommodate the poem as I, a female reader, read it. On my reading the man is not sympathetic or "reasonable," but rather emotionally deficient and inclined to violence when "reason" fails. Neither, however, is the female character representative of any enlightened value. The text ironizes both speakers and sympathizes wholly with neither. The conclusion, with its menace of domestic violence, remains open, since the advent of an unknown visitor is likely a destabilizing, perhaps catastrophic, intrusion into the man's enclosed world. Perhaps this portrait of a failed relationship on the brink of dissolution is the textual voice's portrait of marriage (marriage does not figure in Vergilian pastoral)—a "dark" modern pastoral, indeed, as Brodsky says (see Chapter 2 of this volume), in which there is no idyllicism and no generosity, although there is a new fence and the new grave mound.

If the subject of the poem, the pastoral design, is the relationship of these two, we see that the child, the fence, and the marriage are all rotting. There has been no illuminating exchange between the speakers, and no possibility for a generous coming together is suggested. The narrator's departure from the poem suggests the absence of any higher or controlling insight. For Brodsky the mind of the poet that conceived this poem is dangerously detached from his characters, indifferent to their fate, as if on a trajectory out of the earth's orbit, never to return. Here, as a reader of Vergilian pastoral, I would agree. The absence of deep appeal in either speaker, along with the absence of hope for any insight on the part of either or of possible resolution to their conflict, may well imply the poet's felt separation from their fate. But he is sufficiently engaged, if only by despair, to write the poem.

## VERGIL'S ENGAGEMENT IN THE HUMAN CONDITION

It has been the purpose of this chapter to suggest how Vergil's pastoral questions not only the values of the world of power, but also the choices of the poet-figures, with whom Vergil himself might readily be identified. These figures are, perhaps carelessly, impotent in the world of power. In *Eclogue* I the finer poet is passive with respect to the great world, indulging instead in haunting songs of sorrow and loss. In *Eclogue* X, Gallus concedes (if only ironically) the weakness in the great world of his version of elegiac pastoral, while the Eclogue poet implicitly concedes its ultimate irrelevance for him by leaving pastoral behind. Again, in the *Georgics*, the poet-figure Orpheus is defeated as much by his own actions as by what Aristaeus represents. Vergil concludes the *Georgics* with the only mention of his own name in all his poetry, as he makes a partially ironic, certainly self-deprecating comparison of himself, flourishing in leisure, without fame,[29] playing at poetry, to the *magnus victor* Caesar, who is making his way to Olympus:

> Haec super arvorum cultu pecorumque canebam
> et super arboribus, Caesar dum magnus ad altum
> fulminat Euphraten bello victorque volentis
> per populos dat iura viamque adfectat Olympo.
> illo Vergilium me tempore dulcis alebat
> Parthenope studiis florentem ignobilis oti,
> carmina qui lusi pastorum audaxque iuventa,
> Tityre, te patulae cecini sub tegmine fagi. (IV.559–65)

> (This song of the husbandry of crops and beasts
> And fruit-trees I was singing while great Caesar
> Was thundering beside the deep Euphrates
> In war, victoriously for grateful peoples
> Appointing laws and setting his course for Heaven.
> I, Virgil, at that time lay in the lap
> Of sweet Parthenope, enjoying there
> The studies of inglorious ease, who once

> Dallied in pastoral verse and with youth's boldness
> Sang of you, Tityrus, lazing under a spreading beech.
> (Wilkinson, p. 143)

The poet, maker of moral and aesthetic value, is juxtaposed to the *imperator* as maker of empire. Readers are invited to compare their kinds of power. Vergil thus explicitly locates himself within the set of contradictions that his poems represent as inhering in human experience. Perhaps Vergil does sense in himself an inclination to self-defeating inwardness with respect to the world of power. Yet his poems also point to the morally elevating potential of the poet's imagination. Pastoral values may, then, have influence in the world of power if readers are moved to enact them.

# Chapter 4

# ARISTAEUS, ORPHEUS, AND THE *GEORGICS*
## Once Again

### GIAN BIAGIO CONTE

Some years ago I proposed an interpretation of the story of Aristaeus and Orpheus, and I was quite satisfied with it. Quite—but I still felt a little like the rabbi in the Jewish joke Arnaldo Momigliano once told me. One rabbi goes to see another rabbi and finds him immersed in the reading of the Torah. "What are you doing?"—"I'm trying to interpret a passage that I've been studying for years and can't explain completely to myself." "Let me see, I'll try to explain it to you myself." "That won't do any good. I can explain it to *other* people; what I can't do is explain it to myself."

I would like to see whether this time I can explain the close of the *Georgics* to myself. This time I shall try to be less elliptical, more nuanced, more open to the difficulties. Even if, in a certain way, with adjustments and additions, I end up offering a second time the basic outlines of my first interpretation, I would still prefer to be considered not an inveterate sinner (*perseverare diabolicum*), but only a stubborn rabbi.

More or less simultaneously with my own interpretation, which appeared in 1980, Jasper Griffin published a fine essay on the subject, remarkable for his balanced discussion of the problem and his solid erudition.[1] The simultaneity prevented either of us from knowing of the other's work. When I look back, Griffin's article always appeals to me more than the numerous studies others have devoted to the passage. I find a significant harmony between us above all in the aim which underlies his interpretation: he, too, is looking for an *organic* interpretation, one that connects the *fabula Aristaei* with the whole system of ideas which sustains the *Georgics*. Setting aside all other methodological considerations, this is certainly the way to proceed, the method which treats Vergil's text as an entity delimited by a "classical" closure, as an organic construction composed of various parts, whose closure in fact constitutes its seal of significance.[2]

For my own part, I cannot help but consider less than satisfactory the inter-

44

pretations of those scholars who prefer to read these verses as a decorative exploit on the part of the poet, an ornamental *tour de force* to which he has given the form of an etiological narrative (even though such readings can of course be appreciated for individual felicitous observations). For these critics the final narrative of the *Georgics* is nothing more than a highly elegant and fascinating appendix, a structurally almost autonomous excursus, introduced with the simple aim of furnishing an *aition* (cause) for the *bugonia*, the birth of bees from the corpse of a bull.[3]

It is simply not true that the bees' miraculous reproduction has the same prominence in relation to the poem's doctrinal substance, which is made up of instruction and description, as does "an *aition* in analogous cases in Ovid's *Metamorphoses*."[4] On the contrary: Ovid, who constructs a linear, homogeneous collection of *aitia* by linking one story to another and by inserting one story within another, is one thing; the Vergil of the *Georgics*, who sets his seal upon a didactic exposition—a genre which, properly speaking, is descriptive and not narrative— by means of an appropriate story, is quite another. If one wishes, one can invoke Ovid for a comparison of the *surface technique* (the story of the *bugonia* is contextually motivated as an *aition*: a custom is explained by reference to its mythic antecedent); but the literary function performed by Vergil's narration cannot be compared with that in Ovid's stories. For the relations of context differ too much—at least as much as the *Georgics* and the *Metamorphoses* differ from each other. In Vergil the etiological move with which the epyllion is introduced is merely an "Alexandrian" garment—a fashionable garment—superimposed upon an impressive story which serves to provide a significant conclusion for a doctrinal exposition.

Servius claims that Vergil revised Book IV of the *Georgics* on the death of Cornelius Gallus (27 or 26 BCE), eliminating praise of his recently disgraced friend and substituting the story of Aristaeus (or the section about Orpheus, according to a much less plausible version). This information cannot be simply accepted as fact, but on the other hand it cannot be rejected with absolute certainty. If Servius' information is accepted as a whole, two large problems remain unsolved. First, what happened to the original passage if it was deleted after circulating freely in the years between 29 and 27/26 BCE? Must it not have been a highly desirable sacred relic for the legions of Vergil's admirers? What abyss swallowed up the copies already in circulation? That the *Georgics* were not "published" until Gallus' death seems most unlikely: the work had been finished for three years, it was already known to Augustus and to Vergil's circle of friends, and it was being imitated by other poets. Why then keep it in the drawer? Second, Vergil is alleged to have devoted to Gallus (perhaps in his role as prefect of Egypt) an

encomium lengthy enough to require compensation and replacement by an epyllion more than two hundred verses long—and this in a poem which grants only
a few dozen verses to the celebration of Augustus and four brief mentions to the
addressee and patron Maecenas. But if the praise of Gallus was brief—like, let
us suppose, that of Pollio in the Bucolics—then what else did the fourth book
contain? On the other hand, one can imagine that Gallus was praised less as a
political figure than as a poet, perhaps in an elaborate poetic reflection like the
one offered us by the tenth Eclogue.[5] But in that case the necessity of deleting him
becomes less intelligible, unless one wishes to regard the Augustan regime (what
is more, in its very first years) as a quasi-Stalinist tyranny.[6]

One can add—even if only as an initial suggestion, which we shall try to
substantiate later—that the Aristaeus epyllion, as we read it, presents a strong
internal organic unity and above all is linked by a profound thematic continuity
with the rest of the poem. This renders more unlikely the idea that in essence it
is merely an improvised addition.[7] In any case, even if the authenticity of Servius'
notice and hence of the presumed revision could someday be demonstrated rig-
orously, this would in no way justify an interpretation which ignored the semantic coherence
of the new text.

Let us proceed by looking for meanings in the story of Aristaeus and Orpheus
which enter into free and complex interaction with the didactic part of Book IV
and, more generally, with the economy of the whole poem. We shall try to show
that there is a profound harmony between the meaning suggested by the final
mythic narrative and the ideological construction of the Georgics as a whole. At
the deepest level, the two discursive forms—the expository, didactic form and
the mythic, narrative form—will turn out to be complementary, two different
representations of the very same theme.

In the same way, Plato's dialogues often conclude the exposition of doctrine
with a myth. It should suffice to recall the Gorgias, the Phaedo, and the Republic,
but in almost every dialogue the reader encounters more or less extended mythic
narratives. In these extended "similes"—let us call them this to make the point
clearer—Plato reflects upon his literary works. This is the case, for example, in
the comparisons with the statues of Silenus in the Symposium and with the gardens
of Adonis in the Phaedrus. They form part of that "language by means of images"
which characterizes Platonic discourse and therefore should not be separated
from the metaphors, similes, and easily understood examples with which at every
step in his dialogues Plato vividly illustrates the matter under discussion.[8] These
myths illustrate the Truth in a form accessible to intuition. The mythos completes
the logos but is not opposed to it: it completes it per imaginem (by representation).
The doctrinal discourse, which proceeds by analysis and argumentation, and the

mythic discourse, which proceeds in the condensed and paradigmatic form of narrative, are complementary. Both discourses approach the truth by different but equally legitimate paths; neither form can be substituted for the other. *Logos* has the advantage of exact thought and subtle distinctions, but it lacks the force to represent its contents with realistic vivacity—precisely what *mythos* can do, thanks to its symbols and concrete images. The truth will be found at the point where *mythos* and *logos* accord or converge.[9]

As we have said, Plato often uses a myth to provide the doctrinal exposition with a climax, a final suggestive frame in which he bids his reader farewell, the perceptible representation of a philosophical "truth." Thus the *Phaedo* closes with the "myth of the souls after death" (107d–114c) and the *Gorgias* with an eschatological myth (523–27). Indeed, the words that introduce the myth in the latter dialogue are particularly significant: "Listen to a very fine story: ('Άκουε δή, φασί, μάλα καλοῦ λόγου) you will consider it a fable, I suppose, (ὃν σὺ μὲν ἡγήσῃ μῦθον) but for me it is a story (ἐγὼ δὲ λόγον), since the content of what I am about to tell you is true, according to me." This myth exhibits many elements drawn from the Greek literary tradition (Homer, Pindar, Aeschylus); but its function within the *Gorgias* is to convey a superior revelation, so that it becomes the only form of discourse to which Plato can entrust the loftiest—and for that very reason the most elusive—contents of the philosophy expounded in the preceding part of the dialogue.

In the same way, Plato's long and complex exposition of his ideal of society and the state in the ten books of the *Republic* is concluded by a grand illustrative epilogue, the myth of Er of Pamphylia. This is a structure which Cicero chose to emulate in his *De republica* when he decided to represent the doctrinal content of his thought suggestively—*per imaginem*—and closed the dialogue with the *Somnium Scipionis*. Like Er's, Scipio's voyage, too, is a philosophical voyage, not only because the respective contexts are philosophical but also because the narrative contents are strongly ideological.

The dream-voyage is substantially a form of revelation. Here the addressee of the Ciceronian political project receives a moral lesson which is fully congruent with the political doctrine expounded and discussed in the *De republica* as a whole. In the form of an intuitive and almost initiatory vision, the narrative of the *Somnium*—a mythic excursus illustrating emblematically Cicero's political ideal— condenses and sublimates the dominant theme of the *De republica*, that is, the *princeps*, the political figure to whom Cicero assigned the task of healing the wounds of the Roman republic. The other world Scipio dreams of is certainly the universe of Plato and Pythagoreanism (which we shall find once again, differently elaborated, in Book VI of the *Aeneid*), but it is also another world which is supposed to serve the *princeps* as a model to which he must conform. Scipio, the dreamer-voyager, is merely the prototype of the Ciceronian *princeps*.[10] We shall try to show that—analogously—Vergil's Aristaeus is the prototype of the perfect *agricola* (farmer), or rather, in other words, that the mythic narrative of Aristaeus and of what happens to him is a significant and paradigmatic illustration of the theme which underlies the whole of the *Georgics*.

By its very nature, didactic discourse cannot help but have a form which is, so to speak, "static": it accumulates information and precepts, it instructs and admonishes. The proper form of the didactic mode is not the story but the description. Its fundamental stance is gnomic and could be summarized in the formula "This is how things are; I teach you them and you learn them." So, too, in the model text, Hesiod's *Works and Days*, the farmer's "virtues" are expounded as incontestable truths, like entries in a catalogue: the *georgos'* (farmer's) stubborn effort, the value of human labor and justice, must be learned. The narrative discourse, on the other hand, has a "dynamic" form: it flows in a succession of events and actions and is constructed according to a line of development. An initial situation is followed by a new situation, and meanings result from the attitudes, actions, and reactions of the characters involved in the narrated events.

The only reason I am recalling these elementary differences between didactic and narrative forms is that I suspect the disorientation of many interpreters of the story of Aristaeus arises in some way from a misunderstanding of this radical diversity. Just like Plato and Cicero, as indicated above, so, too, at the close of his own poem Vergil chooses to illustrate emblematically the fundamental theme of his teaching by permitting his poetic discourse to take on temporarily the linear movement of a narrative. The poet changes discursive form and passes from the prescriptive-descriptive code to the epic-narrative code. The story he narrates "deposits" at the end the very same moral message advocated throughout the poem. But it does so this time *sub specie mythica* (under the guise of myth).

Almost everyone who interprets the epyllion of Aristaeus and Orpheus as a narrative endowed with a meaning that in some way coheres with the general meaning of the poem starts out by acknowledging an opposition between the story of Aristaeus (the framing narrative) and the story of Orpheus (the inserted narrative). Above all, one must recognize that this opposition corresponds to a significant contrast between two different types of content; it is a way to make a statement by dramatizing two opposed models of behavior. The comparison demonstrates paradigmatically that behaving oneself in one way produces one outcome (and hence means one thing) while behaving oneself in the opposite way produces a different outcome (and hence signifies the opposite). But it is evident that, even if the narrative is articulated dialectically, its meaning is unified, that is, it arises as a result of the two components which are contextually opposed to each other.

It is no less evident that this opposition between Aristaeus and Orpheus, like any other opposition, must necessarily be based upon an analogy between the two heroes' constitutive features: only because these are shared can the two characters be compared and their significant differences emerge. I believe that, even when interpreters have recognized that the meaning of Vergil's poetic composition is based upon an organic conception of the story, nonetheless when it has come to indicating the analogous elements they have sometimes lacked the analytic rigor which alone permits the truly pertinent narrative features to be identified and set in significant relation to one another. What sense does it make, for example, to treat the contrast between the epyllion's two stories in terms as abstract as, for example, "Death" and "Life"?[11] But reducing the significant correspondences to an entirely general oppositional matrix—one valid for much poetry, for too much poetry—dilutes the epyllion's meaning almost to the vanishing point. At the most, one ends up saying with triumphant fervor that "the myth of Aristaeus is the myth of resurrection and salvation, contrasted with the myth of Orpheus, which is the myth of death—and resurrection, naturally, conquers death."[12]

In contrast, the detailed correspondences between the two episodes which go to make up the epyllion have been studied with greater care: this approach has revealed a minute system of connections and contrasts.[13] Understanding this aspect of the epyllion has been enhanced by comparison with Catullus 64, which is unmistakably constructed as a story that includes another story as a kind of inverted mirror image: the frame (the wedding of Peleus and Thetis) and, on its inside, the inserted episode (Ariadne abandoned).

In the story of Aristaeus and Orpheus, too, the embedded structure is only an external feature of the narrative technique peculiar to epyllion. But it should be noted that an articulation of this sort is merely a *superficial* narrative mode, since it serves to transform the opposition between two mythical events into a continuous narrative, one which continues on the inside of another narrative. It is dangerous to assign to what is merely an external articulation of the narrative a meaning which goes beyond the superficial structure of the text. The technique of embedding has the function here of giving a hypotactic, subordinating structure to a discourse whose content has in its substance a paratactic, coordinating structure. The narration, in fact, defines two opposite attitudes, and it places them precisely in comparison with each other. In reality there is a parallelism between the stories of Orpheus and Aristaeus; the true relation between the two stories is one of comparison.

Even if, for reasons of narrative technique, the superficial structure has taken on the formulation "Aristaeus because of Orpheus" (or even, if one wishes, "Orpheus because of Aristaeus"), the logical structure of the discourse requires the formulation "Aristaeus differently from Orpheus," "Aristaeus as the opposite of Orpheus." The external form of the discourse is causality (hypotactic); the internal form is opposition (paratactic). And it is precisely because some scholars have failed to distinguish in their analysis the different levels of the text and have treated the merely external artifice of embedding as though it were in fact a substantial nexus linking cause and effect that they have even gone so far as to claim that Aristaeus derives from the story of Orpheus and his troubles, simply by listening to it, a lesson capable of overcoming death.[14] But there is not the slightest trace of this sort of *Bildungsroman* in Vergil's text.

The most promising line of interpretation, I believe, tries simultaneously both to analyze the details of the text (which are like the epidermal symptoms of larger meanings) and to reveal the skeleton of the epyllion (that is, the configuration which the story's fundamental points have taken on)—to look from afar in order to ascertain the general outline of the text's meaning, to look from close up because the discourse's very soul often manifests itself (or is condensed) in a detail. In practical terms, we should first try to identify clearly the constitutive elements of the two parts of the epyllion, those which by their very presence qualify each of the two characters and the events of the narrative, and then look for a confirmation of this qualification in the linguistic form in which the idea has found expression.

Let us begin by establishing that both episodes tell the story of a particularly excellent hero (a) stricken by an extremely painful privation (b): death deprives Aristaeus of his bees, the pride of his life, and Orpheus of his wife Eurydice, his deeply beloved companion. Both try to overcome their respective privations by means of an ordeal (c), of which the "voyage to another realm" is an essential feature. The ordeal has different outcomes (d): Aristaeus is successful and transforms the death of the bees into life, Orpheus fails and adds his own death to Eurydice's. In this way the two heroes are linked in the end by a contextual opposition which conveys a profound significance.

We shall deal later with this significant difference between Aristaeus and Orpheus; let us instead cast light now upon the ways in which they are analogous, the features which make it possible to assimilate them in some way, and hence to compare them. It is evident that Vergil decided to construct his narrative in such a way as to establish a comparison between his two parallel characters and that his inventiveness permitted him both to exploit certain preexisting elements of comparability and to introduce new ones.[15]

Outside of Vergil's narrative, too, the two heroes have a functional affinity, a series of significant features which qualify them both as *cultural heroes:* they are like two *protoi heuretai* (first inventors), discoverers of two inventions devised for the benefit of mankind. The work of acculturation they perform is linked to two quite distinct domains: Aristaeus moves exclusively in the agricultural sphere and promotes civilizing activities like stock-breeding and apiculture; Orpheus is the inventor of music and poetry, and in this domain he also fosters the passage from the primitive to the civilized state. The one appears as the prototype of the farmer-shepherd, the other as that of the poet-musician.

Obviously, the mythic complexity of these two figures is not exhausted by this feature: this is merely the *facies* (outward appearance) they present in Vergil's text for the purposes of the roles they are supposed to play in his narrative. Nor should it be forgotten that in ancient culture Orpheus' scope and importance were incomparably greater than Aristaeus'; it is enough to think of Orphism and of Orpheus' literary and religious diffusion. Nonetheless, many critics have tried to interpret Vergil's epyllion by functionalizing only one arbitrarily privileged set of Orpheus' mythic and historical characteristics, or even the *totality* of them— as though a customer in a good restaurant were not supposed to select certain dishes and wines from the ample menu of food and drink in order to have a decent meal but had to eat and drink everything available. This has led such critics to forget the salient feature of Vergil's technique: the *partiality* with which he read and used the myth of Orpheus, once he decided to make him a character in his poetry.

Of course, every myth (with its variants) possesses a plurality of meanings which aggregate around a fundamental thematic function. But when a poet utilizes a myth or a mythic character, he operates by *selection*, reorienting the story in the direction of his own text. If I may permit myself an example, I would refer to the most popular hero of the Greeks. Hercules is celebrated by the poets for innumerable exploits and for the most various characteristics: a civilizing hero, he frees the earth from dangerous wild animals and monstrous creatures; invincible in his physical force and an impeccable warrior, he is extraordinarily exuberant in sexual matters (to the point of becoming Omphale's slave) but he is also an insatiable eater and an intemperate drinker of wine; a tragic figure, he goes mad and kills his wife and children; the mythic progenitor of the Spartan kings, he is the founder of the Olympic games and also the protector of *gymnasia* and ephebes. In Roman culture, he becomes a divinity who protects both the fertility of the soil and also armies in the field, and who guarantees oaths in commercial transactions. I have presented this playful *enumeratio chaotica* only in order to ask: Would you have expected that the sophist Prodicus (as Xenophon reports in his *Memorabilia* II.1.21–34) would one day invent a fable whose protagonist was Hercules, but this time as an exemplar of wisdom and self-control, a paradigm of moral virtue? Certainly Prodicus was able to do this, and perhaps Heracles' mythic tradition also contained elements which lent themselves to such a treatment; but it is evident that Prodicus must have decided to reject many fundamental features of the myth when he chose Hercules to be the protagonist of his story.

In short, Vergil necessarily reduced the significant features of the myth of Orpheus, or, rather, has *activated some of them at the expense of others and adapted them* to his own text. For poets, myth is like a word contained in a dictionary: when it leaves the dictionary and enters their text, it retains only one of its possible meanings. Myth, too, like a word, must be modified by "declensions" and "conjugations" in order to conform to the discourse's global meaning: its function is determined by its context.

Every Greek poet (and *a fortiori* every Latin poet, who inevitably found himself confronting a richly stratified set of variants and adaptations) felt authorized to intervene in the tradition and "conjugated" freely the mythic paradigm. In all probability Homer already did this; certainly Hesiod did.[16] It is well known, to take only a single example, that in his sixth *Paean* Pindar told the story of the death of the hero Neoptolemus in a way completely different from the seventh Nemean (one time accusing him of villainy, the other time treating him with honor and respect). The contexts were different, and so, too, were the functions which the myth of Neoptolemus fulfilled in each text.[17]

In terms which are typically idealistic but which we can nonetheless accept, Werner Jaeger recalled that "myth is like an organism whose soul is constantly being renewed and changed. The person who produces such changes is the poet; but, in doing this, he does not merely obey his own caprice. The poet is the creator of a new norm of life for his age and he interprets the myth on the base of this new norm. . . . Myth can only stay alive thanks to the incessant metamorphosis of its idea, but the new idea rests upon the secure vehicle of myth."[18]

In short, the text of Vergil's epyllion leaves out much of the myth of Orpheus. Vergil's Orpheus is not a seer or a revealer of mysteries, nor is he a demiurge of human progress. And yet, as we shall see, the single qualification that the poet chooses to render pertinent, at the expense of all the others contemplated by the tradition, does grasp something essential.

In Vergil's representation, Aristaeus is the most complete hero of the georgic realm and possesses all the significant attributes of the agricultural art.[19] His initial lament is filled with intertextual references which recall the themes of the didactic part of the poem: *hunc ipsum vitae mortalis honorem / quem mihi vix frugum et pecudum custodia sollers | omnia temptanti extuderat* (*Geo.* IV.326–28: Even this crown / Of my earthly life which skilful husbandry / Of crops and herds and every enterprise / Has hardly fashioned for me) (Wilkinson, p. 135), which refers directly to the exposition of Books I and II (*fruges*: crops) and Book III (*pecudum custodia*: care of herds). An industrious experimenter, Aristaeus must be considered a great benefactor of mankind and hence worthy of the reverence which would belong to a god—Diodorus Siculus IV.81 says that Aristaeus had received ἰσόθεοι τιμαί (god-like honors) for his services as "universal inventor" of the farmer's techniques. And note *ut varias usus meditando extunderet artis* (I.133: That step by step practice and taking thought / Should hammer out the crafts) (Wilkinson, p. 61), and *divini gloria ruris* (I.168: the country's heavenly glory) (Wilkinson, p. 62).

But Vergil had already signaled Aristaeus' emblematic importance as the heroic benefactor of the georgic life even more emphatically when he promoted him to become a tutelary divinity of his incipient poem, innovating significantly with respect to the model constituted by the prooemium of Varro, *De re rustica* (I.1.4–6). And, even more important, Vergil drew the reader's attention to Aristaeus by designating him with an erudite periphrasis of Alexandrian taste: *et cultor nemorum, cui pinguia Ceae | ter centum nivei tondent dumeta iuvenci* (I.14–15 : [and you] Haunter of Woods, for whom in Cea's brakes / Three hundred snow-white bullocks crop rich pasture") (Wilkinson, p. 57).[20] By presenting him as the hero of his georgic poem, Vergil makes Aristaeus an emblematic figure of the farmer's culture and the prototype of the perfect *agricola*: Ἀρισταῖον, ὅν φασι γεωργικώτατον εἶναι ἐπὶ τῶν ἀρχαίων (Aristaeus, who, they say, was the most skilled in farming of the ancients) (pseudo-Aristotle, *De mirabilibus auscultationibus* 100.838b)—an ancient definition which would serve well as an epigraph for the Vergilian character.[21]

When Aristaeus is stricken by disaster and sees his bees die, he searches for the reason for his misfortune and lets himself be instructed so that he can find the remedy. With obedient trust he will perform his ordeal. Once he has been warned (*ut omnem | expediat morbi causam eventusque secundet*, IV.396–97: If you would bring him to reveal the cause / Of this disease and prosper thus the issue) (Wilkinson, p. 137), he finds in "tenacity" the most effective means for success, and he will be able to learn from Proteus the origin of his misfortunes and to receive from his mother the divine injunction of a ritual he must perform without deviating in the slightest detail. The two virtues required for his venture are first tenacity, in order to know, then obedience, in order to enact. The ordeal is difficult because Proteus refuses to answer his questions, transforming himself and striking terror into anyone who lacks the force to "hold firm" (*tenere*) both the terrifyingly metamorphic, struggling prophet and his own heart, which would gladly surrender. His mother, Cyrene, tells him: *vinclisque tenebis* (IV.405: and hold him / In fetters) (Wilkinson, p. 138), and then she repeats, *tu, nate, magis contende tenacia vincla* (IV.412: The more, my son, you must constrict the bonds) (Wilkinson, p. 138). *Tenacitas* (persistence), a humble but effective virtue, is exactly the same force as that of the farmer who combats the reluctance of the miserly earth. Cyrene, warning her son of the ordeal that awaited him, admonished him: *nam sine vi non ulla dabit praecepta, neque illum / orando flectes; vim duram et vincula capto / tende* (IV.398–400: For only by constraint will he give answer: / He bends to no entreaty; capture him / With ruthless force and fetters) (Wilkinson, pp. 137–38).

*Durus*, another key word in these lines, indicates the other, complementary aspect of "tenacity." It often appears in the *Georgics* to signify the "hard" reluctance of nature, which can be overcome only by toil. Thus, *labor omnia vicit / improbus et duris urgens in rebus egestas* (I.145–46: Toil mastered everything, relentless toil / And the pressure of pinching poverty) (Wilkinson, p. 61); *durus uterque labor* (II.412: both causing heavy labour) (Wilkinson, p. 90); *ipse labore manum duro terat* (IV.114: himself must harden / His hands with rugged work) (Wilkinson, p. 127); and in the end the farmers too must be "hard" themselves, "resistant to toil": *dicendum et quae sint duris agrestibus arma, / quis sine nec potuere seri nec surgere messes* (I.160–61: Now for the weapons the hardy farmer needs, / Essential for the sowing and raising of crops) (Wilkinson, p. 62). Resistance to toil, knowing how to persevere in an arduous task with faith and obstinacy—these are Roman virtues. They are ancient virtues but remain relevant, and it is these which obtain success for Aristaeus when they are wedded to scrupulous obedience to divine dictates.

Orpheus, on the other hand, fails. He fails because he contravenes the rigorous conditions imposed by the god of the dead: *rupta tyranni / foedera* (IV.492–93: void the pact / Made with the ruthless tyrant) (Wilkinson, p. 141). To respect the orders he has received would require tenacity and firmness, but Orpheus lacks these virtues because he is a lover. He is possessed by his love, which makes him, so to speak, light-headed. He turns his eyes to look upon the object of his love, and thus violates the *lex* (condition) dictated by Proserpina (487). Love carries him away and makes a fool of him. He yields to love just as any lover can yield all too easily to the illusion that *omnia vincit amor*—as though this sentence could be truer than the one that says *labor omnia vicit*, which contains a large part of the ideology of the *Georgics*.

Thus a slightly more systematic comparison between the two heroes obtains a first result. It seems clear to me that the parallelism between Orpheus and Aristaeus (obtained by means of the Alexandrian-Catullan expedient of embedding) has the function of indicating a pertinent opposition between two attitudes and two ways of life: on the one hand the submissive and scrupulous *georgos* (farmer), the perfect paradigm of religious obedience; on the other the lover, who, even if the force of his love can carry away and convulse other people, is nevertheless carried away himself by the very same *furor* (495) that animates him. Love is a powerful force, but it is *dementia* (*cum subita incautum dementia cepit amantem*, IV.488: When suddenly a madness overcame / The uncanny lover) (Wilkinson, p. 141). The madness of love deceives Orpheus: as its prisoner, he does not preserve obedience to the will of the gods. The exemplary truth that the narration leaves behind—like a sediment which precipitates from the comparison between the two contrasting attitudes—is that only he who gives full recognition to the power and will of divinity wins. And this is in evident harmony with the general ideology and didactic economy of the *Georgics*.

We have spoken of the morphological parallelism between Orpheus and Aristaeus, indicating in this the essential procedure with which the two stories are set in significant relation to one another in Vergil's text. Each of the two narrative structures is made up of some corresponding elementary features, but (it is well to remember) this is done in such a way that the constitutive elements of the one story are demarcated and oriented by those of the other story. That is, each story's narrative skeleton is similar enough to the other's, but neither story is conceived for its own sake. Each is modeled on the other, but the parallelism is adroitly veiled by the technical artifice of embedding one story within the other. Technique, too, calls for fantasy and expressive freedom.

The structural parallelism, in short, dialectically mediates the story's emblematic meaning; but the epyllion's poetic fascination can obviously not be reduced to this naked skeleton. Instead, the extraordinary artistry of Vergil's story consists precisely in the pathetic force with which each of the two stories (in particular, that of Orpheus) acquires expressive autonomy and is elaborated into a complex narrative. Perhaps no other Latin epyllion, not even Catullus' poem on the wedding of Peleus and Thetis, has attained a more complete artistic expression; probably there is no other Latin epyllion in which the art of the "miniature epic" has reached such high levels of perfection.

One explanation is that in a certain sense, Vergil wished to leave unstressed the comparative (contrastive) project connecting the two parts of his epyllion. He let his discourse's illustrative value be glimpsed as an ultimate content, but he also made sure that his liberty of invention was not oppressed by its emblematic function. His capacity of poetic representation and his stylistic vigor superimposed themselves upon the ideological, programmatic scheme and filled it with all the enchantment of a fable. In fact, the story has a strong sense of the tragic, the lightness of fables, and also the customary empathetic and sympathetic participation which is the true mark of Vergil's style.[22]

This might be a good explanation, but it certainly omits something important. The extraordinary seduction that Vergil's myth of Orpheus exerts upon the reader is not an uncalculated result of the text but is a significant effect which it exploits. I mean that this effect is an essential part of the idea that the poet wants to represent. The degree of sympathy the story of Orpheus receives in the text suggests to the reader how painful it is for the poet to permit his character's love to be condemned to failure. Let us put it in these terms for now; later we shall see the meaning of this idea more clearly.

We have said that the two stories are constructed according to a reciprocal and parallel determination of their elements. Both heroes lose their most precious possession: the farmer-breeder loses the object of his most lively care, the poet-lover the object of his passionate song. Aristaeus' offense belongs to the story's prehistory: rather than being an important element in the narrative it is the indispensable premise for the hero's loss, his search for the remedy for the loss he has sustained, and his final success. In fact, Aristaeus is not only unaware of the fault he has committed but also inadvertently the cause of Eurydice's death. The other parallel and analogical element linking the two heroes is the difficult ordeal which unites them in a voyage of search and recovery: both must descend into another realm, the one performing a catabasis to the origin of the waters and the other a catabasis to the Underworld. Both enjoy success in this first phase of their exploits, but in the end one will succeed in his aim while the other will fail.

The difference in outcome, as I have said, corresponds to the difference in attitude maintained by the two heroes. Let us examine the matter in more detail. Aristaeus asks for help: his desperate lament corresponds in some way to the plaintive song of Orpheus, the lover-poet who sings his pain. But the farmer hero *resolves to learn* from the very beginning: he does not go beyond the orders he has received, and he makes himself the scrupulous performer of the divine dictate. The linguistic clue for this attitude is the presence in the text of an archaic and almost sacral style: *haud mora, continuo matris praecepta facessit* (IV.548: Without delay he did his mother's bidding) (Wilkinson, p. 143). Here the formulaic structure reproduces—at the level of the verbal expression—Aristaeus' prompt and respectful response to the ordinances which have been imparted to him and the rigorous precision of the liturgical procedure. The clausula *praecepta facessit* has an epic coloring,[23] but Mynors, comparing Ennius *Annales* (57 Skutsch) *dicta facessunt*, rightly notes in his commentary that "both words seem to suggest active compliance."[24]

Aristaeus' attitude is in perfect harmony with his passive appearance: the text leaves no room for his emotional reactions or development. He is simply an executor: obedience is his virtue. He opens himself up docilely to the revelation of a secret which will save him. In his attitude of pupil Aristaeus fully embodies the status of the *Georgics'* ideal recipient: the farmer who is master of techniques and is ready for *durus labor* but who above all is strong in religious observance.

Beyond the parallelism of the two stories, Vergil's Orpheus has an additional feature which, precisely because it is so evident—the text insists upon it—seems to be strongly significant. Orpheus is not only an unfortunate lover: he is above all a *poet*, a passionate singer of his love. Does this marked characterization as poet have a meaning, a reason? Certainly, it might be sufficiently motivated by extratextual considerations: in the traditional paradigm of the myth Orpheus is the singer *par excellence*. But I want to emphasize now what I said earlier: in a literary work, certain values of a myth are activated at the expense of others; the meaning the myth acquires is determined by its representative function, the orientation the context impresses upon it. Again, in Jaeger's words, "The poet is the creator of a new norm of life for his age and he interprets the myth on the base of this new norm" (pp. 172–73). The myth is conjugated like a grammatical paradigm and permits new discourses when it enters into new contexts. In the present case the fact that Orpheus is represented as a poet is significant: we shall see that this whole finale is dominated by poetry—or, rather, by poetry as the problem of choice between different ways of writing poetry.

Then again, it is perhaps too general to call the Orpheus of Vergil's epyllion simply a poet. What type of poetry does this Orpheus sing? On the basis of the mythic background, we would expect a traditional orphic song, one about cosmogony or nature. In Apollonius Rhodius' *Argonautica* (I.496–511), Orpheus allays a quarrel among his sailing companions by singing a scientific (Empedoclean) poem on the genesis of the cosmos; such an almost Lucretian mode would not be at all extraneous to a didactic, georgic poem like Vergil's. But instead this Orpheus sings of love, the pain of parting, the loss of the woman he loves. In short, this is poetry made up of personal vicissitudes, of unhappy passion.

In this way we have identified another reason for Orpheus' intrinsic weakness: he is not only a lover, he is a lover-poet, a character who turns love, or rather the suffering of love, into the exclusive object of his song. He is indeed a prototype of the poet-singer, but of the singer of an *erotikon pathema* (amatory suffering) made up of heartrendingly painful notes. It has been said that Orpheus' *labor* is spent in vain (*omnis / effusus labor*, IV.491–92: All his endeavor foundered) (Wilkinson, p. 141)[25] because his tactic is different from Aristaeus'. It is not that he evades the more difficult ordeal, for the risk he runs is in fact grander and more audacious than Aristaeus'. But he works *alone*, animated by the pain that fills him: *te, dulcis coniunx, te solo in litore secum* (IV.465: and you, sweet wife, / You on the desolate shore alone [he sang]) (Wilkinson, p. 140). Isolated, he cannot help but turn to himself and dissolve everything into song; the erotic *furor* which is the very source of his poetry (his song is nourished by the passion that blinds him) ends up destroying him.[26]

The same paradox stands at the origin of much elegiac poetry. Poetry is born as a means of consolation, for overcoming the unhappiness of the passion of love: *solans aegrum . . . amorem* (IV.464: He himself sought. . . . To soothe his love-sick heart) (Wilkinson, p. 140). In the final instance this same poetry must become a *reflection* of the lover's suffering, for it cannot help but derive its theme from the very pain of the passion. And so Orpheus sings and weeps alone with himself: *flesse sibi, et gelidis haec evoluisse sub antris* (509: he wept . . . under the chilly stars, / And sang his tale of woe) (Wilkinson, p. 141)—and in the comparison of lines 511–15: *qualis . . . maerens philomela . . . flet . . . miserabile carmen | integrat . . . maestis . . . quaestibus implet* (as the nightingale / Mourning . . . weeps . . . Repeats her piteous plaint . . . Fills all the air with grief) (Wilkinson, pp. 142–43). How can an elegiac poet be defined exactly in a mordant epigram? Domitius Marsus (*ex incertis libris*, verse 9 Morel corresponds to fragment 7.3 Courtney) defines Tibullus as *elegis molles qui fleret amores* (an elegist who laments over tender loves), a definition which could well be applied to elegy in general. In singing his *erotikon pathema* (amatory suffering), Vergil's Orpheus sings in the mode of an elegiac poet, just like Gallus, the founder of Latin elegy, suffering from love in the tenth *Eclogue* (14–15).[27]

It did not escape Horace's notice that Vergil's Orpheus had the elegiac poet's unmistakable lineaments. In *Carm.* II.9 he turns to his dear poet-friend Valgius Rufus with a smile of affectionate criticism: *tu semper urges flebilibus modis | Mysten ademptum, nec tibi Vespero | surgente decedunt amores, | nec rapidum fugiente solem* (II.9.9–12: not always do the rain and wind rage, sometimes the bad weather too stops; but you on the contrary never stop lamenting your lost love and constantly compose tearful elegies). Without bothering to conceal his cards, Horace designates Valgius' kind of sentimental elegy by alluding to the very same verses with which Vergil had represented Orpheus: *ipse cava solans aegrum testudine amorem | te, dulcis coniunx, te solo in litore secum, | te veniente die, te decedente canebat* (IV.464–66: He himself / Sought with his lyre of hollow tortoiseshell / To soothe his love-sick heart, and you, sweet wife, / You alone on the desolate shore alone he sang, / You at return, you at decline of day) (Wilkinson, p. 140). Horace's ode offers a felicitous example of *urbanitas*, made up as it is of elegant irony and at the same time of affectionate seriousness. The poet makes a display of consoling his friend by reminding him of the virtue of moderation, but in fact he wishes to touch upon literary themes; he invites Valgius to commit himself to more serious literary themes but in fact asserts his distance from a type of love poetry closed in its obsessive repetitiveness.[28]

When poetry adheres totally to life (when the poet is also a lover and can sing only of his unhappy love), pain becomes its sole, indispensable nourishment, the substance of its contents.[29] Thus, in the end, of Orpheus only the tongue and voice will remain, surviving as the minimal, indestructible residue, the nucleus of Vergil's representation of Orpheus. At the end of the process of reduction (poetry = song of suffering; poet = afflicted voice), singing a love song will be nothing more than calling the beloved's name: *Eurydicen vox ipsa et frigida lingua, / a miseram Eurydicen! anima fugiente vocabat* (IV.525–26: "Eurydice!" the voice and frozen tongue / Still called aloud, "Ah, poor Eurydice!" / As life was ebbing away) (Wilkinson, p. 142). The residual lamenting voice, the quintessence of this way of composing poetry, is the seal that symbolizes the ultimate meaning of the elegiac Orpheus Vergil invented.

The poetry of love fails because it is constitutively divorced from action; it is entirely and merely egotistic. Its form of existence, at least insofar as it is opposed to the "active" form, is "contemplative." Though endowed with immense force, it is good only for trying to console its singer (without, however, succeeding in this intent) and for sweeping its listener into an enchanted stupor.

In conclusion, the finale of the *Georgics* juxtaposes Aristaeus, the prototypical hero of the *pius agricola*'s toilsome life, and Orpheus, the mythical figure of the poet-singer, deprived of any feature irrelevant to this specific characteristic. What does the reader think at this point? Let us begin by noting that the epyllion's very position, so close to the poet's farewell, is the same as the location in the *Bucolics* occupied by the tenth *Eclogue*, which sets the seal upon pastoral poetry by reflecting upon the borders of the bucolic genre and defining them in a direct comparison with the love elegy of Gallus, the character-protagonist of that eclogue.

Is it legitimate to see in this similarity of contextual functions a suggestion that we consider Vergil's story of Orpheus as his reflection upon the function and modes of composing poetry? More precisely, I mean that the story of Orpheus' love song—his ordeal and his failure—becomes *indirectly* a discourse about the limits that this kind of poetry encounters when it tries to become a practical activity, to engage with "reality."

We have said that the two stories of Aristaeus and Orpheus are constructed in a system of reciprocal relations which coordinate them with each other. They have a rather limited number of shared or corresponding features—those entailed by the narrative model of an ordeal difficult to overcome—and they are opposed to each other above all in their final outcomes. This is the level of description which analysis must hold onto without getting lost in the superficial narrative modalities; only in this way can we grasp the meaning of the comparison-opposition between the stories of the two prototypical heroes.

But in opposing the singer of love to the georgic hero I do not intend to introduce some form of allegorism. I firmly reject the familiar realistic allegorism of those critics who look for improbable historical personages behind the figures of Aristaeus and Orpheus (someone has even thought he could see Augustus in Aristaeus, or else a prefiguration of Aeneas). Nor do I wish to claim that the epyllion's function is to "stage" a genuine (self-reflective, metapoetic) literary-critical discourse which opposes two different forms of poetry, as though the Georgics intended in some way to allegorize its own genre—for then the only reason the epyllion stands in the poem would be to allow room for a treatise on poetics conducted in the form of a contrast.

Let me clarify. There is indeed an opposition between georgic poetry and love poetry arising from the opposition between a "practical dimension" and a "contemplative dimension," in which the latter turns out to be ineffective and is defeated. But the opposition that orients the meaning of this text does not, properly speaking, set in contrast two forms of poetry in order to delimit their proper contents and language in terms of their differences in the way that (as I have said) in the Bucolics the last Eclogue measures the boundaries between the elegiac and pastoral genres. Here the comparison is instead between two different dispositions which produce poetry, and it has the function of mediating symbolically the irreducible difference between two *ways of life*.

Aristaeus is the representation, *sub specie narrationis* (in the guise of the narration), of the *georgos'* (farmer's) life. He identifies and embodies the fundamental theme of Vergil's work, namely the laborious victory obtained by the farmer, trusting in divine aid and with an obedience capable of redeeming his own errors, against the evils of history and of nature—different manifestations, at the end of the first and third books, of the same hostile disorder in the world. Aristaeus, as an agricultural hero, is the model of the perfect farmer, the final representation of an instruction which the poet has dispensed throughout the four books of his poem. But he himself appears as a farmer who needs to be instructed so that—by learning, just like every addressee the poet's words contemplate—he can win his daily battle.

Aristaeus, the ideal model *who* receives and performs teaching, is at the same time the complete model *for whoever* is intended to receive and perform it. He is a farmer in whom farmers can see their reflection. One could say, then, that the *fabula Aristaei* is simply the translation into a dynamic narrative form of the literary stance which underlies the entire poem and foresees its reception. In order to make this meaning stronger and more definite, the text evokes both the "didactic" model represented by Aristaeus and another model—one which configures an entirely different relation between poetry and reality (indeed, the most distant one possible). Orpheus provides a model mediated by the enchantment of a poetry which is heart-rending and passionate but unproductive, unable to prevail in practice. Thus it has come about that a poetic discourse of a properly preceptive mode, namely the didactic form, has taken on the formulation and dynamic rhythm of a narrative, a sequence of events recounted so that an exemplary and instructive story can emerge from them.

Modeled by contrast upon Aristaeus, Orpheus, the character in the epyllion who embodies the other pole of the opposition, fails his ordeal because he does not know how to yield to obedience toward the will of the gods. His way of life is capable of extraordinary miracles, but (as I have said) it lacks practical effectiveness. The song of lament is the very substance of the life the love poet chooses, and it is also the necessary condition of his existence, since the poet's song can exist only by virtue of the suffering of love. So, too, for the elegiac poet, whose poetry is nourished by love and the sufferings deriving from it; without these, the elegiac poet would cease to be a poet. But this uncompromising loyalty to his own suffering cannot succeed where other forces, other spiritual dispositions, are required.

Solitude removes the love poet from the real world, commits him to himself, makes him egotistically indifferent to every external solicitation. Locked into this autonomy of his, he is not able (nor is he willing) to break the closed circle outside of which alone there can be salvation. This is the paradox of the elegiac poet, and it is the paradox of Orpheus, a powerful singer but a powerless agent.

On the other hand, the georgic song, too, is a way of composing poetry, but the life it promises is different. It communicates a secret of possible happiness to anyone willing to accept the tenacious *labor* of an existence docile to simple and holy rules, open to the teachings that can give it help. And in the end the force of this life, which is capable of overcoming the most difficult obstacles, will be revealed to be nothing other than the awareness of a bliss possessed unconsciously until now: *O fortunatos nimium, sua si bona norint, | agricolas* (II.458–59: How lucky, if they know their happiness, | Are farmers, more than lucky) (Wilkinson, p. 91). The farmer Aristaeus testifies to a choice of life. Upon this choice, the poet Vergil constructs the meaning of his own choice of poetry.

The difficult task to which Maecenas challenged Vergil (*tua, Maecenas, haud mollia iussa*, III.41: No soft assignment by your will, Maecenas) (Wilkinson, p. 100) turned him into a "poet-*vates*," a "useful poet," one dedicated to a song which would be able to serve the collectivity, to instruct it and make it participate in positive suggestions and shared values. Lucretius' example carries Vergil toward poetry aspiring to the same seriousness as his Latin predecessor's but confronting him with material of an inferior level. A lesser *vates*, Vergil knows that Lucretius has gone beyond the Alexandrians' preciosity to refound the central intention of the didactic genre by charging it with passion and ardor.

This commitment he makes his own. In a certain sense he goes beyond Lucretius, at least by continuing his example in a different field, but at the same time he takes a step back because he offers knowledge which is less cosmic and more mundane. He accepts the responsibility of speaking to the conscience of his contemporaries and embraces an ambitious cultural program. He seeks, and finds, Hesiod's grand distant voice and chooses for himself the grand myth of the Italian countryside, the land of Saturn, inhabited by men whose hearts are simple and who love justice. In order to declare this vocation with even greater force, Vergil opposes his own poetic choice to the most fascinating poetry of his day, love elegy. On the one hand is Vergil and the world of his Aristaeus, on the other is an entirely private poetry which obeys only the law of *servitium amoris*, invents a closed and absolute "form of the world," and in fact advocates an autarchic ideology indifferent to the values of the collectivity.

Certainly, in Vergil's text the opposition between didactic and elegiac is configured as a bitterly dramatic experience because its substance is made up of *renunciations*. I said earlier that the sympathy which the story of Orpheus encounters in the text shows the reader how great a sacrifice it cost Vergil to permit dedication to love, that great force hidden in nature, to be condemned to failure. The love that holds Orpheus prisoner and the individualism that characterizes him and makes him behave in a way so different from Aristaeus are not valueless. On the contrary, Vergil knows how to render homage to elegiac poetry as the poetic form best adapted to representing human weakness and capable of winning sympathy for the pain of anyone who suffers an existential failure. His is a grand homage. He agrees to expose himself to the risk of that genre and succeeds perfectly in this test—perhaps he does so with the pride of a poet who thereby demonstrates what he could have achieved if only his choice had gone in that direction. But he has to renounce that possibility.

While showing all the force and fascination of the poet Orpheus' destiny, Vergil simultaneously denounces the costs of the "weak" choice, that of elegy, and the bitter price of his own "strong" choice, the mission of a didactic commitment which exalts the simple and solid values of the farmer's life. His *arator* is *durus*, and the virtues that guide him must be indifferent to the mournful complaint of the poor nightingale deprived of its nest; but this is the *dura* law of the world Jupiter willed for men, the world of labor.[30] Consider once again lines 511–15: *qualis . . . maerens philomela . . . | amissos queritur fetus, quos durus arator | . . .*

detraxit; at illa / flet noctem, ramoque sedens miserabile carmen / integrat, et maestis late loca questibus implet (as the nightingale / Mourning . . . Laments lost young ones who a heartless ploughman / Has . . . plundered. She / Weeps all night long and perched upon a bough / Repeats her piteous plaint, and far and wide / Fills all the air with grief) (Wilkinson, pp. 141–42). The nightingale sings and laments, just as the poet-lover Orpheus sings and laments; and the nightingale—since Catullus 65, at least[31]—is the emblematic figure of the elegiac poet. *Durities* (toughness) is a constitutive feature of the *arator*'s character, an indispensable aspect of that perseverance which will help him to pass the test. His choice of life does not know failure, but its price is high. This is the same price the didactic poet Vergil must pay for his refusal of the poetry of love.[32]

An aestheticizing criticism often leaves interpreters dissatisfied because it tends to turn every great poetic work into an absolute individual whose existence is placed miraculously outside of time and space. To be sure, literary historians always take care to react against this tendency by making an undeniable claim for the historicity of the poetic text; but often this claim serves only to demand that the meaning of the individual work be relocated within the opaque body of history.

The right way to consider a poetic work is not to dilute it in history but rather to see history flash like lightning in it. Incorporated in the text's final structure are a poet, a language and an imagination, meanings and addressees capable of receiving them. This is why in every work there is also, necessarily, history. Here, too—in the *Georgics*, and in particular in the story of Aristaeus—there is history, and it has become part of Vergil's poetry: Maecenas and the program of his circle, everyone's anxieties and hopes after the "great fear," the dramatic commitment of a poet who becomes a *vates* in order to transmit strong values and ancient truths, the magnificent ambition of a grand new Latin literature which chooses to direct itself to the conscience of a national collectivity.[33]

Chapter 5

# SOME OBSERVATIONS ON
# *AENEID* BOOK VI

## MARK STRAND

### I.

There are four embraces in epic literature that are remarkably similar. In Book
XI of the *Odyssey*, which takes place in the Underworld, Odysseus embraces the
ghost of his mother, Anticlea. This is the way it is described in Robert Fitzgerald's
translation:

> I bit my lip,
> rising perplexed, with longing to embrace her,
> and tried three times, putting my arms around her,
> but she went sifting through my hands, impalpable
> as shadows are, and wavering like a dream.
> (*Od*. XI.204–8)

In Book II of the *Aeneid*, Aeneas embraces his wife Creusa's ghost in the ruins of
their abandoned home in Troy.

> ter conatus ibi collo dare bracchia circum;
> ter frustra comprensa manus effugit imago,
> par levibus ventis volucrique simillima somno.
> (*Aen*. II.792–94)

> (Three times
> I tried to put my arms around her neck,
> Three times enfolding nothing, as the wraith
> Slipped through my fingers, bodiless as wind,
> Or like a flitting dream.)
> (Fitzgerald, II.1028–32)

In Book VI of the *Aeneid*, Aeneas embraces Anchises, his father.

sic memorans largo fletu simul ora rigabat.
ter conatus ibi collo dare bracchia circum;
ter frustra comprensa manus effugit imago,
par levibus ventis volucrique simillima somno.
(*Aen.* VI.699–702)

(At this his tears brimmed over
And down his cheeks. And there he tried three times
To throw his arms around his father's neck,
Three times the shade untouched slipped through his hands,
Weightless as wind and fugitive as dream.)
(Fitzgerald, VI.938–42)

In Canto II of *Purgatory*, Dante embraces his old friend, the singer, Casella. This is how it is described in the original and in Mandelbaum's translation:

Io vidi una di lor trarresi avante
per abbracciarmi, con sì grande affetto,
che mosse me a far lo somigliante.
Ohi ombre vane, fuor che ne l'aspetto!
tre volte dietro a lei le mani avvinsi,
e tante mi tornai con esse al petto.
(*Purg.* II.76–81)

(I saw one of those spirits moving forward
in order to embrace me—his affection
so great that I was moved to mime his welcome,
O shades—in all except appearance—empty!
Three times I clasped my hands behind him and
as often brought them back against my chest.)
(Mandelbaum, II.76–81)

## II.

Odysseus' embrace of his mother comes after they tell each other what each has been doing. She asks, "Have you not seen your lady in your hall?" (*Od.* XI.162). He says that he has not been home yet, and he wants to know, from his mother, how things are in Ithaca. She is able to fill him in, despite not having known anything of his whereabouts. When she confesses that it was loneliness for him that killed her, Odysseus embraces her. But it is an embrace without conviction. Too much casual conversation preceded it and will follow it for us to feel that it means much to Odysseus. Though he accuses Persephone of setting him up with a hallucination to make him groan again (*Od.* XI.214), he casually concludes his conversation with his mother by remarking, "So went our talk" (*Od.* XI.225). This Underworld domesticity is convincing and is rich in what it says about Odysseus, but it tends to empty the embrace of meaning and to leave it without resonance. Epic does not allow much time for reflection. No sooner does Odysseus say goodbye to Anticlea's ghost than he turns his attention to interviewing other souls. And then he utters one of the poem's best lines, "Here was great loveliness of ghosts" (*Od.* XI.239).

III.

Toward the end of Aeneas' account to Dido and her court of his escape from the blazing city of Troy, he talks about losing his wife, Creusa, along the way, and doubling back at great risk, at least according to Aeneas, to find her. What he finds when he returns to the palace is her ghost, larger than life (*nota maior imago*) (*Aen.* II.773). He says,

> obstipui, steteruntque comae et vox faucibus haesit.
> tum sic adfari et curas his demere dictis:
> (*Aen.* II.774–75)

> (I could feel the hair
> On my head rise, the voice clot in my throat;
> But she spoke out to ease me of my fear.)
> (Fitzgerald, II.1004–6)

What Creusa does is release Aeneas from any further obligation to her. It is a speech of willing self-erasure:

> quid tantum insano iuvat indulgere dolori,
> o dulcis coniunx? non haec sine numine divum
> eveniunt; nec te comitem hinc portare Creusam
> fas, aut ille sinit superi regnator Olympi.
> longa tibi exsilia et vastum maris aequor arandum,
> et terram Hesperiam venies, ubi Lydius arva
> inter opima virum leni fluit agmine Thybris.

illic res laetae regnumque et regia coniunx
parta tibi; lacrimas dilectae pelle Creusae.
non ego Myrmidonum sedes Dolopumve superbas
aspiciam aut Grais servitum matribus ibo,
Dardanis et divae Veneris nurus;
sed me magna deum genetrix his detinet oris.
iamque vale et nati serva communis amorem.

(*Aen*. II.776–89)

(What's to be gained by giving way to grief
So madly, my sweet husband? Nothing here
Has come to pass except as heaven willed.
You may not take Creusa with you now;
It was not so ordained, nor does the lord
Of high Olympus give you leave. For you
Long exile waits, and long sea miles to plough.
You shall make landfall on Hesperia
Where Lydian Tiber flows, with gentle pace,
Between rich farmlands, and the years will bear
Glad peace, a kingdom, and a queen for you.
Dismiss these tears for your beloved Creusa.
I shall not see the proud homelands of Myrmidons
Or of Dolopians, or go to serve
Greek ladies, Dardan lady that I am
And daughter-in-law of Venus the divine.
No: the great mother of the gods detains me
Here on these shores. Farewell; cherish still
Your son and mine.)

(Fitzgerald, II. 1007–25)

Aeneas to Dido and her court then says:

haec ubi dicta dedit, lacrimantem et multa volentem
dicere deseruit, tenuisque recessit in auras.
ter conatus ibi collo dare bracchia circum;
ter frustra comprensa manus effugit imago,
par levibus ventis volucrique simillima somno.

(*Aen*. II.790–94)

(With this she left me weeping,
Wishing that I could say so many things,
And faded on the tenuous air. Three times
I tried to put my arms around her neck,
Three times enfolded nothing, as the wraith
Slipped through my fingers, bodiless as wind,
Or like a flitting dream.)

(Fitzgerald, II.1026–32)

And that is the end of Creusa. She did her job, allowing Aeneas to pursue his destiny without having to look back, which, as it happens, he is in the midst of doing. Her departure is magnanimous, to say the least, but for all its nobility it seems too convenient, too subservient to narrative considerations, to be a source of lyric passion. Creusa leaves nothing in her place; she is absorbed into the destiny of Aeneas. Her speech is coincident with her disappearance and will never serve as a memorial; the sublime retrievals of elegy are absent.

## IV.

In Canto II of *Purgatory*, a crowd of souls arrives on the mountain island of purgatory and gathers around Vergil and Dante, who were watching. One of them moves forward to embrace Dante, and Dante returns the welcome, but with disappointing results:

tre volte dietro a lei le mani avvinsi,
e tante mi tornai con esse al petto.

(*Purg.* II.80–81)

(Three times I clasped my hands behind him and
as often brought them back against my chest.)

(Mandelbaum, II.80–81)

Only when the spirit steps back does Dante see that it is his old friend, the singer and musician, Casella. At Dante's request, he begins to sing, but before he can finish, he and the other newly arrived spirits are urged on by Cato, the Guardian of Purgatory, in their climb toward God. Of all the embraces, we feel that this is the least, perhaps because it is the most accidental. Casella is not a family member and is not central to Dante's own spiritual quest. Whatever power his embrace has comes from the embraces it reminds us of.

## V.

In Book V of the *Aeneid*, the floating image of Anchises appears out of the darkness to speak to Aeneas. He advises Aeneas to meet him in the Underworld, where the future of Rome will be revealed. In Book VI the meeting takes place. Aeneas asks Musaeus, the son of Orpheus, where Anchises is. Musaeus replies:

> 'nulli certa domus; lucis habitamus opacis,
> riparumque toros et prata recentia rivis
> incolimus. sed vos, si fert ita corde voluntas,
> hoc superate iugum, et facili iam tramite sistam.'
> dixit, et ante tulit gressum camposque nitentis
> desuper ostentat; dehinc summa cacumina linquunt.
> (*Aen.* VI.673–78)

> ("None of us
> Has one fixed home. We walk in shady groves
> And bed on riverbanks and occupy
> Green meadows fresh with streams. But if your hearts
> Are set on it, first cross the ridge; and soon
> I shall point out an easy path."
>         So saying,
> He walked ahead and showed them from the height
> The sweep of shining plain. Then down they went
> And left the hilltops.)
> (Fitzgerald, VI.900–909)

This is a brief, disengaged passage, but it establishes an air of great dignity. An immense space, a pastoral setting of significant proportions, has been created for what is about to happen. Vergil continues:

> At pater Anchises penitus convalle virenti
> inclusas animas superumque ad lumen ituras
> lustrabat studio recolens, omnemque suorum
> forte recensebat numerum, carosque nepotes
> fataque fortunasque virum moresque manusque.
> isque ubi tendentem adversum per gramina vidit

Aenean, alacris palmas utrasque tetendit,
effusaeque genis lacrimae et vox excidit ore:
(*Aen.* VI.679–86)

(Now Aeneas' father
Anchises, deep in the lush green of a valley,
Had given all his mind to a survey
Of souls, till then confined there, who were bound
For daylight in the upper world. By chance
His own were those he scanned now, all his own
Descendants, with their futures and their fates,
Their characters and acts. But when he saw
Aeneas advancing toward him on the grass,
He stretched out both his hands in eagerness
As tears wetted his cheeks.)
(Fitzgerald, VI.910–20)

Anchises turns from this vision to Aeneas, who says:

da iungere dextram,
da, genitor, teque amplexu ne substrahe nostro.
(*Aen.* VI.697–98)

(let me have your hand, let me embrace you,
Do not draw back.)
(Fitzgerald, VI.936–37)

Then Vergil, in a passage of extraordinary beauty, describes the embrace of Aeneas and Anchises:

sic memorans largo fletu simul ora rigabat.
ter conatus ibi collo dare bracchia circum;
ter frustra comprensa manus effugit imago,
par levibus ventis volucrique simillima somno.
Interea videt Aeneas in valle reducta
seclusum nemus et virgulta sonantia silvae,
Lethaeumque domos placidas qui praenatat amnem.
hunc circum innumerae gentes populique volabant:
ac velut in pratis ubi apes aestate serena

floribus insidunt variis et candida circum
lilia funduntur, strepit omnis murmure campus.
horrescit visu subito causasque requirit
inscius Aeneas, quae sint ea flumina porro,
quive viri tanto complerint agmine ripas.
(Aen. VI.699–712)

(At this his tears brimmed over
And down his cheeks. And there he tried three times
To throw his arms around his father's neck,
Three times the shade untouched slipped through his hands,
Weightless as wind and fugitive as dream.
Aeneas now saw at the valley's end
A grove standing apart, with stems and boughs
Of woodland rustling, and the stream of Lethe
Running past those peaceful glades. Around it
Souls of a thousand nations filled the air,
As bees in meadows at the height of summer
Hover and home on flowers and thickly swarm
On snow-white lilies, and the countryside
Is loud with humming. At the sudden vision
Shivering, at a loss, Aeneas asked
What river flowed there and what men were those
In such a throng along the riverside.)
(Fitzgerald, VI.938–54)

Of all the embraces, this one strikes me as the most moving. It is the only one
that accommodates the forward motion of epic to a vision of pastoral. None of
the other embraces compels our attention the way this one does. In the *Odyssey*,
a brief explanation by Odysseus' mother of what happens when one dies follows
the embrace; in turn, it is followed by the homely injunction to remember to tell
Penelope of the strange things he witnessed in the Underworld. The embrace is
forgotten, as it is in Book II of the *Aeneid* where Aeneas turns his attention to his
father and to those who have gathered for exile. The event is closed off, existing
as an oddity, an embrace, or near embrace, wholly without resonance. In Dante,
where so many strange and miraculous things happen, it seems little more than
a small detail, a failed attempt at greeting a long-lost friend.

One of the reasons Aeneas' embrace of Anchises achieves greater force is
because it is described in the third person. Vergil can place Aeneas in a context

that only compounds the failure of the embrace, and he can describe Aeneas, report on what he thinks and says, so that finally Aeneas is contained by the scene. Aeneas does not have to speak. He can be silent and the narrative will continue regardless.

VI.

Before I take a closer look at what happens at this point in Book VI, I should make clear one obvious pitfall of doing so. That is, if one's reading of Vergil depends entirely upon translation there is only so much that can be assumed about the original. The translator can be trusted to represent the broad features of the *Aeneid*, but when it comes to details upon which a close reading depends, we should be cautious. For instance, can we assume that the slight difference in English between Aeneas' embrace of Creusa and his embrace of Anchises reflects the same difference in Latin? When Vergil in Book VI says in the Fitzgerald translation, the shade untouched slipped through my hands, is it really different from Aeneas in Book II reporting that the wraith slipped through my fingers? Except for the implication that what slips through one's hands may be imagined as larger in scale than what slips through one's fingers, there is very little difference. And if we compare the lines that immediately follow, a similar difference can be observed. In Book II, we have bodiless as wind, or like a flitting dream. Its parallel in Book VI is weightless as wind and fugitive as dream, which is grander, I think, with both attributes laid down in a single line. The quote from Book II offers us one or the other. Not only that, but the word "flitting," though commonly used in antiquity to describe the motions of the soul, does not seem appropriate in our day as a modifier for "dream," nor does it seem to fit the solemnity of the occasion. Like fingers relative to hands, it seems to diminish the force of what preceded it, whereas the compound line in Book VI only enhances what came before and sets up the lines that follow, inasmuch as they, too, are engaged in a form of enlargement.

The translation has forced us to question subtleties which do not occur in the original. In Latin the several lines describing each embrace are identical. So why does Fitzgerald deviate? Did he consider an exact duplication of words inappropriate to the character of each embrace? Did he feel a distinction should be made between the language of Aeneas and that of Vergil? At any rate, he was not alone in what he chose to do. Dryden deviated from the Latin, and so did Mandelbaum, and it may be that others have as well.

## VII.

When I said earlier that the compound line "weightless as wind and fugitive as dream" (*par levibus ventis volucrique simillima somno*) (*Aen*. VI.702) seemed right for the occasion, I meant that the pastoral scene that follows is in itself a compounding of Aeneas' experience of loss. Having embraced the absence of his father, Aeneas now takes in a whole landscape in which souls of a thousand nations fill the air (*hunc circum innumerae gentes populique volabant*) (*Aen*. VI.706). They are, he says:

> ac velut in pratis ubi apes aestate serena
> floribus insidunt variis et candida circum
> lilia funduntur, strepit omnis murmure campus.
> (*Aen*. VI.707–9)

> (As bees in meadows in the height of summer
> Hover and home on flowers and thickly swarm
> On snow-white lilies, and the countryside
> Is loud with humming.)
> (Fitzgerald, VI. 948–51)

This is both a continuation and an altering of the embrace. The simile performs an act of poetic replenishment. A teeming fullness is described, a flourishing of bodilessness. When Aeneas asks Anchises in the lines immediately following to tell him "What river flows there and what men were those in such a throng along the riverside?" (*quae sint ea flumina porro, | quive viri tanto complerint agmine ripas*) (*Aen*.VI.711–12), the answer Anchises gives him bears directly upon the regenerative properties of Vergil's evocation of pastoral plenitude. Those gathered at the river are souls for whom a second body is in store (*animae, quibus altera fato | corpora debentur*) (*Aen*. VI.713–14). In other words, a new beginning awaits them. This is very different from what happens at the close of Book XI in the *Odyssey*. First, a spectacular image in Fitzgerald's translation tells us that Odysseus' anticipated meeting with some of the great heroes of the past is interrupted by "shades in thousands, rustling in a pandemonium of whispers, blown together" (*Od*. XI.632–33). Then a terrifying premonition that Persephone is about to bring from darker hell a saurian death's head has Odysseus running as fast as he can to exit the Underworld and safely board his ship. Here an interesting comparison could be made between the simile of the bees mentioned above and what happens at the beginning of Book II of the *Iliad* when the Greek soldiers, at the urging of Nestor, run to arm themselves for an assault:

> From the camp
> the troops were turning out now, thick as bees
> that issue from some crevice in a rock face,
> endlessly pouring forth, to make a cluster
> and swarm on blooms of summer here and there,
> glinting and droning, busy in bright air.
> Like bees innumerable from ships and huts
> down the deep foreshore streamed those regiments
> toward the assembly ground—and Rumor blazed
> among them like a crier sent from Zeus.
>
> (*Il.* II.86–94)

## VIII.

Let me go back to the embraces. What they have in common is that they signify possession and loss at the same time. And, of course, each embrace is actually three embraces, a fact which, besides the likelihood of its making numerological or mystical sense, makes psychological sense. Simply speaking, one attempt at an embrace would be insufficient; a second attempt would merely confirm the strangeness of the first; but a third establishes the utter futility of making further attempts. Anything beyond three would seem either comic or the surreal enactment of repetition-compulsion. But back to possession and loss. Each of the shades is able to speak, and yet each is insubstantial. Each can be moved to tears, tears that we assume are a real manifestation of their joy or sorrow—emotions which we must also suppose are real. Each is an embodiment of speech and feeling, and each might be called, accommodatingly, a figure of speech.

A peculiar doubleness is enacted everywhere in Book VI. Things are present and yet they are not; vision and action are accorded epic scale but they nevertheless suggest the lyric; the future is both itself and the past; Aeneas listens to Anchises but cannot embrace him. Even the reader becomes part of the poem's elusiveness. Like Aeneas, who listens to Anchises but cannot embrace him, the reader reads Book VI but cannot be sure of where Vergil is. He seems as ghostly as Anchises. This suggests, at least to me, that the Underworld and poetry have something in common. When Aeneas, upon hearing from Anchises that the souls he sees will be returning to the body's dead weight (*tarda corpora*) (*Aen.* VI.720–21) asks "How can they crave our daylight?" (*quae lucis miseris tam dira cupido*) (*Aen.*

VI.721), he is in fact questioning the wisdom of accepting the prose of everyday life over the magical properties of poetry. But he also knows that the embrace which ended in failure in the world below would have succeeded in the actual world, that corporeality has its dispensations. The spiritual world of poetry and the spiritual world of Hades permit us to see beyond what our bodies can allow, but they do not permit physical participation. The Underworld embrace offers what a poem does, which is the inseparability of presence and bodilessness.

If the description of the embrace of Anchises and Aeneas is more moving than the others I have touched on, it is because of its lyric character. Even the great catalogue of the future, of the glory that will be Rome, ends up sounding more elegiac than epic, more like a dirge, a slow parade of mortals under the great sky (*magnum caeli . . . sub axem*) (*Aen.* VI.790). Whatever is acknowledged or named into being assumes the sad quality of having been. So that near the end of Book VI, when Anchises is so moved by the appearance of young Marcellus that he wishes to scatter lilies and scarlet flowers before him, it is more than anything like the laying down of a wreath. One feels that Rome's past is being memorialized instead of Rome's future being celebrated. It is this contradiction which may be at the center of Aeneas' puzzling exit from the Underworld through the gate of ivory, which, as everyone knows, is the gate through which false dreams pass on their way to the world above. Could it be that the sanctity of Anchises' revelation has been compromised by its not being a true revelation and by Aeneas not being a true shade? It is not possible to memorialize what has not happened, nor possible to pass off what has already happened as what will happen. Each alternative is false, which is why Vergil in what seems like a judgment of himself and his rendering of the existence of Rome sends Aeneas back to the upper world through the ivory gate. It is the gate at least in this instance where prolepsis and prophecy meet, where elegy imagines a future that mourns the past and epic sacrifices the present to achieve the future. Because we are made to feel, especially in Book VI, epic creating the conditions for elegy, the existence of Rome becomes an occasion for mourning. It is the lyric and not the epic that offers images of continuity which can be set against the fact of mortality.

## Chapter 6

# MORTAL FATHER, DIVINE MOTHER
## Aeneid VI and VIII

### HELEN H. BACON

Aeneas is the son of Venus, a goddess, and Anchises, a mortal. The divine and mortal parts of this heritage coexist in him in an uneasy tension that is played out dramatically in the poem. The encounter with his mortal father in the world of the dead in Book VI and the encounter with his goddess mother in the world of the living in Book VIII are successive climaxes in the process of transformation Aeneas undergoes from reluctant mortal to willing future god in preparation for his role as founder and defender of the first Trojan settlement on Italian soil, the germ of Rome to be.

In Book I Venus denies Aeneas her embrace (*Aen.* I.407–9). An invisible barrier prohibits direct contact between mortal and undisguised divinity. The affair with Dido that follows this episode is only one of many indications of how completely mortal, how bound by longing for ordinary human happiness, he still is. In Book VIII when Venus brings him the divine armor she freely grants her embrace. The barrier that separated mortal and divinity in Book I has given way. The embrace signals that Aeneas, destined for godhood after death, is already well on the way to achieving divine status. Since the events of Book I, a series of ordeals and revelations have empowered him to renounce one by one most of his merely human ties and aspirations and dedicate himself wholeheartedly with no further holding back to the superhuman task laid on him by destiny.

The final act of renunciation occurs a little earlier in Book VIII when he accedes to Evander's injunction to dare to repudiate pomp and wealth (*opes, Aen.* VIII.364) and make himself worthy of godhood (*te . . . dignum finge deo, Aen.* VIII.364–65) by entering the humble dwelling on the Palatine where Evander had entertained Hercules, another future god. Shortly thereafter he openly accepts godhood, rather than mortality, as his ultimate destiny when he greets Venus' portent of lightning and thunder in a clear sky accompanied by the spectacle of dazzling, clashing arms with the cry "I am summoned on Olympus" (*ego poscor Olympo*) (*Aen.* VIII.523–36); the long withheld embrace between him and his mother and the gift of divine armor that follow signify divine recognition of the culmination of his spiritual transformation.

It is my view that the status of future divinity is accorded to Aeneas and all his divinized successors in the Julian line, beginning with Romulus and including Augustus, more for the quality of the *labores*, the struggles to bring Rome into being, than for their outcomes. The insistence of Anchises, in the first of his two great speeches in Book VI, on the corrupting effects of matter implies that outcomes of all these great struggles are necessarily partial and flawed. If we are to take this part of Anchises' message seriously, not even Augustus can bring about in this world the golden age of universal harmony that Jupiter, in Book I, promises to Venus the descendants of Aeneas will achieve (*Aen.* I.286–96). This moment of flawless peace can be fully realized only in the world of the spirit expounded by Anchises. Jupiter's prophecy of godhood for Augustus, as for Aeneas, will be the acknowledgment that the *labores*, the only partially successful efforts to achieve an ideal, give transcendent meaning to human life.[1]

The actual story of the *Aeneid* covers the period from the fall of Troy to the establishment of a Trojan settlement in Italy. But through visions, prophecy, and dreams it encompasses all that follows from those adventures. It will be three hundred and thirty-three years before Aeneas' descendant, Romulus, will found Rome itself, and hundreds more to the age of Augustus and Vergil. The action of this story of Rome's beginnings falls meaningfully into three groups of four books each. Books VI and VIII are part of the central tetralogy, V through VIII, which separates the first four books of wanderings at sea, presided over by his father, Anchises, from the last four books of battles on Italian soil, presided over by his mother, Venus. Compared with the stirring events of the first tetralogy— the fall of Troy, the adventures at sea, the affair with Dido—and of the last tetralogy—the passionate resistance of the Italians, the victories and defeats in battle—the central tetralogy is relatively static and lacking in action: interminable funeral games for Anchises in Sicily, long didactic speeches by the Sibyl and Anchises in Hades, the catalogue of all the Italian tribes marshaled against the Trojans, the description of the episodes of (future to Aeneas, past to Vergil) Roman history inscribed on the shield Venus brings Aeneas. And yet this tetralogy is the pivot of the action of the whole poem. For in it Vergil shows that through a series of visions, portents, and revelations Aeneas finally relinquishes his Trojan and Carthaginian past and with them all his personal hopes and desires and accepts his role as initiator of the process that will culminate in a new golden age.

In Books V through VIII, Venus and Anchises function in parallel and with one goal, the forwarding of the fate of Aeneas. At two particularly significant moments Aeneas himself expresses some sense of a distant pairing between his two parents, one a dead mortal in the Underworld, and the other a goddess in Olympus. Near the end of Book V, when the wanderings are about to come to an end, after founding the city of Acesta in Sicily where he will leave behind the aged and the weary, he establishes a cult for each parent near the city: a shrine to Idalian Venus on the top of Mt. Eryx "near the stars" (Aen. V.759–60) and beside Anchises' tomb on the plain below a sacred precinct and a priest (Aen. V.760–61). As though Vergil wished to emphasize the linking of the parents, he frames this act of double consecration with interventions by both Anchises enjoining his son in a dream to leave the weak and weary in Sicily and persevere with the young and strong to confront the appalling challenges of the hostile Italian tribes and the journey to Hades (Aen. V.721–40), Venus successfully petitioning Neptune to protect Aeneas on the last leg of his sea journey (Aen. V.779–826). In Book VII, when Ascanius' chance remark about eating their tables makes his father recognize that he is at the place where he will establish the first settlement in Italy, Rome's forerunner, the city of the future, Aeneas wreathes his temples with leaves and prays first to local and to Trojan gods and finally to "his two parents in the sky and in Erebos" (et duplicis caelo Ereboque parentis) (Aen. VII.135–40). The mother on Olympus and the father in Hades are jointly invoked to preside over both the Sicilian city founded to mark the end of the struggles at sea, and the settlement on the banks of the Tiber founded to mark the beginning of the struggles on land. Though at the opposite limits of creation, the parents' powers are somehow joined.

The formal parallels between the scene with the father in Book VI and with the mother in Book VIII are further evidence that Venus and Anchises function as parts of one whole. In each account the son leaves a city behind him and enters a new region of fields, groves, and streams where people are collected. Each parent's message to the son is delivered in a special part of this region into which the son descends after viewing it from above, a hollow in the hills characterized by the same phrase, in valle reducta (Aen. VI.703, VIII.609) by a stream near a grove. The parent sees the son first, greets him and offers an embrace, and then delivers a lengthy and complex message that has a powerful impact on the son. These similarities are balanced by profound differences.

First, Book VI. Aeneas, after leaving behind him the city of Persephone, proceeds on foot in the company only of the Sibyl through the Underworld to Elysium, a landscape of woods and fields and streams diffused with the radiance of its own sun, moon, and stars, where the happy spirits stray and disport themselves without restraint (nulli certa domus) (Aen. VI.673). Guided by the poet Musaeus, he descends from a hilltop into a green valley, where his father is reviewing the souls of his descendants to be.

Anchises' spirit sees his son approaching in the distance and, arms extended, greets him with tears and passionate words of joy mixed with longing and grief. Aeneas' response is equally passionate and even more grief-stricken as he tries three times and fails to embrace his father. Even though his outstanding *pietas* has overcome the barriers that prevent the living from entering the kingdom of the dead in the flesh, and have enabled him to cross Acheron, appease Cerberus, placate Persephone, this last barrier between the living and the dead remains unbreachable. Anchises instructs his son in two lengthy speeches explaining what the souls gathering at Lethe in this secluded valley are preparing for, first in general philosophical terms and then in relation to future Roman history. He points out, names, and characterizes individual souls who will be reborn to play an important part in the founding or growth of Rome. Then, when he has fired (*incendit*) (*Aen.* VI.889) his son's soul with the future glories of Rome, he instructs him specifically about "wars that he must fight, about the people of Laurentum and the city of Latinus, and how to avoid or endure every ordeal (*laborem*)" (*Aen.* VI.890–92). Aeneas leaves the Underworld with several kinds of necessary information, but without the solace of his father's embrace.

The father's message is almost entirely verbal. The two great speeches have a visual component only to the extent that they are explanations of what Aeneas sees around him. The briefly summarized instructions about the immediate future are exclusively verbal. These instructions are Anchises' final act of parental guidance.

As Aeneas is driven by portents, dreams, and prophecies from burning Troy to Sicily, Anchises has been at his side as cherished companion and chief interpreter and guide. Even after death he visits his son in dreams—in Book IV to remind him of his mission and wrench him away from Dido and in Book V to urge him to found a city in Sicily for the weary, and to make the journey to the Underworld.

After his father's revelations in Elysium, Aeneas no longer blunders or hangs back. He willingly pursues his fated mission. And he is no longer dependent. In Books VII and VIII he assumes his father's role as interpreter of the omens, dreams, and prophecies, which help him to make the crucial choices in the next stages of his mission: to establish a settlement, to choose a bride, to accept command of local allies in a joint war against the Latins.

In this last stage of Aeneas' preparation for the battles of Books IX through XII Anchises drops into the background and Venus comes to the fore, not with companionship, advice, and guidance, but with practical help: a prearranged signal from heaven, the gift of divine armor. In the battles on land that follow Book VIII, her role of keeping things going in the right direction parallels that of Anchises in the wanderings. But unlike Anchises' interventions, hers are not verbal and are often without her son's knowledge. They continue to take the form of practical assistance, timely intervention in battle, healing Aeneas' wound, freeing his captive spear at the crisis of his duel with Turnus.

The meeting with the mother closely follows the pattern of the meeting with the father. Again, Aeneas leaves behind him a city, this time Pallanteum, a city of this world, the city of Evander. No longer on foot, he gallops forth at the head of a mounted troop of armed Trojans and Arcadians. His mother has sanctioned this mission by her portent of thunder and armor (*Aen.* VIII.524–36), just as she sanctioned the Underworld mission with the golden bough. Her star shines over the departing contingent, and she will greet him with an embrace near his destination. But all he knows is that he is on his way to Caere in search of allies. Again, he arrives in a region of woods and fields and streams. Here his troops encamp, and, as in Book VI, he descends after viewing the encampment from above. This landscape forms a somber contrast to the airy, light-filled regions of Elysium. It is dark and mysterious, filled with the religious awe associated with the ancient cults of prehistoric peoples. The groves are of black fir trees, the streams are cold, the hills confining. They are frequented not by the freely straying souls of the blessed (compared to bees in a summer meadow, *Aen.* VI.707–10) but by Aeneas' armed followers encamped and battle ready. As in Elysium, Aeneas receives his parent's "message" apart from the throng, *in valle reducta* (*Aen.* VIII.609).

Venus, undisguised and radiant, arrives bringing the gift of arms. Like Anchises, she sees her son in the distance, but unlike Anchises, it is *she* who approaches *him* as she greets him. Her words, again unlike Anchises' personal and impassioned welcome, as befits the solemnity of the ritual transfer of the divine arms, are few (three lines versus nine) and distant, sacramental in tone. "Behold the promised gifts accomplished by my spouse's art. So that you may not hesitate, my son, to challenge in battle either the proud people of Laurentum or Turnus" (*Aen.* VIII.612–14). Then she leans the arms against an oak tree and, without further words, she more than permits, she actually seeks (*petivit*) her son's embrace. Aeneas says nothing, apparently lost in speechless wonder, though in Book I (405–9) he can address her with articulate reproaches when she denies him her embrace, revealing her identity only as she vanishes.

In the radiant world of the blessed spirits, Anchises is a partly sorrowing figure, irrevocably barred from embracing the son who has overcome nearly insuperable forces to be reunited with him. Among the living warriors encamped in the forbidding and mysterious valley of this world, Venus appears unannounced. A visitor from another sphere, she brings her own radiance, as she joyfully sweeps her son into her arms. The strong contrasts in settings, in mood and tone, and in the initial actions of these two scenes are as striking as are their close parallels. They link the mortal and immortal parents in a complex relationship that suggests their roles are both distinct and inseparable.

In contrast to what takes place between father and son in the Underworld, communication between mother and son, except for her three-line greeting, is wordless. It consists of a mutual embrace and of the message which he receives visually in his wondering contemplation of the divine armor, particularly the shield. While each element in Anchises' message is verbally explained and made relevant for Aeneas, nothing in Venus' gift is explained. Aeneas is overcome with wonder and joy at the beauty and radiance of "the indescribable fabric" (*non enarrabile textum*) (*Aen.* VIII.625) of the shield. At the end of his eager perusal of every detail, as at the beginning, still full of wonder and joy, he remains completely uncomprehending of what the images on the shield refer to. "He marvels and rejoices at the image in ignorance of the events" (*miratur rerumque ignarus imagine gaudet*) (*Aen.* VIII.730).

After leaving his father in Elysium where he found him, Aeneas returns to this world fortified to face future ordeals with actual knowledge of great events, in which he and his posterity will participate, in the context of the cosmic cycle of deaths and rebirths—knowledge that "fires his spirit with love of renown to come" (*incenditque animum famae venientis amore*) (*Aen.* VI.889). The encounter with his mother inverts this experience. She comes to him in this world and leaves him where she found him, equipped with divine armor for the war that has already begun, inspired but without specific knowledge of the future events represented on the shield. In the last line of Book VIII, Aeneas joyfully, wonderingly, blindly, "taking on his shoulder the renown and fate of his descendants" (*attollens umero famamque et fata nepotum*) (731), assumes the burden of the Roman future (already past for Vergil's audience), as he prepares to defend the city coming into being.

The pervading imagery of Book VI draws attention to the importance of words. From the gates (*fores*) of the temple of Apollo to the gates (*portae*) of sleep through which Aeneas and the Sibyl leave Hades, Book VI throngs with images of gates, doors, mouths, thresholds, and the interior spaces to which they give access. In the capacity of mouths to engulf and devour like those of three-headed Cerberus or to produce guiding and enlightening words like those of the Sibyl that may guide a soul past the devouring dangers in Hades, these images actualize two opposing aspects of the Underworld. In keeping with the positive aspect of this imagery, after Aeneas and the Sibyl have safely passed the barred gate of Tartarus and the doors of Persephone's palace, Orpheus, poet and man of words, is the first figure they see as they approach Elysium; poets, *pii vates*, are nearby among the benefactors of humanity, and the poet Musaeus guides them to Anchises (*Aen.* VI.664–78), whose words will both fortify and inspire Aeneas and enable him to avoid or overcome the dangers he is about to encounter in Italy.

The father's words to the son, like the Sibyl's words to Aeneas, are delivered in person. His first speech (*Aen.* VI.724–51) provides a cosmic perspective for the development of Rome—an account of the relation of matter and spirit, and of the ordeals of once embodied human souls, contaminated by matter, struggling to purify themselves through many cycles of births and deaths in order to regain their pristine state as pure spirit and escape further reincarnation. It is a message of hope, but also of prolonged suffering and struggle with an uncertain outcome. Anchises' second speech (*Aen.* VI.756–853) deals more specifically and factually with the Roman future, as he points out and names descendants of Aeneas among the souls crowding around Lethe waiting to drink and be reborn, future builders of Rome whose achievements will be glorious, but like those of Aeneas himself repeatedly marred by *furor* and premature death.

The message fires the son with love of renown but also confronts him with the inescapable pains and griefs of the human condition in this world and the next, the enormous price of human achievement. It is the message of a father strengthening—perhaps I should say hardening—his son for the ordeals of manhood, and the long struggle of the human soul to regain its lost innocence. It is a message brutally brought home at the beginning of the scene by the irreversible reality that separates the living and the dead and forever bars the son from the human comfort of embracing his dead father—the message of the inexorable conditions of mortality, often reaffirmed by the events of the war in Italy in the last tetralogy. Aeneas brings back from Hades his father's words of enlightenment to guide him through the ordeals ahead, and Anchises' injunction to his descendants to practice not the arts refined by other peoples, such as sculpture, oratory, astronomy, but the specifically Roman arts (*hae tibi erunt artes:* "these will be your arts"), the art of war, and, above all, the supremely verbal art of ruling with justice (*Aen.* VI.847–53). In this section of Book VI, so directly evocative of Plato's vision of souls waiting to drink of Lethe before being reborn in his myth of Er at the end of the *Republic*, it seems legitimate to assume that Vergil, like Plato, would think of the statesman lawgiver as the supreme craftsman with words (in many parts of his work, but very explicitly in *Symp.* 208e5 to 209a1-b4 and a5-e4, Plato puts lawgivers even above poets in the sphere of human creativity).

Words, the medium of Anchises' message, prepare the reader for the ambivalent and pervasive imagery of mouths in Book VI. In Books VII and VIII, lyrical scenes of pastoral peace and harmony alternating with scenes of actual or implicit violence prepare the reader for the possibility of transcendence of violence that dominates the representations on the shield. The early inhabitants of Italy live in innocent harmony with nature in a still unspoiled landscape. But this apparently idyllic world also harbors easily triggered rage which culminates in the violence and chaos of war. The vivid depiction of these two sides of early Italian life in Books VII and VIII introduces Venus' wordless message on the shield. Vulcan, *ignipotens* (firemaster), brings them together both in his person and in the creation of the shield. He is the father of the fire-breathing underground monster, Cacus, that preyed on the early settlers at the site of Rome to be, but he is also the artist, the harnesser, and harmonizer of volcanic fires in his underground workshop. Only at the end of the description on the shield of the pacified nations does Vergil call him *Mulciber*, the soother, caresser, reconciler. Inspired by sexual love, described as flame and compared to lightning, he creates a weapon of war that depicts scenes of violence but also, as we shall see, suggests some possibility of pastoral peace and of transcendence. The creative and destructive aspects of sexual love and of volcanic fire are joined in Vulcan, the creator of the message Venus brings Aeneas.

Venus' only words when she meets her son are the brief hieratic greeting as she presents the divine arms and then leans them against a nearby tree. In contrast to the inexorable law that forbids physical contact between the living and the dead and prevents the embrace of father and son, the law which forbids physical contact between mortal and god, the source of such grief and frustration in Aeneas' encounter with Venus in Book I and with Anchises in Hades gives way as she hastens to embrace him in Book VIII. This act, as I have already suggested, acknowledges that by accepting the summons on Olympus he has begun to transcend the limits of mortality. Almost her first gesture is the intimate wordless comfort of a physical embrace that confirms the possibility, never explicitly contemplated in Anchises' message of mortality, of transcending the established order of the cosmos. The gift of arms will be of immediate practical use. Their brilliance and beauty will also inspire Aeneas and his followers and intimidate their enemies. The arms are as wordless as the embrace, and the scenes on the shield are accompanied by no explanations such as Anchises provides for the procession of his descendants. The shield is the product of one of those arts which Anchises would leave to non-Romans: *excudent alii spirantia mollius aera* (Others will hammer out the gently breathing bronze) (*Aen.* VI.847). The beauty and radiance of this non-Roman art without context is half Aeneas' legacy. It inspires him, though he knows nothing of the events it represents. He responds to the shield with serenity, confidence, trust in the face of the unknown, whereas his father's specific and intelligible words leave him both grieving at inescapable mortal anguish and keyed up and intent on entering the struggle that will lead to the glorious Roman future.

The historical events depicted on the shield, unlike those narrated by Anchises, though mainly military in character, are not infused with tragedy. They are referred to as Roman triumphs, but their fortunate outcomes are not achieved by military skill alone or by other merely human effort. They repeatedly suggest that the forces of nature or the gods or both rally to support the exertions of those who revere *pietas* against those who violate it. The miraculous deliverances of Horatius and Cloelia, and the spectacles of Tullus passing judgment on Mettus in this world and of Catiline suffering in Tartarus while Cato sits as judge in Elysium, all in their different ways exemplify this reassuring idea. The initial scene—the wolf gently suckling Romulus and Remus—has no aspect of human effort at all. It is a crowning emblem of this principle of miraculous transcendence of the laws of nature in the scenes that follow. The unbreakable natural law that separates predator from prey is transcended in the pastoral scene of the wolf tenderly cherishing the helpless offspring of her natural enemy.

In a similar way, before the *pietas* of Aeneas, the barriers that normally prevent the living from penetrating into the Underworld give way. But the barrier that stands between him and his father does not yield even for him. The shield illustrates this principle with images of critical episodes in the history of Rome in chronological order from the nurture of Romulus and Remus to the battle of Actium and the subsequent triple triumph. Its message is an appropriate prophecy for a people of whom Jupiter predicts to Juno at the end of Book XII, "You will see them [the Romans] go beyond humankind, beyond the gods in *pietas*" (*supra homines, supra ire deos pietate videbis*) (Aen. XII.839). One may imagine that though Aeneas understands nothing of the actual incidents represented on the shield, their more confident and hopeful tone, as contrasted with Anchises' message of mortal limitations, has something to do with the wonder and joy they inspire in Aeneas.

In the events of the last four books as both messages are played out, we see that they are not contradictory but complementary, that they express two distinct but inseparable aspects of one reality that both Aeneas and Rome will actualize. This reality includes both the tragic and inescapable limitations of the human condition—the brutal and gratuitous deaths of young and old, the indiscriminate havoc wreaked by *furor* on both sides—but *also* the mysterious possibility that, against all expectation, unseen forces will rally in support of the hero who commits himself completely to destiny. In a Roman future not known to Aeneas, the Sabine women will reconcile their fathers and their husbands, the geese will save the Capitol, Apollo will stand with drawn bow over the rout of the forces of darkness at Actium. In Aeneas' own immediate future, Tiber will reverse his current, timely interventions in battle will occur, a wound will be miraculously healed, a spear retrieved at the crisis of his duel with Turnus.

The encounters with father and mother mirror each other so closely and yet differ so profoundly that one feels they must be equally necessary aspects of Vergil's vision of Rome, and of the spiritual preparation of Rome's founder for the culminating ordeals of the last four books. The encounter with the father says, "Steel yourself, earn renown by learning to accept the finality of death, the limitations of mortality, the gratuitous grief and violence that are an inevitable part of great human achievement." The encounter with the mother, wordlessly, mysteriously urges, "Trust life and yourself who have become worthy of a goddess' embrace."

Chapter 7

# VERGIL'S *AENEID*
## The Final Lines
### MICHAEL C. J. PUTNAM

Cunctanti telum Aeneas fatale coruscat,
sortitus fortunam oculis, et corpore toto                              920
eminus intorquet. murali concita numquam
tormento sic saxa fremunt nec fulmine tanti
dissultant crepitus. volat atri turbinis instar
exitium dirum hasta ferens orasque recludit
loricae et clipei extremos septemplicis orbis;                        925
per medium stridens transit femur. incidit ictus
ingens ad terram duplicato poplite Turnus.
consurgunt gemitu Rutuli totusque remugit
mons circum et vocem late nemora alta remittunt.
ille humilis supplex oculos dextramque precantem                      930
protendens 'equidem merui nec deprecor' inquit;
'utere sorte tua. miseri te si qua parentis
tangere cura potest, oro (fuit et tibi talis
Anchises genitor) Dauni miserere senectae
et me, seu corpus spoliatum lumine mavis,                             935
redde meis. vicisti et victum tendere palmas
Ausonii videre; tua est Lavinia coniunx,
ulterius ne tende odiis.' stetit acer in armis
Aeneas volvens oculos dextramque repressit;
et iam iamque magis cunctantem flectere sermo                         940
coeperat, infelix umero cum apparuit alto
balteus et notis fulserunt cingula bullis
Pallantis pueri, victum quem vulnere Turnus
straverat atque umeris inimicum insigne gerebat.
ille, oculis postquam saevi monimenta doloris                         945
exuviasque hausit, furiis accensus et ira
terribilis: 'tune hinc spoliis indute meorum
eripiare mihi? Pallas te hoc vulnere, Pallas
immolat et poenam scelerato ex sanguine sumit.'
hoc dicens ferrum adverso sub pectore condit                          950
fervidus; ast illi solvuntur frigore membra
vitaque cum gemitu fugit indignata sub umbras.

(As [Turnus] hesitates Aeneas brandishes his fateful spear. He sought out fortune with his eyes and from afar twists [his spear] with his body. Never do stones hurled from a siege engine roar so loudly nor do such crashings burst from the thunderbolt. The spear flies like a black whirlwind bringing dread destruction and lays open the fringes of the corselet and the outermost circles of the sevenfold shield. Whizzing [the spear] passes through the midst of his thigh. Stricken, mighty Turnus sinks to the ground, his knees doubled under. The Rutulians rise up with a groan and the whole mountain round-about roars and the lofty groves send back the cry far and wide. He, a suppliant, with eyes humbled, and stretching forth his right hand in prayer, says "Indeed I deserved [it] nor do I pray it away. Use your lot. If any care of a sad parent can touch you, I pray you (for even such was your father Anchises), take pity on the old age of Daunus, and return me, or, if you prefer, my body despoiled of light, to my own [people]. You have conquered and the Ausonians have seen me, conquered, stretch forth my palms. Lavinia is your wife. Don't stretch your hatreds further." He stood fierce in his weaponry, Aeneas, rolling his eyes, and he held back his right hand, and now, even now [Turnus'] speech began to bend him more as he hesitates, when the unfortunate baldric appeared high on [Turnus'] shoulder and the belt of the youthful Pallas gleamed with the studs he knew, [Pallas] whom, conquered, Turnus had laid low with a wound and whose hateful sign he was wearing on his shoulders. He [Aeneas], after he had drunk in with his eyes the memorials of his savage grief and the spoils, inflamed by furies and terrible in his anger: "Are you, clothed in the plunder of my own, to be snatched from me? Pallas sacrifices you with this wound, Pallas takes punishment from your criminal blood." Saying this he buries his iron [sword] under the chest opposite him, blazing; but [Turnus'] limbs are undone with cold and his life flees, resentful, with a groan under the shades.)

I would like to survey in detail the concluding thirty-four verses of the *Aeneid*. One motive for such an appraisal lies in the fact that Vergilian criticism still harbors the view, prevalent among those who disapprove of what happens in the last lines, that the epic is unfinished and that, if Vergil had lived longer, he would have concluded with a happy ending—with the marriage of Aeneas and Lavinia, say, and with reconciliation between the terrestrial enemies. But such was not the poet's intent. Rather, he shows his hero killing in an act of anger, and he does so in some of his most polished verse. The twelfth is not only the longest book in the epic, it is also one of the richest and most multivalent. There is no question in my mind that the finale which Vergil left us is what he wanted us to have, and to ponder.

We should keep in mind some significant areas of concern as we go through this exercise. There are, for instance, the problematics of closure, especially closure vis-à-vis the epics of Homer and, in particular, the *Iliad*. We might also think about circularity versus linearity as ruling principles of the poem. Complementary to such means of structuring are reversals in the role of Aeneas, from suffering Trojan to the embodiment of Achilles at the end where in several respects he mirrors the Greek hero, who kills Hector and who listens to Priam's prayer, in *Iliad* XXII and *Iliad* XXIV. And then, of course, there is the prominence of violence throughout the poem and the connection of irrationality with the feminine, especially, and the role such fury plays in the ending. We will also confront the myth of the Danaids, the most brutal segment of which is depicted on Pallas' baldric, in discussing aspects of civil war residual at the conclusion. We should bear in mind as well the notion of ideal versus real as a major dichotomy in the poem and, conspicuously, in the last lines.[1]

*Cunctanti telum Aeneas fatale coruscat* (As [Turnus] hesitates Aeneas brandishes his fateful spear). The first word is key when considering the pattern of the last lines. We have within forty lines or so three instances of this notion of delay, of hesitation. We find Turnus here twice over in this position, for only three lines before he is also hesitating, and then we watch Aeneas doing the same at a crucial point in the lines to come. Heroes aren't supposed to hesitate. They go ahead and forthrightly follow their intent. So to begin with an act of hesitation and to have another major example occur shortly after is a careful part of the poet's design. Turnus delays before facing up to what he thinks is his immediate death or, one might guess, because the possibility might remain to postpone or even to alter his destiny. Aeneas momentarily defers action for other reasons, as we shall see.

*Cunctanti telum Aeneas fatale coruscat,* / *sortitus fortunam oculis, et corpore toto* / *eminus intorquet* (he sought out fortune with his eyes and from afar twists [his spear] with his whole body). These are wonderful lines. Aeneas stands in the middle of the first hexameter, with its initial four spondees complementing the momentary pause in action. The hero is centered between his weapon and its connection with fate, and he "shakes" (*coruscat*) the spear that brings destiny to Turnus, whose wariness opens the line. We admire how the music of *coruscat* is furthered, first, in the next line, with the sounds of "sor," "for," and "cor" running through *sortitus fortunam oculis, et corpore toto*, and then, in the subsequent two verses, with *intorquet* and *tormento*. The noise of the quivering weapon resonates throughout and sonically pulls together the continuum of narrative excitement. So also *telum* and *fatale*, the spear and the destiny it brings, are linked by assonance, as are *fatale* and *fortunam*, for kindred reasons.

Another detail to watch closely in these and in the following lines is the extraordinary amount of enjambment to which Vergil has recourse. There are few end-stopped lines. In fact, in the sweep of verses from 919 through 952 we discover fewer than a dozen where sense-pause (whether during or at the end of a sentence) and the conclusion of the hexameter line are coterminous. In the rest we are tugged along in an exciting and excitable way from one line to the next. Through concentrated use of enjambment, meaning is constantly bursting the bounds of formal metrical patterning at this, the most intense moment of the plot. The arrangement of the hexameter line suggests regularity and therefore ordered, contemporaneous completion of meaning and meter. In contrast enjambment, by postponing the reader's expectation of pleasurable fulfillment at line's end in forced anticipation, fosters a disordering, unsteadying, questioning effect which here unremittingly pits the feverish energy of ongoing narrative against the methodical delimiting effect of meter.

Let me put the observation in another, more metaphorical way. As the *Aeneid* draws to its agitated conclusion, the rigidity of end-stopped, stichic statement is more than ever challenged by the rhythmical fluidity that enjambment causes. This friction arises from no mere virtuoso display of rhetorical counterpoint on the part of the poet but from a linguistic acknowledgment that, as the epic's conflict between order and disorder comes to a head, in the plotline itself emotionality triumphs over discipline, passion over decorum. Heightened action and sharpened doing, whether physical or metaphysical, take precedence over the halts in, or conclusions to, meaning that might in turn define the abatement or even arrest of the passional proceedings.

The first climax, we notice, leads up to *intorquet*, with a halt in the middle of the line, but sense-pause and metrical incompletion are at odds. For a moment we stop, rhetorically, just as Aeneas stops dramatically, but the pressure of the hexameter, complementing the hero's plunge into action, soon urges us to read on. We focus on the word *oculis* also, at the center of line 920: *sortitus fortunam oculis, et corpore toto*. The amount of emphasis on parts of the body in these thirty lines is extraordinary. We have *oculos*, for instance, again in line 930, *oculos* in 939, and *oculis* once more in 945. Through the use of the word "eyes" we find ourselves observing the observers. And with our own inner eye we sometimes empathize with Turnus or Aeneas watching, or with the observant narrator, or with the poet creating all these contemplators. Meanwhile the notion of quivering and twisting, which we also hear as well as see, takes us from the end of line 919 to the virtual midpoint of 921, at *intorquet*.

Vergil then offers us two analogies for Aeneas' spear in flight: *murali concita numquam / tormento sic saxa fremunt nec fulmine tanti / dissultant crepitus* (Never do stones hurled from a siege engine roar so loudly nor do such crashings burst from the thunderbolt). The two lines beginning at *murali* and going down to *dissultant crepitus* are in essence unnecessary in the Latin. Vergil could have gone right on from *eminus intorquet* to the subsequent *volat atri turbinis instar* without any break in the beat of the line or any apparent loss in meaning. So we're made to examine closely these analogies that the poet offers us as Aeneas' *telum* goes on its way. The comparisons are important and form curious points of reference for the spear, ones I think we have to view with some irony. Comparing the hero's weapon to rocks hurled against city walls makes the role in which Vergil now casts Aeneas disconcerting. Why create a parallel between this spear, used in the wounding of Turnus, and an implement that destroys cities (the etymological link between *intorquet* and *tormento* reinforces the connection)? Vergil is preparing the reader here for one of his most prominent ambiguities, namely the use of *condere* in the anti-penultimate line of the poem, where the verb occurs when Aeneas finally plunges his second weapon, a sword, into the chest of Turnus (*condit*, 950). This, we recall, is the word that appears twice in the opening lines of the poem to describe the establishing of Rome. The resulting double entendre is by design. *Condere* means both to found and to bury, and there is a hint of this multivalent import in the first part of the analogy we have been discussing. To some ways of thinking, Aeneas' actions, as the poem draws to a close, hint that, metaphorically at least, he could destroy as well as establish cities.

Aeneas also takes on the role of Jupiter (*nec fulmine tanti*). With the rarest of exceptions, nobody controls the lightning bolt except the king of the gods. Such complementarity is interesting because it makes us return to the epic's preceding episode, in particular to recall the reconciliation in heaven between Jupiter and Juno and to rethink its significance for the context that follows. Some who like to see the ending in a positive light assert that, because we have been witnesses to apparently renewed harmony in heaven, we must now have concord on earth. Such an interpretation is open to doubt not least because the major concession that Juno makes in her dealings with Jupiter, were she to forgo her anger, is that the Trojans must renounce their world—the Trojan name, the Trojan mode of dress, the Trojan language—in favor of everything that is Latin. Yet this final action on Aeneas' part is perhaps the greatest single display of self-assertion in the poem. This is not a Trojan yielding his identity but one strongly responding to events in terms of his feelings and passions as his epic reaches its climactic, memorable conclusion. So we must worry about this Juno, smiling happily because she has agreed to give in to Jupiter's requests. Juno, in fact, metaphorically asserts dominion over the end of the poem, as we shall see.

In addition to analogies that suggest the destructive power of Aeneas' spear and that propose a parallel between him and Jupiter, there remains one further comparison: *volat atri turbinis instar / exitium dirum hasta ferens orasque recludit / loricae et clipei extremos septemplicis orbis* (The spear flies like a black whirlwind bringing dread destruction and lays open the fringes of the corselet and the outermost circles of the sevenfold shield). This third correlation, which anticipates the immediate return to direct narrative, likens the spear's flight to a black whirlwind. The last time that Vergil used a parallel simile in the poem was in connection with the unnamed Dira (Fury), who had not long since come down from the throne of the king of the gods to drive Juturna from the battlefield. Aeneas thus adopts not only the role of Jupiter but also the destructive, irresistible force of his servant, a force that disastrously limits Turnus' ability to function and makes the final conflict terrifyingly unequal. The last extended simile of the poem, which we find shortly before the present passage and which Vergil adapts from *Iliad* XXII, is extraordinary in its power because it is drawn from the moment that Hector is being chased by Achilles. As if in a dream (so goes the comparison of Aeneas pursuing Turnus) one person tracks another, and the first nearly catches the second, who almost, but not quite, escapes. Vergil humanizes this description in an extraordinary way. He turns third-person narrative—one man chases, one flees—into first-person. It is now we, the readers, who suffer the dream, we who follow. This is not in Homer. We are drawn deeply into a world that sympathizes with Turnus and Turnus' inability to react to his circumstances. The effect of the Dira's dramatic appearance is parallel. Vergil now challenges the reader by appropriating the same language to delineate Aeneas' spear. The conquering hero's weapon is associated with a city-destroying catapult, with omnipotent Jove's thunderbolt, and with the black whirlwind of the latter's Fury.

We marvel also at the manner in which words are deployed in line 925: *loricae et clipei extremos septemplicis orbis*. We notice, first, the iconic use of double elision to vivify the spear shearing its way through Turnus' protective armor. Then there is the a-b-a-b order of "shield," "outermost," "sevenfold," "circle." Such verbal intertwining, in grammatically alternating order, gives one a sense of the plaiting of the narrative and of its layers evolving. Vergil makes a strong point of this by playing on the Latin root *-plic*, which simply means "fold." He begins with *septemplicis* in line 925, picks it up again in the word *duplicato* (927), as Turnus' knee folds in under himself, and then in place of climax, and, most brilliantly, with *supplex* (930), because the meaning passes from concrete to abstract, from literal to metaphysical. This is the final use of *-plic*, when Turnus' sevenfold shield has yielded to his knee doubled beneath him and finally to the conquered hero's being forced into the posture of suppliant—*supplex*. Not *superbus* anymore, he is underneath, not on top, in the final illustration of this enfolding. Our eye, pursuing the poetic narrative at work in the Latin, gains enormous excitement from this interweaving of words that takes us through folding and enfolding, finally, and here I anticipate, to the picture of Turnus humbled before his vanquisher.

The next line likewise lays vivid claim to our inner vision: *per medium stridens transit femur. incidit ictus* (Whizzing [the spear] passes through the midst of his thigh. Stricken he sinks). Meter demands a momentary but chilling stay at *incidit ictus*, preceding which the poet masterfully interrupts the deployment of *medium femur* with the phrase *stridens transit*. We are forced to follow the spear going through the thigh, as *stridens transit* separate *medium* and *femur*, a phrase which receives particular stress because of the powerful sense-pause it brings two-thirds of the way through the line. We read on to complete the potential of the dactylic hexameter line, but, as in the case of *intorquet* (921), fulfillment of meaning makes us dwell on *femur*, the thigh where Aeneas has wounded Turnus. Such a halt not only emphasizes the urgency of the Latin but also asks us to linger on the site of the hero's injury before the line is finished and to contemplate as well the crucial difference between what occurs here and what happens in *Iliad* XXII. We remember that Hector, though wounded in the throat, yet manages to utter one final speech to his slayer. Nevertheless he is fatally hurt, whereas Turnus is not. This difference is vital for understanding Vergil's narrative as it builds to a climax.

Then we have the extraordinary arrangement of words in lines 926 and 927 that shows Turnus in spatial terms—Turnus laid out in front of us by means of the dimensionality of language: *incidit ictus / ingens ad terram duplicato poplite Turnus* (Stricken, mighty Turnus sinks to the ground, his knees doubled under). Vergil is astonishingly adept at deploying words on the page to recreate for the reader his narrative's portrayal of physical action. The ending of line 926 and its enjambment is especially telling: *incidit ictus / ingens*. We have assonance and alliteration that begin in one line, jump to the next, and then move our ear and eye from *ingens* to *Turnus*, words which surround the line but also coopt the preceding hexameter. Such figuration helps bring into strong focus the picture of Turnus himself, now overwhelmed before his victor. So even after the stress on *femur* from the sense-pause, and even though meter, too, would urge a further stop after *incidit ictus*, nevertheless Vergil carefully keeps the momentum going. We are taken into this highly particularized world of Turnus and his chastened posture, as he is literally and metaphysically "humbled" by being pressed toward the ground.

The next two lines, of which the second is end-stopped, could, like 921–23, also have been omitted from the narrative. But, not unexpectedly, they serve an extraordinary, powerful purpose as well: *consurgunt gemitu Rutuli totusque remugit / mons circum et vocem late nemora alta remittunt* (The Rutulians rise up with a groan and the whole mountain round-about roars and the lofty groves send back the cry far and wide). The first line here is wonderful because it takes the sounds in the name of Turnus—"u," "ur," and "us"—from the preceding verse and spreads them over the subsequent hexameter. *Consurgunt gemitu Rutuli totusque remugit:* we linger on the many "u"s and "tu"s, as if the hero's death were now permeating his world at large. And we hear the "m" sounds as well, which begin with *gemitu* and *remugit* (the latter a near anagram of the former) and which hold together the subsequent line: *mons circum et vocem late nemora alta remittunt.* Sound effects mimic at once both bellowing and its reverberation while sonically supporting the pathetic fallacy as nature, too, responds to Turnus' fall.

Again we observe the way in which Vergil makes us aware of space through words. We sense the lofty groves, but we also cast our eyes far and wide, absorbing both the horizontal and the vertical dimensions. For a brief moment we enter a grand, all-embracing expanse which abstracts us from the immediate presence of Turnus laid out before us and into the thoughts of those beholding the drama as it unfolds. The purpose of this extension of the eye outward is manifold, but one of its primary reasons is to help us visualize the relationship between Turnus' wounding and his people's dependence upon him. The theatricality of the occasion is important, too. The event is made highly visual, and Vergil wants to have us deliberate on its meaning by enlarging our sight to absorb the whole incident, and to imagine how it affects its larger surroundings in a public fashion.

The very openness of the event is worth further consideration. For years it was fashionable in criticism to equate the public aspects of the *Aeneid* with the glory of Rome and Augustus to come, and to connect its private side with personal suffering and hurt, with the individual losses that somehow generated the collective, cumulative gain of Roman grandeur. The duel we now join the Rutulians, and implicitly the Trojans, in witnessing may bring some future splendor in its wake, but it is not mentioned in Vergil's text. What we, and the onlookers within the epic story, can attest to is the centrality of vengeance both to the final lines of Vergil's poem and to the monumentality of Augustan art. Revenge figures prominently as a motif in the events portrayed on the doors of the emperor's temple to Apollo and in the very title of the shrine central to his forum dedicated, some years after Vergil's death, to Mars Ultor (Mars the Avenger).

*Ille humilis supplex oculos dextramque precantem / protendens 'equidem merui nec deprecor'* inquit (He, a suppliant, with eyes humbled, and stretching forth his right hand in prayer, says "Indeed I deserved [it] nor do I pray it away"). We've examined the word *supplex* before and how through it we move from literal to figurative. It is important, as the context continues to unfold, to remember always Turnus' posture as someone lower and underneath, with Aeneas looming over him. *Humilis*, as we saw, plays on this positioning, with its etymological punning on *humus*, on the "ground," toward which the victim has been lowered. So the role of suppliant and the notion of being humiliated gain both literal and symbolic aspects from the language. "And stretching forth his right hand in prayer": again notice the powerful enjambment of *protendens*, especially following *precantem*. We go from humbled eyes to praying hand and then, with a suddenness unwonted in Vergil, to a second use of *precor*, now as a compound in the beginning of Turnus' speech. "I don't pray this from me," says Turnus. "I don't attempt to imagine away the position into which fate has put me, but I still stretch forth my hands in entreaty." So there are two modes of imploring at work here—one negative, the other positive.

'Utere sorte tua. miseri te si qua parentis / tangere cura potest, oro (fuit et tibi talis / Anchises genitor) Dauni miserere senectae / et me, seu corpus spoliatum lumine mavis, / redde meis' ("Use your lot. If any care of a sad parent can touch you, I pray you (for even such was your father, Anchises), take pity on the old age of Daunus, and return me, or, if you prefer, my body despoiled of light, to my own [people]"). The verb *tangere* is splendidly brought in here. We have been getting closer and closer to a moment of touching, with Turnus' hands spread out before his conqueror. But the result which Turnus wants is something spiritual, something that the victorious hero might grasp in his mind, both complementary and running counter to immediate action. Again we observe the power of enjambment, with its stress given here to *redde meis*: "me . . . give back to my people." Turnus' request is particularly telling because it is novel and unexpected, and the elliptical rhetoric helps again to keep the reader (and presumably Aeneas, too) on edge.

The general vocabulary here is intriguing because Vergil has recourse to similar words when Aeneas begs for mercy from the Sibyl in Book VI so as to gain access to the Underworld and to see his father. A Roman reader would certainly hear the resonances. It is crucial, as we ponder the ethics of Aeneas' behavior at this moment, to have Anchises brought directly before us. The last time we saw him was in the Underworld, and, though his final words, fine and moving as they are, deal with the funeral of Marcellus, the last line of his long disquisition on future Roman luminaries and on Roman artistry is one which we are meant to reflect on again here as a touchstone through which to test Aeneas. "Remember, Roman," says Anchises to his son, "to spare those who have been made subject and to war down the proud" (*parcere subiectis et debellare superbos*) (*Aen.* VI.853). His words remain before us at this, the pivotal ethical moment of the poem. Through them, father assays son and, with him, all future Romans. In these same words, as we hear them in our ear, from *subiectis* to *superbos*, we have reiterated the high and the low, the person beneath and the person above, the one in the posture of pride, the other who is beaten down, with the humbled hero, according to Anchises, being the one who should (now) be spared.

At this moment we also confront an extraordinary difference in ethics between the *Iliad* and the *Aeneid*. In the *Iliad* a hero could spare or not spare. Once, near the beginning of Book VI in Homer's epic, as Odysseus contemplates letting a foe go uninjured, Agamemnon urges against such a course of action. No Trojan, he shouts, should fail to perish, not even one in the womb of his mother. So in the *Iliad*, sparing is possible but its implementation depends on the whimsy of the winning hero. Anchises, by contrast, lays down a more universal, morally demanding rule, which we ponder in the *Aeneid*'s last books. Its presence is felt climactically here, especially with the direct mention of the father's name and with the implicit *pietas* such specificity should arouse in the son. There is no question that Aeneas is in the position of having beaten down the proud. Turnus is in fact called *superbus* at a critical moment in Book X after he has killed Pallas and taken his sword belt. The killing of Pallas is not what is wrong, according to the narrator. Rather it is Turnus' donning of his victim's baldric, which is seen as an overweening gesture and not just part of an ordinary victory on the battlefield. So from several points of view Turnus is now in the position of having been humbled. And what about Aeneas in his role as victor? Notice that he is given a choice: "return me or, if you prefer, my body despoiled of light." There is no question, at least in Turnus' eyes, that there is a possibility of his being spared.

One other aspect of Turnus' words deserves our consideration here. Though his hesitation tantalizes the reader with the possibility that Aeneas might practice *clementia*, the abstraction itself is never mentioned by either speakers or narrator. The virtue to which Turnus directly refers is *misericordia*: he asks pity, not leniency, of his conquering foe (clemency is not an immediate part of the moral dialectic here, and in any case would have been feasible only as a gesture emanating from within Aeneas' psyche). Even the response which Turnus craves from his assailant is in fact deflected. The defeated hero does not seek to summon pity for himself from his victorious opponent. Instead he asks it for his father, and Vergil puts the request powerfully before the reader by personifying Daunus' old age (*senectus*).

It is not so much in his capacity as father that, according to Turnus, Daunus merits pity, though the humiliation or death of a child before their eyes would have been a standard perversity for parents to suffer. It is the father's elderliness that is here featured in the son's words. Neither vanquished son nor distant father per se deserves pity, if we follow Turnus' suggestive words, which is rather owed to the latter's old age with its implicit aura of melancholy at the passage of time and of helplessness. But, whatever its particular focus, the presumption of Turnus' logic here is that Aeneas' sympathy for Daunus, especially given his analogy with Anchises, might initiate an act of *clementia* toward his defeated son or at the least rouse in him the realization that he faces forthwith a dramatic ethical choice.

'Vicisti et victum tendere palmas / Ausonii videre' ("You have conquered and the Ausonians have seen me, conquered, stretch forth my palms"). The double emphasis on Aeneas as victor—active on his part, passive on Turnus'—is brilliantly accompanied by the phrase *tendere palmas*. The words continue the graphic quality of *dextram precantem* but now call special attention to the physical quality of the hands themselves, raised in a gesture of prayer.

And then, finally: 'tua est Lavinia coniunx, / ulterius ne tende odiis' ("Lavinia is your wife. Don't stretch your hatreds further"). Turnus' last word is *odiis*. It also ends a segment of sense in the middle of the line. We are forced to dwell on it and then continue on, but the pause and the sentiments it engenders are especially dynamic here. Cicero defines *odium* (hatred) as *ira inveterata*, anger that is constant and continuous (it is not coincidental that Vergil pluralizes the noun). Hatred is a vice that Vergil associates more closely with Juno and her minions than with any other characters in his epic. Turnus prays to Aeneas that he not continue to cherish a mind-set that the goddess, whose loathing of the Trojans is one of the poem's initial generating principles, seems to have renounced in the epic's preceding episode. We have to ask ourselves whether the narrator partakes in the emotionality of this request and whether we as readers should share in it as well. At the least, our empathy for the suppliant Turnus not only urges an equation, which the subsequent lines support, between Aeneas and Juno but also suggests that the victorious hero now has the opportunity to repudiate any putative similarity.

What happens next is extraordinary: *stetit acer in armis / Aeneas volvens oculos dextramque repressit* ("He stood fierce in his weaponry, Aeneas, rolling his eyes, and he held back his right hand"). Once more, enjambment, enhanced by the alliterative sequence from *acer* to *armis* to *Aeneas*, adds its special stress, here on Aeneas himself and on the fact that he remains motionless. Moreover, for characters in the *Aeneid*, rolling the eyes occurs only at moments of debate, not of assurance. We witness Dido, in Book IV, behaving in similar fashion as she deliberates whether to kill Aeneas. Should she attack his forces and burn his ships? In Book VII Latinus rolls his eyes when pondering the reception of the Trojans as allies, with all the consequences of such a decision. If a Vergilian character has made up his mind, he exhibits *fixos oculos*. We will remember, from Book I, the scene in the murals of Dido's temple to Juno where Athena is asked for help by the Trojan women and proffers in response *fixos oculos*, a signal that she intends to offer them no aid. Hence at the poem's end Vergil leads us to believe, at least for a moment, that several responses to Turnus' supplication are available to Aeneas as he ponders his course of action.

This deliberately unsettled situation raises a major concern for all readers of the poem. If any villainy on Turnus' part were foremost in Aeneas' mind, we would expect him to slay his vanquished opponent forthwith while proclaiming the justice of the deed. Now is Aeneas' opportunity for response: "you shouldn't be spared; you broke the treaty; you don't deserve to continue living, much less to have Lavinia offered to you in marriage." But Aeneas does not so react. He hesitates. And at this moment, when you expect Aeneas or the narrator of his tale to come forward with reasons that Turnus should be killed, Vergil doesn't seize the occasion but teases his reader by failing to suggest what might happen next. For the moment, Aeneas' hesitation is accompanied by a lack of physical response as he "held back his right hand" (*dextramque repressit*). Again the reader looks at eyes and hands, now turning from Turnus' humbled eyes and hands stretched forth in prayer to the unsure eyes of Aeneas and his right hand, hindered from its use in force at the most critical ethical juncture in the poem.

*Et iam iamque magis cunctantem flectere sermo / coeperat* ("and now, even now [Turnus'] speech began to bend him more as he hesitates"). Again we have an enjambed verse, and the figuration forces the reading eye (and the ear attentive to the rhythm of the hexameter) to plunge forward from one line to the next. Again Vergil doesn't want us to stop at the line's end but moves us inexorably ahead. The pause at *coeperat* is particularly impressive, as Vergil's handling of words mimics the indecision of his hero. And, at this culminating moment, it is well to remind ourselves about the hesitations throughout the poem, which come to a climax here. Dido hesitates in her *thalamo*, her marriage chamber, before leaving with Aeneas on the hunt, with all the resulting consequences. The helmsman Palinurus hesitates before his fatal plunge. The golden bough hesitates, even though we are told by the Sibyl that it will be plucked easily (*facilis*) or not at all. Aeneas will either break it off immediately, or else never. Why does it hesitate? What gives it this personified power? What does its momentary nonaction tell us of Aeneas' mission? What does its hesitation reveal of the way we are supposed to "read" the bough? As something both positive and negative, or merely grudging? At the end of Book VI, the last person on Anchises' list of heroes is also someone who hesitates, Fabius Maximus Cunctator, the delayer, who saves by nonaction. And, finally, Vulcan hesitates before he makes Aeneas' arms. Why? Again we must ponder Vergil's intellectual designs. Is there really a need for the god to hesitate? What is wrong with making splendid, indestructible weaponry for a half-immortal hero who is in the process of founding Rome? Why, at the moment when Venus seduces her husband into making the arms, does Vergil have the goddess laugh at her *doli*, the wiles that she had to exert over her husband, the fire-god? Vergil uses the same language there that he does of the wooden horse and of Sinon in Book II, an alliterative combination of gift and guile, *dona* and *doli*. Through Vulcan's delay he thus calls in question, as he does so often throughout the poem, the absolute certainty and authority of a gesture symbolically connected with future Roman grandeur. Aeneas' is the final hesitation, at an extraordinary moment of complex balance as the poem comes to an end.

*Flectere sermo*, "[Turnus'] speech [began] to bend him." How often we have observed the same scenario in the poem when, for a moment at least, words appear to triumph over deeds. We find it in the poem's first simile where Neptune is compared to a man "heavy with piety" (*pietate gravem*), and the winds, irrational and animalized through the metaphor of horses, are likened to an angry mob which the god bends with words. In Book VII Latinus tries to behave in similar fashion against the passions of Amata, Turnus, and the Latins but he doesn't succeed. So, here in Book XII, as last resort, we have one final exemplar of another motif that runs through the poem, reaching a climax at the end. Will *sermo* work? Will the possible remembrance of his father's dictum "to spare the subjected and beat down the proud" triumph in Aeneas' thoughts? What arguments carry weight with Aeneas as he ponders his reaction to Turnus' plea? The alternatives are the reader's to weigh as well.

Aeneas stands in contemplation *infelix umero cum apparuit alto* / *balteus et notis fulserunt cingula bullis* / *Pallantis pueri* ("when the unfortunate baldric appeared high on [Turnus'] shoulder and the belt of the youthful Pallas gleamed with the studs [Aeneas] knew"). We should read these lines out loud to observe the extraordinary way in which sound and sense go together. We have *balteus* and *bullis* framing their hexameter and therefore "outlining" the belt rhetorically just as we saw *ingens* . . . *Turnus* display the wounded hero "extended" toward the ground. But this progress begins in the preceding line: *umero* . . . *apparuit alto* / *balteus*. Assonance (*alto* / *balteus*) reinforces the height of the sword belt on the shoulder of Turnus as he kneels. Our eye follows that of Aeneas, moving from Turnus' pleading hands to the baldric attached to his body, just as our thoughts, and presumably his, turn from suppliant hero to Pallas, the young warrior Turnus had previously killed. Assonance and alliteration likewise mark the continuum from *alto* / *balteus* . . . *bullis* to *Pallantis*. So it is that Pallas, protégé of Aeneas and victim of Turnus, and his sword belt, associated closely with Turnus' pride, become the special focus in this interpenetration of words. And *apparuit* ("it appeared") is as surprising a word as the image of which it tells. The belt had been on Turnus' shoulder all the time, as any reader of Book X would well know, but only now does Aeneas notice it and only now does Vergil directly recall it to our memory. Aeneas suddenly sees the piece of armor as if it were the apparition of a *monstrum*, and he, and we, are pressed to react accordingly. How are we supposed to read this magic sign with its spectral flash, which Turnus was wearing on his shoulders, an *inimicum insigne*, a piece of insignia belonging to Turnus' enemy who was Aeneas' friend?

We must pause here for a moment to remember the Danaids, the daughters of Danaus, whose murder of their husbands on their wedding night, as engraved on the baldric, Vergil describes in a two-line *ekphrasis* in Book X. This is one of the rare instances where the poet makes a reference to Greek tragedy that is both direct and pointed, not least because the myth was much in the air through its highly visible manifestation in a major Augustan artistic monument. The emperor built a portico next to the temple of Apollo (dedicated in October of 28 BCE), which contained statues of the daughters of Danaus poised to kill their husbands. Their posture does not, as has been suggested, signify repentance. They were not imagined by Augustus' artisans, as they often were in Roman literature and art, in the Underworld, carrying leaky water jugs as emblematic punishment for their misdeeds. Rather, according to all the literary evidence, they were shown actually about to slay their spouses. In choosing poetically to depict the murderous women as Augustus does in his sculpture, Vergil enters into a dialogue with his great friend and contemporary poet, Horace. The lyricist has a splendid ode dedicated to Hypermestra, to the one Danaid who spares her husband, in which he also uses much of the vocabulary which Vergil gives to Anchises for his definition of *clementia* quoted earlier. For the epic poet, however, revenge is what the Danaids emblematize. Moreover, the two groups of husbands and wives were each offspring of brothers; therefore, it was their cousins the women murdered. Their action, then, serves as a prototype for civil war. *Clementia* comes strongly into the Horatian ode and remains much in our mind, too, as we ponder the meaning of the sword belt, first in Book X and now at the epic's end. For Vergil, as for Augustus in the statuary of his portico, the Danaids, with one exception, personify vengeance. But the myth's tension between treacherous, quasi-fratricidal killing and the possibility of sparing is meant to remain with us as, along with Aeneas, we contemplate the meanings of Pallas' baldric for the last time.

It is also essential to remember that the story of the Danaids was the subject of a trilogy by Aeschylus. Luckily we have the first part, the *Supplices*, but we remain in ignorance of the full plotline of the following two plays. At some point, either on stage or off, the Danaids dispatched their husbands. We do, however, have words of Aphrodite preserved from the final segment of the trilogy, which preach the importance of marriage and reconciliation. Vergil, throughout his epic, when he makes explicit references to tragedy, is careful never to give his reader any Aeschylean resolution. He never shows us, as does the author of the *Oresteia*, the metamorphosis of *Furiae* into *Eumenides*. He compares Dido, during her madness in Book IV, to the frenzied Orestes of the *Choephoroi* with no changed Furies in the offing. In another one of his brief *ekphrases*, this time toward the end of Book VII, we watch Io, on the armor of Turnus and therefore implicitly connected with Turnus himself, being turned into an animal but not back into human form. Again, as at the end of the poem, there is no positive resolution. In sum, we are meant to think of several aspects of the Danaid myth. One is the presence, or lack, of clemency. Another is the fact that Vergil gives us no reversal of tragic inexorability. We end with a physical act of violence with no hint of redemption. Such is what Aeneas sees, and such is his reaction to the sight.

The alliterative connection between *Pallantis* and *pueri* that begins line 943 is also pointed. Pallas is purposefully apostrophized as *puer* twice before in the epic—by his father in Book VIII, as he departs for battle, and by Aeneas, as he lies on his bier, in Book XI. Here the word "boy" has special force in contrast to the old age of Daunus and, implicitly, of Anchises, to whom Turnus had called attention in his preceding speech. And if mention of Anchises reprojects the high moral tone which Aeneas' father had assumed in Book VI, allusion to Pallas and his youth brings forward once again the beauty and the strong responses to it that were his in life (he is compared to Venus' star in Book VIII) and in death (the narrator is at pains in Book XI to present Aeneas gazing on his corpse—snow-white, like the once living youth himself, in its radiance with smooth chest).

Hence if reference to Anchises suggests patriarchal control of man's passional side, mention of Pallas here brings with it the emotionality that he had constantly aroused in others. We have seen it detailed in the two episodes which contain the apostrophes noted above: in Evander's agitated farewell to his only child in the eighth book and in Book XI, in the preparations for the youth's funeral, whose elaborate detail is unparalleled elsewhere in the poem and highlighted by Aeneas' affective response to the death. The pathology of eroticism reaches its climactic moment five lines later as Aeneas, in the heat of his rage, reiterates the name "Pallas" as would-be killer of Turnus, with Aeneas himself claiming only to stand as his surrogate, the mere instrument of Pallas' vendetta.

The word *bullis* (studs) in line 942 stands out because of its infrequency in Vergil's lexicon. It appears elsewhere in the poet's corpus (along with one of only two other instances of the word *cingula*) only at *Aen.* IX.359–60, where the poet uses the phrase *aurea bullis / cingula* (a belt golden with studs) to describe a baldric which Euryalus, in his pursuit of spoils, snatches from the body of Rhamnes, whom his lover Nisus has just slain. "He fits it," Vergil continues, "in vain to his brave shoulders" (*atque umeris nequiquam fortibus aptat*) (364). Turnus, at the epic's end, echoes the Homeric paradigms of Patroclus and Hector, each slain in the armor of Achilles, which was given by the latter to his companion and snatched from Patroclus' corpse by Hector. But he also replays the part of Euryalus, a youth wearing the armor of another youth and dying as partial consequence. The parallel with the events of Book IX also implies a more immediate eroticism in the *Aeneid*'s finale than anything Vergil found directly in his Homeric model.

In this regard I should make one further comment on the participle *notis* (942), which, together with *bullis*, absorbs Vergil's readers into the processes of Aeneas' thinking and readies us for his reaction to the vision which has suddenly come his way. Here, too, the poet guides us to an appreciation by means of self-allusion. I mentioned earlier Vulcan's hesitation (*cunctantem*) (VIII.388) before making weaponry for Aeneas, a hesitation overcome only by Venus' wily sexuality. In Book VIII it is "the well-known warmth" (*notus calor*) (VIII.389–90) the goddess of love arouses in her husband that overcomes his reluctance and brings to fruition both his desire and hers. At the conclusion of the epic it is likewise something "known," now palpable, with which the eye alerts the mind, that impels Aeneas to seek revenge after his moment of delay (*cunctantem*) (940). The parallelism once again underscores the eroticism implicit in the hero's final deed. On this last occasion in the epic where hesitation anticipates action, Aeneas in his thinking brings Pallas momentarily alive by claiming to become his replacement. But his declaration only thinly masks the emotion behind the intensity of his response as tangible merges with irretrievable and the immediately evidential conjures up the dead.

*Ille, oculis postquam saevi monimenta doloris | exuviasque hausit, furiis accensus et ira | terribilis* (He [Aeneas], after he had drunk in with his eyes the memorials of his savage grief and the spoils, inflamed by furies and terrible in his anger). The words *saevi . . . doloris* are carefully echoed from the opening of the poem where the *saevi dolores* (*Aen.* I.25) of Juno receive pride of place, while the word *ira* is also associated three times with her during the epic's first twenty-five lines. So Vergil is purposefully not pushing us into a glorious Roman future, but, in one way of reading these lines, taking us back in circular fashion to the poem's beginning once more, now applying words such as *saevitia*, *dolor*, and *ira*, which he associates with Juno at the start, to Aeneas himself. The resulting parallelism forms a major part of his final message.

The word *monimenta* is also salient. *Moneo* constitutes the active use of *meminisse* (to remember). Its force here is to bring something to mind, to reactivate the memory through *monimenta*. It, too, retrojects us again to the beginning of the poem, where memory also plays a vital role. We hear of it three times at the poem's start. Vergil twice refers to the remembering wrath of Juno, and in between we have his own prayer, *musa mihi causas memora* (*Aen.* I.8: bring to my mind, O Muse, the reasons). Any close reader of the language of the opening lines of the epic is caught watching the poet in his desire for the ability to recollect, being complemented strongly by Juno's active memory. It is Juno's rage that sets the plot of the poem in motion, with the storm scene and its aftermath. It is her mindful wrath that is symbiotic with the poet's prayer to the muses to remember, to recall. Both motivate each other. And these *monimenta* at the end, of Pallas and of the Danaids, are closely connected with Juno's *ira* and *saevus dolor*. The link, by summoning us back to the weighty acts of memory which initiate it, brings the epic full circle. We also have another vivid enjambment, tugging *ira* and *terribilis* together, the anger of Aeneas with the terror it produces both within and without the story, for Turnus and for the reader.

'*Tune hinc spoliis indute meorum / eripiare mihi?*' ("Are you, clothed in the plunder of my own, to be snatched from me?"). The implications of the phraseology are not fully patent and are perhaps not meant to be. What does angry Aeneas mean by *eripiare*? Who is doing the snatching? What is going on in Aeneas' mind as he, and we, contemplate the situation before him? The answers are unclear. If we accept the suggestion that we are meant to remember Anchises and his exhortation of clemency toward a fallen foe as well as the notion that words can, on occasion and in the hands of the wise, take precedence over deeds, then all such ideas can be seen as potential agents for snatching Turnus' body away before it is made lifeless. My suspicion is that here, too, the possibility of practicing *clementia*, of sparing the humbled foe, lurks in the background, and that Aeneas, in his fury, can have none of it. For the vengeance-driven hero, in his wildness, sparing seems an act of violence.

The language from *exuvias* to *indute* is also echoed from *Aen.* II.275, where Hector, after besting Patroclus, is portrayed by Aeneas as "clothed in the spoils of Achilles" (*exuvias indutus Achilli*). The parallelism in language reinforces for one last time the complementarity of Turnus and the Trojan hero and, therefore, implicitly of Aeneas and the Greek Achilles, each seeking retribution for loss.

Aeneas' thoughts, as the anadiplosis emphasizes, rest with Pallas and with revenge: '*Pallas te hoc vulnere, Pallas / immolat et poenam scelerato ex sanguine sumit*' ("Pallas sacrifices you with this wound, Pallas takes punishment from your criminal blood"). One of the key words here is *immolat*. It is used three times in the poem—twice elsewhere of Aeneas in Book X when he goes on the rampage after the death of Pallas. He first takes eight living warriors to serve as human sacrifice.

(We never actually see them killed, as we do in the parallel moment in the *Iliad*, and they are mentioned again in Book XI. But the implications of *immolat* are clear enough.) He then kills the priest, Haemonides, and in describing that deed the narrator also utilizes the word *immolat*, again with the connotation that we are witnessing a human sacrifice. Turnus is Aeneas' final blood offering to Pallas. If we choose to interpret this action positively, the dead hero becomes a kind of scapegoat, the victim who has to be sacrificed and killed so that order can be reestablished and so that a new, rational dispensation can be achieved to act as model for the Roman future. Such a view is supported by René Girard's conception of the scapegoat whose elimination purges the community of evil. Vergil's text, however, lends such a view little support. We certainly cannot find in Turnus a victim who willingly offers his life for the betterment of his world. Nor is Turnus a version of the animal sacrifice which earlier in the book had been offered as the short-lived treaty was put into place by king Latinus and Aeneas. Rather, his role as human offering complements Aeneas' now unpatriarchal savagery. Vergil concentrates on Turnus at prayer and on Aeneas in a final bout of anger, suffering from *saevus dolor*, not on larger social concerns such as are operative, for example, at the end of *Oedipus Rex* where society is given the chance to be relieved of the evils that the newly punished, soon to be exiled, tragic protagonist had brought to it and to suffer renewal. If such implications lurk in Aeneas' ultimate words, they are deeply hidden.

*Hoc dicens ferrum adverso sub pectore condit / fervidus* (Saying this he buries his iron [sword] under the chest opposite him, blazing). *Fervidus* completes the final enjambment of the poem. Its force is even more salient than that allotted *terribilis* three lines earlier, in that it draws attention to the last adjective allotted Aeneas in his epic. He is terrifying in his wrath before he kills Turnus and still seething after he accomplishes the deed.

I have already mentioned the irony of the word *condit* and its connection with the beginning of the poem. I would like also to show how Vergil plays further with *fervidus* as the epic's penultimate line continues on: *ast illi solvuntur frigore membra* (But [Turnus'] limbs are undone with cold). Aeneas is boiling with rage as Turnus suffers death's chill. Images of hot and cold distinguish the conqueror from the conquered, the killer from the killed, and life from death. Once more, any reader of the poem who has been following the Latin carefully will think back to the early part of the epic's first book and remember that this very phrase, *solvuntur frigore membra*, is used of Aeneas when he is suffering the horror of Juno's storm and his limbs are undone with cold. So we come full circle, once more, in the language. We return not only to Juno in the beginning of the first book, but to Aeneas himself at his epic's start—to the suffering Trojan, the passive hero, the person that T. S. Eliot admires so much as the proto-Christian, uncomplaining endurer of fate, the embodiment of *pietas* who bears his father on his shoulders and leads his young son out of burning Troy. It is he who now, at the end, becomes Juno the victimizer, embodiment of a spiritual wildness now made visible in the hero's fervid act of killing. And in switching his final representation away from Aeneas to Turnus Vergil for one last time complicates his text and asks us to meditate on why he chooses the victim, not the victor, for his last words.

The epic's final line—*vitaque cum gemitu fugit indignata sub umbras* (and his life flees, resentful, with a groan under the shades)—is repeated from Book XI, where the death in question is that of the warrior-maiden Camilla. So once more we are propelled not so much out into a grand future as back toward a world of repetitions, a world which has revealed to us an Aeneas transformed from suffering Trojan into brutal, raging actor.

The predominant analogy (through his allusions to Homer) that Vergil applies to Aeneas—from the middle of Book X up to this point—is that of Achilles as conquering Greek hero, not passive Trojan wanderer. There are abundant, careful allusions to this psychological change, beginning with Aeneas' rampage after Turnus has killed Pallas. Also, we have Turnus twice over associated with figures in the *Iliad* who are at Achilles' mercy, first Hector and then Priam, pleading for Hector's body. Thus Aeneas also, in these concluding lines, doubly adopts the part of Achilles. But instead of any whole or partial reconciliation, such as Homer offers us in *Iliad* XXIV—with the old man and the killer of his son eating together and with the ransom accepted—we have no intimations of harmony as the poem concludes. The *Iliad* comes to an end with the funeral games for Hector—not necessarily a happy event but at least a way of pulling society together. Or, remember the end of the *Odyssey* where Odysseus wants to go on a further rampage of killing and Athena and Zeus instead insist that he seek reconciliation and bring a halt to violence. There is no attempt at harmony here. We are taken full circle back to Juno, back to the death of Camilla, and, by the very act of repetition, we are made to dwell not on a golden future but on the fact that the past reiterates itself. There is nothing simple or reassuring about the vision with which Vergil leaves us—either of Aeneas or consequently of Rome—as his epic comes to an end.

Chapter 8

# THE END OF THE *AENEID*

ROSANNA WARREN

In the last lines of the *Aeneid*, a vast chord is swelling. Almost every word has some complex harmonic relation to the preceding twelve books. I want to look at one word in particular—*immolat*—as it appears in line 949: '*Pallas te hoc vulnere, Pallas / immolat et poenam scelerato ex sanguine sumit*' ("Pallas sacrifices you with this wound, and Pallas demands payment with your criminal blood"). In turn, *immolat*—from the verb "to sacrifice"—draws into its magnetic field a sequence of earlier scenes and variations, and exerts its own pressure on the triumphant and civilizing goals of the Roman race as announced in the prophecies of Jupiter in Book I and of Anchises in Book VI.

I think most readers agree that the conclusion of the *Aeneid* is shocking. The shock derives partly from narrative pace. In effects imitated, and transformed, from *Iliad* XXII, the long delayed duel of the two heroes plays itself out in agonizing detail: Turnus' sword shattering in his hand, a circular chase of figurative hound and stag, weapons lost and restored to each combatant, and a time-out

This chapter was originally presented as a paper at the colloquium *After Grief and Reason: Poets and Critics Read Vergil* at the University of Georgia in March 1995. At the time, I was unaware of T. P. Wiseman's superb book, *Remus*, which had appeared in 1995 from Cambridge University Press. Whereas the figure of Remus, for me, remained a literary and mythological intuition, Wiseman integrated a full array of Roman source material with archaeological and historical evidence to produce a richly suggestive and (to my mind) convincing explanation of Remus. For him, Remus personifies distinct political and religious forces in distinct periods of Roman history. His argument is too complex to be summarized easily, but to put it in the simplest terms, Wiseman associates the mythological twins with the struggles of plebeian-patrician power-sharing in the fourth century BCE, and in pointing to an unusual grave beneath the altar of the Temple of Victory on the Palatine he associates Remus with a specific if obscurely attested instance of human sacrifice to ward off the threat from Samnites, Etruscans, and Gauls in 496 BCE. Wiseman traces the vagaries of the later Romulus and Remus myth as political iconography through vicissitudes in the reign of Augustus: in the earlier years Remus was celebrated in association with Augustus' colleague Agrippa, and was later suppressed after the death of Agrippa and the murder of Agrippa Postumus, the rival heir with Tiberius. Wiseman's book is a model of erudition dynamically organized in the service of argument; it would seem to command the field in any further investigation of Romulus and Remus.

on Mt. Olympus where Jupiter and Juno come to terms and determine Turnus' fate. By the time the scene shifts back to the battlefield, the winged fiend has driven Juturna from her brother Turnus' side, and the Rutulian hero faces his death alone. And now the poem grinds massively into slow motion. The nightmare of immobility, transferred from Achilles' pursuit of Hector around the walls of Troy, here freezes Turnus as he tries to hurl the boulder, which is not any old stone, but by a sad irony a boundary stone set to prevent quarrels over property. He cannot complete the throw, and, most eerily, this huge and powerful man does not "know himself": *sed neque currentem se nec cognoscit euntem / tollentemve manu saxumve immane moventem* (*Aen.* XII. 903–4: But he did not recognize himself running nor going nor lifting with his hand nor moving the huge stone). The drag of spondees in these lines, the hallucinatory piling up of ineffectual participles, and the gluing alliteration of N's and M's all suggest that Turnus' paralysis has impeded the verse itself. That undertow of delay gathers force in the simile of the dream which follows the boulder sequence, in Turnus' strange inward and outward vision as he stands in a trance facing Aeneas' spearcast, and in the repetition of the verb *cuncti*, "to hesitate." Aeneas seems to throw in slow motion; the spear takes eight lines to leave his hand and pierce Turnus' thigh. Even Death hesitates in this scene, and that hesitation, as Aeneas stands (*cunctantem*) over the wounded Turnus and "represses" his own sword arm, seems to hold in balance all the mighty values of justice, clemency, and *pietas* the poem has celebrated. When the scales tip in favor of *ira*, rage, the poem goes into fast-forward: three lines for Aeneas' infuriated speech, three lines for him to plunge his sword into Turnus' chest and for that abused spirit to flee to the Underworld. End of poem.

The shock of shifting velocities in this scene, the lurch from almost frozen motion to savage swiftness, recapitulates the suddenness and shock of an actual death. Nor is there an aftermath. Here is Turnus, whom we have known and followed since Book VII, whose courage, fears, desires, and delusions we have intimately observed, who was just now breathing and speaking—gone. More shockingly, his "going," the last line of the poem, borrows the precise line of verse from the warrior-maiden Camilla's death in Book XI, 831: *vitaque cum gemitu fugit indignata sub umbras* (and life flees with a groan for [its] indignity into the shades). But Camilla, in her dying, has about fifteen lines in which to slip away from life, whereas Turnus is quenched instantaneously. To compound the abruptness, memories of the *Iliad* crowd in. The originating scene, the duel of Hector and Achilles, occurred in Book XXII, leaving two more books for the consequences of Hector's death to eddy and take their course in shapes of grief, rage, reconciliation, and foreshadowed doom. Vergil allows no such space for imaginative absorption of Turnus' death. A noble if deluded creature is killed in a fit of fury; the act that founds the city in blood also closes the poem. If the word *indignata*, used for Camilla's death, described the protest (her own and possibly the poet's) at young and brilliant life cut off—a life that would have no place in the Roman order—*indignata* in Turnus' case carries a far more somber cast of outrage at the *way* he dies: at the failure of supplication, the failure of enlightened mercy.

A shock of pacing, that is, bears a deeper, moral shock. It is one of the weird brilliances of Vergil, not unnoticed by his devotees, to have used the same verb for *founding* the city of Rome in the opening lines (*dum conderet urbem*) (*Aen.* I.5) and for Aeneas *planting* (or *founding*) his sword in Turnus' chest at the poem's conclusion: *hoc dicens ferrum adverso sub pectore condit / fervidus* (*Aen.* XII.950–51: saying this he planted his sword in the opposing chest in fury). Vergil will not let us gloss over the cost of this founding: its price was blood, and, it appears, blood spilled in rage, not justice. Rage (*ira*) presides over the opening and closing of the poem just as the verb *condere* does: Juno's rage sets things in motion— *saevae memorem Junonis ob iram* (*Aen.* I.4: because of the relentless rage of cruel Juno)—but Aeneas' rage, the rage of the *pius* hero who was to found a city dedicated to the arts of peace, with Furor chained in the temple, brings it all to a savage halt. If the reader feels taken aback at Turnus' death, it is partly at the contradiction between the scene itself and the values of moderation and justice associated with Aeneas and the city he is to father. *Ira* and *furor* have been the insatiate forces of evil throughout the poem; they have been linked with the female violence of Juno, Allecto, and Amata, and with the monstrous Cacus, and both Jupiter and Anchises have laid out for their earnest hero a blueprint for a city that was to repress such rage. But *ira* also helped Hercules to defeat the monster Cacus in Book VIII, and from Book X onward, fluctuations of *ira* seem to fuel Aeneas' heroism on the battlefield. It is as if a Latin poem of *dolor*, of *lacrimae rerum*, had been invaded by Iliadic *mènis* (wrath).

The noun *ira*, the participle *indignata*, and the verbs *cuncti* (to hesitate) and *condere* (to found) help organize any reading of Turnus' death. But the word I want particularly to examine, as I have said, is *immolare* (to sacrifice). It is not a word used often in the poem, and a feel for its weight and valence may help us chart the forces which join in Turnus' death. In what sense is Turnus a sacrifice? Does his death ritually sanctify the imperial destiny the poem projects? How does his immolation extend and complicate the pattern of the many previous sacrifices the poem has presented? Looking at the death of Turnus, we see a multiple exposure of immolations, some animal, some human, all of which color Aeneas' final act in the poem. The offering up of Turnus draws its power not only from association with the poem's many recorded acts of sacrifice, but, even more eloquently, from one unrecorded one: the death of Remus at the hands of his brother, Romulus. That murder haunted the mythic founding of Rome, but is never explicitly mentioned in the *Aeneid*, though Romulus and Remus enter the prophecies of the poem as figures of law and imperial power. In more than one way, Rome is founded on ritual bloodshed; how we interpret that fact will depend partly on how we read the silence at the heart of the poem, the unacknowledged but central murder of Remus.

To say "ritual bloodshed," of course, is to beg the question. The death of Remus is not technically a sacrifice, and we would have to admit that Aeneas is using the word *immolat* in a metaphorical sense when he vents his fury on Turnus: *Pallas te hoc vulnere, Pallas / immolat et poenam scelerato ex sanguine sumit (Aen.* XII.948–49: Pallas sacrifices you with this wound, and Pallas demands payment in your criminal blood). Strictly speaking, Turnus has not been offered ritually to the gods but has been killed in single combat. Aeneas' figurative use of *immolat* needs to be heard in the context of a taxonomy of deaths, ranging from the bulls, sheep, and boars offered ceremonially at altars, through the eight young men Aeneas destines for Pallas' pyre, through Priam murdered at his altar in Troy, Dido on her pyre, Palinurus and Misenus (who seem to pay the price of Aeneas' entry to the Underworld and arrival in Italy with their lives), Silvia's stag, the loss of Anchises, and on up to the great scenes of warrior deaths in battle, particularly the young, like Nisus and Euryalus, Lausus, and Camilla. The list culminates in Turnus himself. As the idea of sacrifice widens in range, one can see whole panoramas as sacrificial offerings: Troy in flames in Book II, and the weary burning of the Italian and Trojan war dead in Book XI. To return for a moment to *immolat* as Aeneas uses it, we need to note that as a figure of speech it has ambiguous rhetorical and moral consequences. In an immediate sense, it seems to absolve Aeneas of wrongdoing in his slaying of Turnus: that death is claimed as a price justly paid for the death of Pallas. In a larger sense, it justifies the invasion of Latium. At the same time, however, that holy word uttered by a man enraged, *furiis accensus et ira / terribilis* (kindled in fury and terrible in rage) (*Aen.* XII.946–47), casts doubt on both the smaller and the larger justifications and sets up a vibration of doubt that reverberates back through the entire poem. When does a sacrifice become a murder?

The place to start would seem to be with the animals, those patient creatures whose blood flows so freely throughout the poem that it almost seems a substitute for ink. The bullocks, sheep, and boars die, their throats slit at altars, at fairly regular intervals. Their deaths serve not only to punctuate august events (prophecy, celebration, funeral rites, truce-making), but to confirm a system of contact and reciprocity between humans and gods, and a sense of regularity and justice in the workings of fate, as well as of sanctity in the shedding of blood. The vocabulary describing sacrifice varies considerably from scene to scene; each rite is individual and unformulaic in presentation, but the essential form remains the same, and a single phrase returns now and again to describe it: the beasts are slaughtered *de more*, according to custom. These scenes combine variation and continuity, the variations displaying a rich choice of words for killing— *mactare* (to slay), *caedere* (to cut, kill), *ferire* (to strike dead), *sacrare* (to dedicate to a god)—and emphasizing transactions of particular intensity between humans and gods. Offerings presented in such a spotlight include the sacrifice to Hecate in Book VI, with details of the bullock's forelock bristles cast on the flames and his blood caught in cups, and the sacrifice to ratify the treaty between the Latins and the Trojans in Book XII. The latter rite has a drama all its own—mingling darkness and light, interior secrets and exterior revelation, the quick and the dead—as it takes place at sunrise and requires that the viscera be ripped from the living sheep to be loaded on platters at the altar flame.

A gulf divides these sacred, sanctioned, customary killings from Neoptolemus' stabbing of Priam in his son's blood at the altar at Troy in Book II. But between these extremes of the sacred and the impious, most of the deaths of the *Aeneid* take place; in that doubtful space, even the purity and justice of the gods may suffer some stain. They, after all, sponsor much of the killing. And this is the acting space of this poem of *pietas*: the highly charged, obscure arena in which piety is not always so clearly discernible from impiety. The poem unrolls, for the most part, in a moral twilight only stabbingly illuminated by the glare of sacrificial flames, pyres, torches, and—more rarely—the radiance cast by a goddess.

Turnus falls heavily, immensely. He tumbles down in an enjambment from the main verb and participle as if the line itself had suffered the jolt of Aeneas' spear: *incidit ictus | ingens ad terram duplicato poplite Turnus* (*Aen.* XII.926–27: Turnus fell, struck huge to the earth, his knee bent). When he falls, what does it mean that he has been compared (just a hundred lines earlier) to a stag? In Fitzgerald's translation:

> As when a stag-hound
> Corners a stag, blocked by a stream, or by
> Alarm at a barrier of crimson feathers
> Strung by beaters, then the dog assails him
> With darting, barking runs; the stag in fear
> Of nets and the high river-bank attempts
> To flee and flee again a thousand ways,
> But, packed with power, the Umbrian hound hangs on,

Muzzle agape: now, now he has him, now,
As though he had him, snaps eluded jaws
And bites on empty air
                    (Fitzgerald, XII.1013–23)

Most immediately, such imagery seems to contribute to the legitimacy of the word *immolat* as used by Aeneas, animals being the designated victims of sacrifice, and appropriately offered to the gods. But a stag is the prey of hunters, not customarily dispatched on an altar. In Turnus' death, then, hunting imagery complicates the claim of sacrifice. Furthermore, Turnus-as-stag inevitably recalls the death of Silvia's tame stag, carelessly, even brutally slain by Ascanius in Book VII in the act of aggression that starts the war between Latins and Trojans. That earlier scene establishes a code we can't help applying to the death of Turnus. Vergil calls our attention to it all the more by altering the analogous Homeric simile. Hector pursued by Achilles in Book XXII was seen as a fawn beset by a hound: "As a hound who has started a fawn from its mountain lair pursues it through the coombs and glades, and even when it takes cover in a thicket, runs on, picks up the scent and finds his quarry, the swift Achilles was not to be thrown off the scent by any trick of Hector's" (in Rieu's version). Casting Turnus as a stag insists on the Latin leader's stature and nobility, not on his weakness, and insists as well on neural pathways of imagery peculiar to the *Aeneid*.

Silvia's stag is hardly the first to be killed in the poem. When the battered Trojan ships draw up on the Carthaginian coast in Book I, Aeneas' first act as a responsible leader is to kill seven deer to feast his crew. He accomplishes this robustly and matter-of-factly, and the narration hints neither at sacrificial ritual nor at pathos in the fate of those deer. But Silvia's stag was half-tame, and we suffer his death from his point of view. In Fitzgerald's version:

Now as he wandered far from home, the hounds
Of Iulus on the hunt, furiously barking,
Started the stag. He had been floating down
A river, keeping cool by the green bank.
Ascanius himself, now on the chase
And passionate for the honor of the kill,
Let fly a shaft from his bent bow: Allecto's
Guidance did not fail his hand or let him
Shoot amiss, and the arrow whizzing loud
Whipped on to pierce the belly and the flank.

Mortally hurt, the swift deer made for home
In the farm buildings. Groaning, he found his stall,
And coated with dark blood he filled the house
With piteous cries, as though imploring mercy.
                                        (Fitzgerald, VII.677–90)

The deer, half-tame, half-wild, had personified the innocent harmony between humans and nature that prevailed in the pre-Roman world of Latium. He is wounded not only in the belly but in the groin, or genitals (*ilia*), so that this pastoral world loses its future, its power of propagation. And he is killed through the direct agency of the fury Allecto, who inflames Ascanius and his hounds in vocabulary contaminated by association with the poem's other infuriated characters, Juno, Dido, the Trojan women who set fire to the ships in Book V, Amata. Allecto rouses *rabiem*—frenzy—in the dogs, so that they would "burn" to chase the deer, *ut cervum ardentes agerent* (*Aen.* VII.481); the killing of the deer ignites the country people to war, *belloque animos accendit agrestis* (*Aen.* VII.482); Ascanius himself is kindled by love for outstanding praise, *eximiae laudis succensus amore* (*Aen.* VII.496); and not for the first time in the poem has *amor* gone up in smoke, fired by some baser passion. At this juncture one might think not only of Dido, but of Brutus in Book VI, putting his own sons to death, conquered by love of the fatherland and immense greed for fame (*vincet amor patriae laudumque immensa cupido*) (*Aen.* VI.823).

To see Turnus as a stag, then, is to contradict the sense of *immolat* on which Aeneas insists: the justification of Turnus' death as the due price for the death of Pallas, and an offering to the destiny of Rome. From the perspective established by the imagery of Book VII, Turnus' death is a needless, infuriated act of aggression, a perverted immolation. Both forces of the word are at work in the last scene, and that huge dissonance endows the scene, and the entire poem, with uncanny, reverberating power. Furthermore, the image of Turnus as a stag culminates an extended metamorphic sequence. Turnus was seen as a lion as he prepared to fight Pallas in Book X, and at the opening of Book XII; fighting with Aeneas he is several times portrayed as a wild bull (and in the simile preceding the stag simile in Book XII, the combatants are both seen as bulls, quite recasting the Iliadic model which gives Achilles overwhelming superiority). Turnus has also been envisioned as Mars, as wind, as fire, and as a mountain crag. Only in his last confrontation does he slip into focus as a stag: no longer a predatory force, no longer enraged, but restored to his original state of natural nobility and peacefulness from which Allecto's torch had hurled him.

If we track the word *immolat* in the poem, it only compounds the perplexities folded into the last scene. With all the variety of words for ritual killing, Vergil never uses *immolare*, which would seem to be the obvious choice, to describe animal sacrifice in the *Aeneid*. He reserves it, bloodchillingly, for human sacrifice, and in contexts that hardly shore up the claims for justice and sanctity in the poem's final act. Dido on her pyre had been acting as a human sacrifice. But in Book X Aeneas literally engages in that grim rite, capturing eight young Latins—four sons of Ulmo, four of Ufens—to be killed at Pallas' funeral:

> Sulmone creatos
> quattuor hic juvenes, totidem quos educat Ufens
> viventis rapit, inferias quos immolet umbris
> captivoque rogi perfundat sanguine flammas.
>
> (*Aen.* X.517–20)

> (Four young sons of Sulmo, as many whom Ufens raised, he took alive, whom he would immolate to the shades of the Underworld, and with whose captive blood he would sprinkle the flames of the pyre.)

Vergil proceeds briskly from those lines to recount Aeneas' further prowess in battle. But the model passage in the *Iliad* calls out in protest. Achilles in Book XXIII throws on the pyre of Patroclus not only countless sheep and cattle but four high-necked horses (for which he grieves), two dogs, and twelve noble sons of great-hearted Trojans, slashing them with the sword: δώδεκα δὲ Τρώων με-γαθύμων υἱέας ἐσθλοὺς / χαλκῷ δηϊόων (*Il.* XXIII.175–76). And, the narrator declares, in doing so Achilles contrived an evil thing in his mind: κακὰ δὲ φρεσὶ μήδετο ἔργα.

The narrator's judgment of human sacrifice as κακὰ is conspicuously absent from—but, I think, obscurely operative in—the *Aeneid*. The events immediately following the capture of the eight sacrificial victims would suggest as much. First, Aeneas refuses the supplication of Magus, who is at his mercy:

> And with this he took
> The man's helm in his left hand, bent the neck
> Backward, still begging, and drove home the sword
> Up to the hilt.
>
> (Fitzgerald, X.751–54)

Then, in the second appearance of *immolare*, Aeneas hunts down and slaughters a priest of Phoebus and Diana:

Next, not far off, he met
Haemonidës, a sacred minister
Of Phoebus and Diana of the Crossroads,
Wearing the holy headband, all in white
And shining priestly robes. Over the field
Aeneas drove him till the man went down,
Then stood, his mighty shadow covering him,
And took his life in sacrifice.

(Fitzgerald, X.755–62)

. . . . *lapsumque superstans / immolat ingentique umbra tegit* . . . (Aen. X.540–41). Here, the moral argument is carried not only by the paradox of a priest in holy regalia presented as the victim of sacrifice but also by the collision of light and dark: the glittering robes of the priest flutter against Aeneas' shadow, which extends hugely over him, and, in a sense, snuffs him out.

By the time the sacred verb *immolare* makes its third and last appearance in the poem, in Aeneas' final speech to Turnus, it carries a burden of implicit desecration. As Aeneas' sword hesitates over Turnus, the vision of Rome hangs in the balance. Jupiter has foretold, in Book I, that in Rome the gates of War will be shut, and unholy Fury (*impius Furor*) chained in the temple. Anchises, in Book VI, has confirmed that vision in his famous definition of the Roman arts:

'tu regere imperio populos, Romane, memento
(hae tibi erunt artes), pacique imponere morem,
parcere subjectis et debellare superbos.'

(Aen. VI.851–53)

("Roman, remember by your strength to rule
Earth's peoples—for your arts are to be these:
To pacify, to impose the rule of law,
To spare the conquered, battle down the proud.")

(Fitzgerald, VI.1151–54)

Aeneas himself has often acted as the agent of such a destiny, displaying self-control and *pietas*. During the funeral games for Anchises in Book V, Aeneas provided the very pattern of enlightened rule, restraining fury (*iras*) when it threatened to break up the community, and in the boxing match between Darës and Entellus, substituting an animal for a human victim in what can be seen as an archetypal sacrifice:

Fatherly Aeneas would not sit by
While this fury went further—so berserk
Entellus was in the rancor of his soul.
He stopped the fight, and saved bone-weary Darës.
(Fitzgerald, V.597–600)

When the victor Entellus receives the prize bullock, Fitzgerald's translation continues,

He set himself to face the bull that stood there,
Prize of the battle, then drew back his right
And from his full height lashed his hard glove out
Between the horns. The impact smashed the skull
And fragmented the brains. Down went the ox
Aquiver to sprawl dying on the ground.
The man stood over it and in deep tones
Proclaimed: "Here is a better life in place of Darës,
Eryx; here I lay down my gauntlets and my art."
(Fitzgerald, X.618–27)

Entellus' rage has almost broken the boundaries of law, and the games—the model of aggression organized and contained—have almost collapsed into fury. But Aeneas imposes order, and the bull's life ransoms Darës.

It is all the more tragic, with this example in view, and with the prophecies of justice and order echoing through the poem, that Aeneas should give way to *ira* at the end. But if we look back at the prophecies, we find precisely that dark potentiality already inscribed there in the story of Romulus and Remus. And here, too, we find an example of the height of Vergil's art, an art which in its most stringent form consists in *not* saying; an art of the unspoken, perhaps of the unspeakable (*infandum*). Versions vary as to the story of Romulus and Remus, and they vary importantly (for our purposes) in justifying or not justifying the fratricide. Plutarch himself in his *Life of Romulus* cites contradictory sources and versions of the tale; genealogies of the twins vary, as do accounts of their bringing up, and in some versions it is not Romulus but his companion Celer who slays Remus. The violent death of the twin brother, however, remains at the heart of the tale. In many accounts, Remus is said to have provoked the murder by leaping over the ditch his brother had ploughed to mark his city wall on the Palatine hill. As we see in Plutarch, uncertainty hangs about the ancient tale, and about the potential curse of a city's being founded on a killing. In a poem roughly contemporaneous with the composition of the *Aeneid*, Propertius refers to the walls of Rome as "established by the slaying of Remus," suggesting a ritual aspect to the slaying: *ordiar et caeso moenia firma Remo* (Ode III.9.50). Vergil handles the problem by shoving it into a black hole and simply eliding the murder in both prophecies. But like a black hole in space, the unspoken murder exerts a magnetic pull on the entire poem.

Jupiter, in Book I, famously promises nothing less than the world to his distraught daughter, Venus:

> Romulus excipiet gentem et Mavortia condet
> moenia Romanosque suo de nomine dicet.
> his ego nec metas rerum nec tempora pono:
> imperium sine fine dedi.
> (*Aen.* I.276–79)

In Fitzgerald,

> young Romulus
> Will take the leadership, build walls of Mars,
> And call by his own name his people Romans.
> For these I set no limits, world or time,
> But make the gift of empire without end.
> (Fitzgerald, I.371–75)

Brother Remus, over whose dead body (so to speak) this glorious future comes to fruition, appears some seventeen lines later, as—paradoxically—a lawgiver, along with the deities Fides, Hestia, and Quirinus, guarantors of social order in the same sentence that shuts the gates of War and enchains Furor. This conjunction of figures is more peculiar and complex than we can explore here, but we need to note, at least, that Quirinus, that ancient Roman god, is sometimes used as another name for Romulus, and he seems in this list to represent Romulus alongside his "brother Remus" (*Remo cum fratre Quirinus*). In a terrific sleight of hand, this dream of future peace has reconciled the brothers and healed fratricide and civil war by promoting both Romulus and Remus to the status of gods. This line gives us a spectacularly bifocal view: through one lens, the dream of peace and restoration, and through the other (more veiled), unassimilable horrors of mythic murder and historic civil war. Anchises, in Book VI, doesn't even mention Remus. Rome is now embodied in the figure of Romulus, who as son of Mars turns the fratricidal force of civil war outward, in the legitimate aggression of imperial conquest.

> Look now, my son: under his auspices
> Illustrious Rome will bound her power with earth,
> Her spirit with Olympus.
> (Fitzgerald, VI.1047–49)

But Remus' death is not so easily exorcised. If his story remains unspoken, it is not unknown. Other hidden murders rise up to haunt the poem: Sychaeus, Dido's husband, cut down by her brother in *furor* at the altar, appears as a ghost and inspires her escape; and in Book II Aeneas recounts to Dido how he tore violently at the bleeding tree in Thrace (in a ghastly prefiguration of his wrenching the Golden Bough) until the voice of Polydorus cried out from the earth to tell how he had been murdered.

Turnus dies, in a sense, *because* of a mythological scene of massacre: the story of Aegyptus' forty-nine sons slain by their brides on their wedding night is inscribed in gold on Pallas' fatal swordbelt. A whole chorus of indignities, not just the deaths of Camilla and of Silvia's stag, resound in the word *indignata* in the last line of the poem: *vitaque cum gemitu fugit indignata sub umbras*. And the choral effect includes the dissonances in the various senses of *immolat*. Like Remus, Turnus is both innocent and guilty. His death, like that of Remus, allows for the founding of Rome. What are we to make of such sorrow? Of a poem that tallies up so grievously, so relentlessly, the cost of the order it celebrates? In one mood, the modern poet W. H. Auden holds the whole dolorous matter at arm's length. In "A Walk After Dark" (1948), he quips,

> Yet however much we may like
> The stoic manner in which
> The classical authors wrote,
> Only the young and the rich
> Have the nerve or the figure to strike
> The lacrimae rerum note

A decade later, Auden resists Vergil more directly in "Secondary Epic," which opens, "No, Virgil, no. . . ." In rejecting the prophetic structure of the *Aeneid*, Auden colludes with the Roman poet in ignoring Remus: "That Romulus will build a wall, / Augustus found an Age of Gold." But in his long last sentence, which unwinds torturously toward its own prophetic revelation, Auden substitutes for the initial sacrifice of Remus a terminal blood offering, the last boy emperor of Rome, Romulus Augustulus, whose names, obviously, could not appear in Anchises' prophecy, but which in their ironic diminutiveness linger in the ear of the student of Roman history: "The names predestined for the Catholic boy / Whom Arian Odovacer will depose."

Auden's sinister prophecy delivered with Modernist hindsight hardly found a redemptive power in that death, except insofar as "Alaric has avenged Turnus." The Augustan empire in "Secondary Epic" prefigured Hitler's Germany. But in "Vespers," composed a few years earlier in 1954, imagining a meeting between himself-as-Arcadian and his Utopian, totalitarian anti-type, Auden seems disposed to accept the price of memory, and mindfulness, that Vergil demanded:

Was it (as it must look to any god of cross-roads) simply a fortuitous intersection of life-paths, loyal to different fibs?

Or also a rendezvous between two accomplices who, in spite of themselves, cannot resist meeting

to remind the other (do both, at bottom, desire truth?) of that half of their secret which he would most like to forget,

forcing us both, for a fraction of a second, to remember our victim (but for him I could forget the blood, but for me he could forget the innocence),

on whose immolation (call him Abel, Remus, whom you will, it is one Sin Offering) arcadias, utopias, our dear old bag of a democracy are alike founded:

For without a cement of blood (it must be human, it must be innocent) no secular wall will safely stand.

Between the poles of Auden's readings of the *Aeneid*, between the cynicism and dread of empire motivating "Secondary Epic" and the acceptance of sacrifice as a political sacrament in "Vespers," we may locate the terms of the debate continuing in our day about the price of peace. Vergil refuses to ease our reading. In that refusal may lie at least part of the secret of the enduring life of his poem.

Part 3

# The Debate, or Stepping out of the Frame

Chapter 9

# THE *AENEID* TRANSFORMED
## Illustration as Interpretation from the
## Renaissance to the Present

### CRAIG KALLENDORF

WHAT else indeed could (say) "Virgil" be other than what readers have made
of him over the centuries?
   —Charles Martindale, *Redeeming the Text*

### I.

In classical studies, as in so many other areas of academic life, things used to be
so much simpler. Interpreting a text, for example, used to be a relatively straightforward affair. Traditional philology provided the model, originating with the
humanists of the Italian Renaissance, refined by German scholars between 1750
and 1850, and applied in essentially the same way a hundred years later. According to this model, each text has one meaning, embedded within it at the moment
of creation, and the role of the interpreter is to recover this original signification,
to see the text as it actually was (and is). To be sure, this process becomes more
difficult as the text and the culture in which it was created recede further and
further into the past, for in time a series of different interpretations of the same
text almost invariably appears. According to the traditional model, however, these
differences arise when interpreters allow their own values and beliefs to come
between them and the text. Philology is the tool by which interpreters set aside
their own values and beliefs in order to see the text clearly and to recover the one
timeless meaning embedded in it.[1]

As we all know, literary theory in one form or another has challenged almost
every part of this traditional model. Many people now believe that the meaning
of a text, for example, is created cooperatively between author and interpreter.
That is, the text may indeed exist in and of itself, but it can never be examined
from a position of complete objectivity. All interpreters have some values and
beliefs that they cannot set aside and take up again at will, and these values and

beliefs enter into the way in which they understand everything they read and see. The text, in other words, functions rather like an orchestral score which contains many potential cues, with each interpreter responding to the cues that he or she can hear. As a result, the single timeless meaning of a text has been replaced by many timebound meanings, created and recreated as cultural change makes some textual cues audible and suppresses others.[2]

$\rightarrow$   Now, I am enough of a traditionalist still to feel a certain amount of longing for the tidy certainties of the older model. Nevertheless, I am forced to admit that I find it very difficult indeed to determine when I am being objective and when I am not, and I find myself increasingly unwilling to dismiss as erroneous many, indeed most, of the previous attempts to interpret Greek and Latin literature through the ages. What is more, many of the interpretations that must be wrong according to the standards of traditional philology strike me as well worth studying in and of themselves.

Vergil's *Aeneid* has stimulated an especially rich variety of interpretations through the centuries. As verbal constructs, these interpretations have taken many forms: commentaries on the text, poems written in imitation of the *Aeneid*, and so forth. Fortunately there are a number of fine studies in this area, so that at this point I do not see any reason to attempt yet another.[3] Vergil's influence on European art, however, has received rather less attention,[4] and, surprisingly, I know of only a handful of efforts to analyze the artistic interpretation of the *Aeneid* on the most basic level: the pictures that accompany the printed texts on which our modern understanding of the poetry is based.[5] Therefore, in this chapter I focus on these woodcuts and engravings, beginning with the first printed editions some five hundred years ago and continuing into the twentieth century. My examples come from the Junius S. Morgan Vergil collection at Princeton University, whose seven hundred fifty volumes include dozens of illustrated editions.[6] My underlying premise is that the same sorts of problems that have recently bedeviled interpretations constructed in words also affect how we should be dealing with visual responses to a text. I show, first, that willingly or unwillingly, artists inevitably end up viewing a poem from the past at least in part through the same stylistic assumptions that govern how they view their own world. I then show through one carefully chosen pair of examples how the artists' political beliefs also determine, again at least in part, what they can and cannot see in the text. Finally, I suggest that attention to the illustrations that accompany the *Aeneid* reveals a constriction in the intended audience, which in turn poses a challenge for us today. I hope you will agree with me that as the results of mediation between text and interpreter, these changing visions *are* Vergil. If instead you find some (or all) of them to be misinterpretations, I hope you will at least find them interesting misinterpretations which retain their value as windows into the culture which produced them.

## II.

As Charles Martindale shrewdly observes, stylistic periods have no greater claim to universal validity than do the interpretations of art and literature fashioned within them; both are cultural constructs, created at a particular point in time and subject to recreation at any time in the future.[7] Nevertheless, I believe that there is at present a certain basic agreement among art historians about how early modern Europe might be divided into periods and about how successive responses to the artifacts of Greece and Rome might provide a rhythm to that periodization. Medieval painters and sculptors, as we all learned in school, tended to see everything in terms of their own culture, to appropriate the "other" and make it their own—hence the late Gothic statues of Jupiter as a monk and Mars as a knight from the bell tower next to the Florentine cathedral. Under the influence of humanist historians, Renaissance artists sought to envision antiquity on its own terms, to preserve its "otherness," so that artists of this period attempted to remove themselves and their values from their works.[8] Baroque artists in turn sought to focus attention on themselves, using classical subject matter as a means to show off their ability to solve technical challenges in a flurry of motion and activity; we might think, for example, of Bernini's *Apollo and Daphne* or his *Rape of Persephone*. It seems that in art, as in physics, actions provoke reactions, so that neoclassical artists responded by shifting attention away from themselves to their subject matter, again attempting to let the grandeur and nobility of their classical past shine forth in the pure vision of, say, David's *Oath of the Horatii*. The romantic vision shifted from public to private, from the mind to the heart—another version of action and reaction—so that classical subject matter now serves as a source for pathos, which must be felt by the artist and communicated to the viewer. In other words, the way in which classical subject matter is appropriated provides a sort of rhythm to this periodization. First the emphasis is on the artist, with the past envisioned in terms of the present. Then the emphasis is on the subject matter, as the artist attempts to suppress the present to see the past on its own terms. Next the artist returns to center stage, then the classical subject matter, then the artist.

Admittedly oversimplified, such a narrative nevertheless seems to me to retain a certain usefulness as a starting point in our inquiry. I shall therefore begin by approaching the woodcuts and engravings from the *Aeneid* within this familiar interpretive construct. I believe, however, that the way the Vergilian material was

treated in the end suggests that this narrative would benefit from a certain re-
finement.

Let us begin with the most famous early printed edition of Vergil, the one edited by Sebastian Brant and printed by Johannes Grüninger in Strasbourg.[9] This
book is anchored into both the Middle Ages and the Renaissance, as we might
expect from its date of publication (1502). Textually it appears to be rather avant-
garde: for example, the commentaries it contains include both those of the Italian
humanists Antonius Mancinellus, Domitius Calderinus, and Christophorus Landinus and that of Tiberius Claudius Donatus, the late-antique writer whose work
was recovered by scholars of the early Renaissance. Visually, however, the book
is anchored firmly in medieval art. For one thing, many of the woodcuts do not
freeze a single moment in time like those of the progressive Italian artists, but
record instead a series of events that must be read in chronological order. This
scene from the beginning of Maphaeus Vegius' fifteenth-century supplement to
the *Aeneid* (Figure 1), for example, begins with the fall of Troy and ends with the
final battle between Turnus and Aeneas—that is, it summarizes Vergil's entire
poem. It should therefore not surprise us that the action Vergil described is seen
through the prism of a much later culture. The characters in this scene are dressed
in costumes from the turn of the sixteenth century, not from ancient Rome, and
the wooden ring in the foreground, along with the helmets and pikes stacked
behind it, suggest that Aeneas and Turnus have just finished fighting according
to late medieval conventions. The cities in the background look like the northern
European cities that Brant and Grüninger knew, and the perspective does not
conform to the emerging canons of Italian Renaissance art. The combination of
textual and visual, in short, makes this book very much the product of one particular cultural moment: the passage from the Middle Ages to the Renaissance.

The blocks from the 1502 Strasbourg edition were copied in Italy and France
and remained very popular for several decades, but after mid-century several other
series of woodcuts began to compete successfully with them.[10] One of these
competing series appeared in an Italian translation published in Venice near the
end of the century.[11] The woodcuts in this book are not of the highest quality,
but they clearly reflect the norms of Italian Renaissance art. The battle scene
depicted here (Figure 2) represents one and only one point of action within Book
XI, and it is rendered in reasonable perspective and a pleasingly balanced composition. Yet even here, the effort to see Vergil's world on its own terms is not
completely successful. The town in the background, for example, is not envisioned in terms of the ancient ruins which humanist scholars had by now been
studying for several generations. Its most striking feature instead is the towers
within the walls, which were a common feature of postclassical Italian cities and

# Eneidos

Maphei Veggi Laudensis Poetę clariffimi Liber Tertiufdecimus Addit⁹ duodecim æneidos libris.

Vrnus'vt extremo vitā sub marte profudit:
Subdunt se rutuli æneę troiana
sequentes;
Agmina:'de hinc superis meriti
redduntur honores.

Cōga udet gnato ac focijs memor;ante malorū

Actorū pater Aeneas.turni inde latinus
Morte dolet.patrię miserāda incendia claunus
Euersæ;& cari deflet pia funera gnati.
Connubiū instaurat gnatę:lætofcę hymengos
Rex socer æneę genero:gens vtracę pacto
Fœdere pacis ouat:tū nomine cōiugis vrōem
Instruit:& laudē placida sub pace regentē
Transtulit ęneā venus astra in summa beatū.

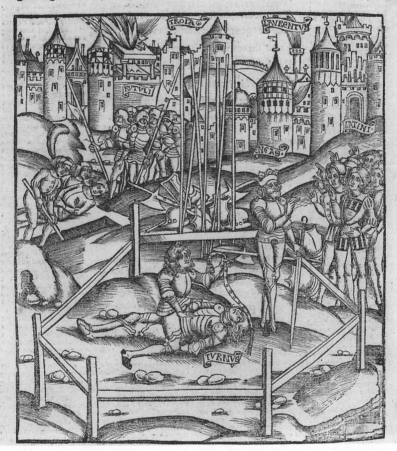

FIGURE 1 Argument to Maphaeus Vegius' supplement to the *Aeneid*. *Publii Virgilii Maronis opera* (Strasbourg: Johannes Grüninger, 1502), fol. 407v. Princeton University Library.

# DELLA

## ENEIDE

# DI VERGILIO
## LIBRO XI.
Tradotto per M. Bernardin Daniello.

*Al Magnifico M. Bernardo Zane.*

### ARGOMENTO.

**M**ORTO che fu Mezentio, Enea uincitore
rizzò un trofeo a Marte, poi con gráde ap-
parato di pompa rimandò il corpo di Pallante mor-

FIGURE 2 Argument to *Aeneid* XI. *L'opere di Vergilio* (Venice: Giacomo Cornetti, 1586),
fol. 221v. Princeton University Library.

which can still be seen today in isolated towns like San Gimignano. In other words, the designer of these blocks appears to have tried to suppress the most obvious signs of his own culture. However, while he has indeed produced an effect different from that of the Strasbourg edition, he has still left enough traces of his own world view that we can place him in the culture within which he worked.

At the end of the following century, John Dryden's monumental English translation appeared, first with the baroque engravings of Franz Cleyn,[12] then with another series published by the same printer in 1716.[13] The scene depicted here (Figure 3), the moment of Dido's death, was obviously selected to allow the flurry of movement so favored by baroque artists:

> ter sese attollens cubitoque adnixa leuauit,
> ter reuoluta toro est oculisque errantibus alto
> quaesiuit caelo lucem ingemuitque reperta.
> Tum Iuno omnipotens longum miserata dolorem
> difficilisque obitus Irim demisit Olympo
> quae luctantem animam nexosque resolueret artus.
>                 (Aen. IV.690–95)

> (Thrice Dido try'd to raise her drooping Head,
> And fainting thrice, fell grov'ling on the Bed.
> Thrice op'd her heavy Eyes, and saw the Light,
> But having found it, sicken'd at the sight;
> And clos'd her Lids at last, in endless Night.
> Then Juno, grieving that she shou'd sustain
> A Death so ling'ring, and so full of pain;
> Sent Iris down, to free her from the Strife
> Of lab'ring Nature, and dissolve her Life.)
>                 (Dryden, IV.989–97)

This engraving is baroque in every respect. For one thing, it is dominated not by Dido, but by Iris, who is depicted at the very moment of descent, which requires the greatest technical skill to render. The foreshortening is not so severe as in, say, Tintoretto's *Miracle of St. Mark,* but the effect is similar as we admire the artist's skill in controlling a difficult composition. The building behind the pyre is typically baroque as well, showing the dissociation of form from function that characterizes, for example, Il Gesù in Rome. In this case, the engraver clearly sees the *Aeneid* through the filter of the baroque aesthetic which dominated his culture.

E.4.l. 990.

54

FIGURE 3 *Aeneid* IV. 690–95. *The Works of Virgil: . . . Translated into English Verse*, by Mr. Dryden (London: Jacob Tonson, 1716), vol. 2, following p. 454. Princeton University Library.

FIGURE 4 *Aeneid* VIII. 209–11. *Picturae antiquissimi Virgiliani codicis* . . . (Rome: Joannes Zempelius 1782), No. 84. Princeton University Library.

It is perhaps not surprising that such a stylistically vigorous presentation would provoke a reaction. In the history of Vergilian illustration, this reaction took a turn we might not have anticipated with the publication of the *Picturae antiquissimi Virgiliani codicis Bibliothecae Vaticanae* . . . , of which I have used an edition from 1780–82.[14] The engravers came up with a different way of illustrating the poetry of Vergil as it would have been seen in its own time (or shortly afterward): they reproduced scenes from two very old manuscripts, the *Codex Vaticanus* and the *Codex Romanus*,[15] along with other scenes from gems, monuments, mosaics, and other artifacts of ancient Rome. Number 84 (Figure 4), for example, is engraved from a gem that depicts Cacus stealing the cattle of Hercules, a story narrated in Book VIII as Aeneas tours the future site of Rome with Evander (204ff.). By illustrating the *Aeneid* from an ancient gemstone, the engraver is trying to let the poem illustrate itself through evidence recovered from its own time, a strategy which should in essence eliminate the role of the modern interpreter.

In a certain obvious sense, it does. But a closer look at these engravings suggests that here, as elsewhere, subjectivity proves surprisingly difficult to banish. Erich Odermann observed over sixty years ago that some of the details of these engravings are "stylized,"[16] although I would explain the matter a little

FIGURE 5 *Aeneid* II. 212–22. *Picturae antiquissimi Virgiliani codicis . . .* (Rome: Joannes
Zempelius 1782), No. 37. Princeton University Library.

differently. Number 37 (Figure 5), for example, "exhibet Laocoontem ante Nep-
tuni aedem taurum mactantem, ac dein ab anguibus impetitum una cum pueris
duobus. Ex iisdem picturis. Pertinet ad lib. II. Aeneid. vers. 201" (shows Laocoön
slaying a bull before the temple of Neptune, and then attacked by the snakes
together with his two sons. From the same group of pictures [i.e., the Codex
Vaticanus], it illustrates *Aen.* II.201). The basic design comes from the manuscript,
but one must admit that it ends up suiting a neoclassical temperament rather
well. The composition, for example, shows signs of symmetricality, with one
child on either side of Laocoön, who has his arms upraised in perfect balance
and the two snakes draped across his body in perfect parallelism. What is more,
the figures maintain their dignity and restraint, even in an agonizing death. It is
impossible not to think of this scene in comparison to the famous Hellenistic
statue of Laocoön, which had been discovered several generations earlier and
moved with great fanfare to the Vatican.[17] Vergil's poem, as we can see, contains
a variety of aesthetic cues, and the ones to which any given interpreters respond
are at least in part a function of the culture in which they live and work.

Just how complex this process can be becomes apparent when we return to
Dryden's translation. Produced in baroque England, the set of illustrations we
have already seen is a suitable accompaniment for the text. However, the trans-

lation itself remained popular for a long time afterward, and over its long publishing history it attracted several additional sets of illustrations. One of these
additional sets, which appeared in 1802 and was republished the following year,[18]
shows signs of a newly emerging romantic sensibility. For one thing, as he
worked through Book IV, the illustrator has chosen to depict not the descent of
Iris, but Dido's dying speech (Figure 6):

> interiora domus inrumpit limina et altos
> conscendit furibunda rogos ensemque recludit
> Dardanium, non hos quaesitum munus in usus.
> hic, postquam Iliacas uestis notumque cubile
> conspexit, paulum lacrimis et mente morata
> incubuitque toro dixitque nouissima uerba:
> 'dulces exuuiae, dum fata deusque sinebat,
> accipite hanc animam meque his exsoluite curis.'
>                (Aen. IV.645–52)

> (Then swiftly to the fatal place she pass'd,
> And mounts the fun'ral pyre with furious haste;
> Unsheaths the sword the Trojan left behind,
> [Not for so dire an enterprise design'd.]
> But when she view'd the garments loosely spread,
> Which once he wore, and saw the conscious bed,
> She paus'd, and, with a sigh, the robes embrac'd,
> Then on the couch her trembling body cast,
> Repress'd the ready tears, and spoke her last:
> "Dear pledges of my love while heav'n so pleas'd,
> Receive a soul, of mortal anguish eas'd.")
>                (Dryden, IV.928–38)

The challenge in this scene is not the technical one of depicting motion, but the
emotional one of conveying feeling. The earlier version was set outdoors, but
this one is set inside, so that nothing can distract us from Dido and the distraught
figures around her. The figures in the earlier version do not appear to be deeply
moved by what has happened, but the ones in this engraving clearly are. The
woman in the foreground rushes toward the collapsed queen, while the one in
the background throws up her arms in grief. This is the point in the story of
greatest emotional force, and the illustrator was clearly drawn to it as a vehicle
for communicating the emotional content he valued in the story.

*Dear pledges of my love, while heaven so pleased*
*Receive a soul, of mortal anguish eased:*

Œn. 4. v. 937.

Published by Verner & Hood. Nov.1.ˢ 1802.　　F. Bartolozzi R.A. sculp.

FIGURE 6 *Aeneid* IV. 645–52. *The Works of Virgil, Translated into English Verse by Mr. Dryden* (London: James Swan, 1803), vol. 1, following p. 160. Princeton University Library.

Thus as we have seen, the conventional periodization of art history offers a reasonable beginning point for tracing changes in the stylistic paradigms through which the Aeneid has been viewed through the ages. This pattern, however, seems to be most helpful for the periods in which the role of the artist is foregrounded: for medieval woodcuts, in which time and space collapse into the universal present of the artist's own culture; for baroque engravings, which serve as a means for displaying the technical skill of the artist; and for illustrations of the romantic period, in which the artist strives to respond emotionally to the text and to transfer that response to the viewer. The conventional pattern, I believe, is less successful in explaining the illustrations from the Renaissance and the Neoclassical Age. These are the periods in which artists and scholars sought to withdraw themselves as much as possible from the process of interpretation, to see the classical past as it really was. This effort seems to fail repeatedly, for even if artists could (for example) depict an ancient city that did not resemble one of their own day, they still betrayed their aesthetic principles in the scenes they chose to depict and in the way they responded both to Vergil's poetry and to earlier renderings of it. In other words, it does not seem to be any easier for the interpreter to disappear completely from an illustration of a poem than it is to disappear completely from a verbal explication of it.

## III.

This principle holds true, I believe, on the ideological as well as the stylistic level. To show how this works, I turn to the illustrations accompanying two French translations of the Aeneid, the first published under the *ancien régime*, the second under Napoleon. I have chosen these two editions quite deliberately, for reasons that should become clear in the discussion that follows.

The first of these two translations is a straightforward, serious work by Pierre Perrin.[19] The first volume was dedicated to Cardinal Mazarin (1602–61), the influential cleric and diplomat who played an important role in shaping the foreign policy of several French monarchs. This dedication, however, is no empty formality, for Perrin draws Vergil and his poetry explicitly into the service of the French state:

En effet, Monseigneur, le siecle fameux de ce grand Autheur ne semble t'il pas revolu dans le present? Qu'est-ce maintenant que Paris, qu'une Rome triomphante, comme elle, immense dans son peuple & dans ses limites, comme elle, Reine des Citez, maistresse des Nations, capitale du Monde? nostre Monarque qu'un Auguste naissant, dans ses premieres années déja

le plus victorieux, déja le plus auguste des Roys? & V. Eminence, Monseigneur, qu'un fidele Moecene; comme luy Romain, comme luy son plus
grande & plus cher Ministre, & le sacré Depositaire de ses secrets & de sa
puissance? Pour achever ces illustres rapports, le Ciel ne devoit il pas à la
France un Virgile François?

(In effect, Sir, the famous century of this grand author, does it not seem
to have come around again in the present? Is Paris not now a Rome triumphant, like her enormous in population and territory, like her queen
of cities, mistress of nations, capital of the world? Is our monarch not a
nascent Augustus, in his first years already the most victorious, already
the most august of kings? And your eminence, sir, are you not a faithful
Maecenas, like him a Roman, like him the most grand and the most
cherished minister, and the sacred depositary of his secrets and his
power? To complete these illustrious connections, does not Heaven require for France a French Vergil?)[20]

Perrin, of course, presents himself as the French Vergil, but in doing so, he
transfers the entire ideological framework of Vergil's Rome to seventeenth-
century France. In one sense, this is simply one more in a centuries-long series
of attempts to use a combined *translatio studii-translatio imperii* gesture to legitimate
national consciousness and governmental authority.[21] And Perrin's version, like
most of its predecessors, is straightforward and unproblematic: as Vergil served
and supported Augustus, so the new Vergil will also serve and support his political successor.

This *Aeneid* is the public one, the poem which was regarded as the founding
document for a western civilization which traced its sense of patriotism and national consciousness back to ancient Rome. That is, it is the literary elevation of
the group over the individual, of the need for the individual to find meaning and
purpose in service to the state. The engravings that accompany Perrin's translation reinforce these values. The one that accompanies Book II (Figure 7), for
example, is at first glance an unremarkable depiction of Aeneas leading his father
and son from the burning buildings of Troy. But Aeneas is dwarfed by the scene
around him; what matters, the artist seems to be saying, is his role as citizen of
the city, as part of a group. In a similar way, the other engravings in this edition
are group scenes: the one accompanying Book IV places Dido's funeral pyre before the city of Carthage, the one accompanying Book V places the athletic games
of the Trojan youth before the assembled army, the one accompanying Book VI
places Charon's boat before the masses of souls in Hell, and so forth. In each

FIGURE 7 *Aeneid* II. 721–25. *Leneide de Virgile fidellement traduitte . . . par* M. P. Perrin (Paris: Estienne Loyson, 1664), vol. 1, following p. 70. Princeton University Library.

case, the engravings situate the individual characters in relation to the social and political units to which they belong, reminding us that individuals have obligations to those who depend on them. The illustrations, in other words, reinforce the dedication in its attempt to highlight those features in the *Aeneid* which can be seen as supporting the claims of the state to the allegiance of its people.

The same poem, however, can also be appropriated by those who stand in opposition to the political order of their day. One such malcontent was Victor-Alexandre-Chrétien Leplat, a Flemish poet who published a travesty of Vergil in his native language in 1802, then in French in 1807–8. His *Virgile en France . . .* is not a translation per se, but rather an effort to adapt the *Aeneid* to the events of the French Revolution of 1789. Lest any of his readers miss the analogies, Leplat supplied a commentary which explains his text in great detail, complete with bibliographical references to standard histories of the period.[22]

In this translation and commentary, the fall of Troy in Book II is rewritten into an account of the overthrow of the French monarchy, beginning with the convocation of the Estates General, continuing with the arrest of the king and the "Sac de Troie par les jacobins," and ending with the death of the king and general ruin. Leplat's sympathies are clearly with the old order:

> On vit toutes les horreurs qui ont lieu dans les guerres civiles; des pères dénoncer leurs fils, des fils accuser leurs pères, des frères trahir leurs frères et des neveux leurs oncles, pour envahir leurs biens et leur succession; des domestiques trahir, calomnier leurs maîtres, etc. Ces crimes étaient regardés comme des actes de civisme qui méritaient des récompenses. Le fanatisme politique produit les mêmes effets que le fanatisme religieux.[23]

> (One sees all the horrors which take place in civil wars; fathers denounce their sons, sons accuse their fathers, brothers betray their brothers and nephews their uncles, to usurp their goods and their succession; servants betray and slander their masters, etc. These crimes were regarded as acts of civic duty which deserve rewards. Political fanaticism produces the same effects as religious fanaticism.)

Leplat sees the revolutionaries not as noble idealists, but as greedy opportunists who would betray anyone and anything for personal gain. The cause of all this is fanaticism, especially in the lower classes:

> La société des jacobins, bonne dans son origine, offre un exemple terrible du danger des sociétés populaires, et de la marche rapide du peuple armé du pouvoir, vers l'anarchie qui est la mère de la tyrannie, qui exerça ses ravages en France pendant quinze mois, avec une fureur dont aucun ouragan politique n'offre l'exemple dans l'histoire des peuples.[24]

> (The society of the Jacobins, good in its origin, offers a terrible example of the danger of popular societies and of the rapid march of people armed with power toward the anarchy which is the mother of tyranny, which exercised its ravages in France for fifteen months with a furor which is not exemplified by any political hurricane in the history of nations.)

According to Leplat, empowering the lower classes leads to anarchy and tyranny, then to a new government which rests in the worst excesses of human depravity.

To illustrate this political vision, the engraver turned to the image of the orator calming the crowd in Book I of the *Aeneid*. In Vergil, the crowd is first agitated by sedition, then calmed by an orator of pious dignity. In Leplat's travesty, however, the focus remains on the first part of the image. The illustrator quotes only the lines describing sedition and its effect on the crowd (148–50), then shows a personification of the state threatened by all sorts of related dangers (Figure 8): hypocrisy, greed, vengeance, treason, impiety, famine, plague, and the like. It is sedition, however, which topples the *ancien régime*, as we see in Leplat's description of the death of Elisabeth, the sister of Louis XVI. She refused to leave her brother's side, and when the "brigands" surrounded his castle, she stood firmly beside the king and queen, "haranguing the seditious with the grandest determination" ("haranguant les séditieux avec la plus grande fermeté"). Handed over in the end to a revolutionary tribunal, she mounted the scaffold with the calmness of virtue and the dignity proper to her rank, perishing (in Leplat's view) as a victim to fraternal love.[25]

From the perspective of the French government at the beginning of the nineteenth century, however, these sentiments were seditious, and agents of Napoleon tried to seize the entire press run and destroy it shortly after the first two volumes appeared. The French translation was never finished, but Leplat responded by publishing a satire on Napoleon and his family, which appeared anonymously in London in 1814 under the title *Les Voilà*.[26] In this case, the French government recognized that Leplat's political vision was dangerously subversive, and that he had appropriated the *Aeneid* in support of his opposition to what the authorities now saw as the legitimate succession of power.

I would like to make two points regarding this pair of translations. First, we must recognize that even after centuries have passed and ancient Rome has given way to the modern nation state, illustrations of works like the *Aeneid* remain ideologically committed, for translators and engravers end up viewing Vergil through the concerns of their own day. Second, Vergil's poetry is open to appropriation by all sorts of interest groups. Modern scholarship has suggested that the *Aeneid* has been used more often to prop up authoritarian governments than to embolden those who challenge them,[27] and I suspect this is probably true. Yet as the example of Leplat shows, the same poem which was explicitly embraced by the French government could be recast less than one hundred fifty years later into a profoundly subversive form. Like stylistic and aesthetic norms, ideological commitments leave their traces in the history of Vergilian illustration.

## IV.

As we have seen, woodcuts and engravings can tell us a great deal about the reception of the *Aeneid*—about the series of interpretations made over time whose history connects the poem and its own culture to modern readers like us. It is

*Ac velute magno in populo cum sæpe coorta est*
*Seditio, sævitque animis ignobile vulgus;*
*Jamque faces et saxa volant, furor arma ministrat.*
V. L. I V 148

FIGURE 8 *Aeneid* I. 148–50. *Virgile en France* (Brussels: Weissenbruch, 1807–08), vol. 1, before p. 1. Princeton University Library.

clear, however, that different kinds of people read the *Aeneid* at different points in the past. Careful attention to the illustrations accompanying the text can also help us here, for I suggest that changes in the audience to whom these illustrations were directed reveal changes in Vergil's position in western culture.

Let us first return to the woodcuts in the 1502 Strasbourg edition. A folio edition containing five detailed commentaries in Latin, this book was obviously aimed at a learned market, and the annotations in the Princeton copies confirm that it was indeed used by educated readers.[28] A poem at the end of the volume, however, reveals that Brant envisioned the widest audience possible for this book, and that he added the pictures to make the poem accessible to the unlearned:

> Virgilium exponant alii sermone diserto.
> Et calamo pueris: tradere et ore iuvent.
> Pictura agresti voluit Brant: atque tabellis:
> Edere eum indoctis: rusticolisque viris.
> Nec tamen abiectus labor hic: nec prorsus inanis.
> Nam memori servat mente figura librum.

(Let others explain Vergil in eloquent speech and be pleased to hand him down to boys in written and spoken form; Brant wished to publish him for unlearned and peasant folk in rustic pictures and drawings. Nevertheless, this task is neither lowly nor wholly useless, for the picture preserves the book in the remembering mind.)[29]

A woodcut from Book VI of the *Aeneid* (Figure 9), for example, would be accessible even to someone who could not read the few words of Latin in it. The figures in it are from Vergil's *lugentes campi* (fields of mourning), and it is not difficult to guess that this might be the underworld and that the people there are not happy. For those who could read Latin, the commentary of Landinus that accompanies the text would develop in detail the parallels between Vergil's underworld and Christian theology. Uneducated readers, in other words, could get the general idea from the pictures, and learned readers could use the pictures to fix key points in their memories. In this edition, the pictures suggest that Vergil's poetry would have attracted readers from a wide variety of social classes.[30]

The next engraving (Figure 10) accompanies an edition of the *Aeneid* published in London in 1753.[31] At first glance, it would seem that this edition should make Vergil more accessible than the Strasbourg one of two hundred fifty years earlier, for here the Latin text is accompanied by the English translation of Christopher Pitt. A closer look at the two books, however, leads me in the end to a different

FIGURE 9 Aeneid VI, 426–51. *Publii Virgilii Maronis opera* (Strasbourg: Johannes Grüninger, 1502), fol. 270r. Princeton University Library.

FIGURE 10 *Aeneid* VIII. 626–728. *The Works of Virgil* (London: R. Dodsley, 1753), vol. 3, following p. 453. Princeton University Library.

conclusion. Brant's woodcuts are accompanied by (among other things) the commentary of Landinus, which was designed to accommodate Vergil to the common Christian values of fifteenth-century culture. The engraving reproduced here is accompanied by a learned treatise, "Observations on the Shield of Aeneas" by William Whitehead, which serves as a commentary to the end of Book VIII. This commentary is necessary because the events depicted on Aeneas' shield, which were once well known to every schoolboy with a basic humanist education, offered little more than antiquarian appeal some two hundred years later. What is more, Whitehead wants to show that the scenes selected by Vergil were not "thrown down at random," but "in reality form a kind of regular whole." To show that these scenes are "actually inconnected with each other,"[32] Whitehead must interpret Vergil's vision of his own past, and he does so from within the Enlightenment paradigm favored by the educated Englishmen of his day. Certain principles, he feels, emerge from Vergil's account: treaties are honored, liberty resists tyranny, public virtues outweigh private ones, and religion protects the state. "Whether this was really the case, with regard to Rome, we are not to consider: It is so represented by the poet," Whitehead writes, "and if we take his word for the truth of it, I am sure we need not wonder at any pitch of greatness to which such a state arrived."[33] In other words, Whitehead starts by claiming that he is merely recording what Vergil thought, but then his own moral optimism creeps in through the back door ("I am sure we need not wonder at any pitch of greatness to which such a state arrived"). This illustration is therefore anchored just as firmly in Enlightenment England as it is in Vergil's text, and this helps explain its somewhat limited appeal, for by this point Vergil had become a concern primarily to a fairly small group of well-educated aristocrats with the time and resources to pursue knowledge which often drifted from culturally central to decidedly antiquarian.

Not all renderings of the *Aeneid* are as serious as Pitt's translation, with its accompanying illustrations and scholarly apparatus. Among the most skillful of the less serious treatments is the travesty of A. Blumauer, which was popular in the eighteenth century and still being reprinted in 1841, when it was accompanied by thirty-six illustrations by Franz Seitz.[34] The one reproduced here (Figure 11) comes at the point in the *descensus ad inferos* when Aeneas and the Sibyl reach the fork in the road. Aeneas asks to see lower Hell first and his wish is granted, at which point he and the Sibyl meet Satan. The entire scene has a distinctly "Alice in Wonderland" quality, with a dandified hero and tiny devils frolicking about. Satan is presented as an infernal cook, with a description of Hell as a kitchen that has more than a little of Dante's spirit as well:

> Die große Höllenküche sah
> > Der Held nicht ohne Regung.
> Viel tausend Hände waren da
> > So eben in Bewegung,
> Um für des Satans leckere
> Gefräßigkeit ein groß Soupé
> > Auf heute zu bereiten.

> Als Oberküchenmeister stand
> > Mit einem Herz von Eisen
> Hier Pater Kochem, und erfand

FIGURE 11 *Aeneid VI. Virgils Aeneis travestiert von A. Blumauer* (Leipzig: K. F. Köhler, 1841), following p. 184. Princeton University Library.

Und ordnete die Speisen.
Er ging beständig hin und her,
Und kommandirt' als Oberer
Das Küchenpersonale.

Hier sott man Wucherseelen weich,
Dort wurden Advokaten
Gespickt, da sah man Domherrnbäuch'
In großen Pfannen braten;
Und dort stieß man zu köstlichen
Kraftsuppen die berühmtesten
Genies in einem Mörser.

Hier böckelt man Prälaten ein,
Dort frikassirt man Fürsten,
Da hackt man große Geister klein
Zu Cervellate-Würsten,
Da hängt man Schmeichler in den Rauch,
Und räuchert sie, dort macht man auch
Aus Kutscherseelen Rostbeef.

Hier steckt ein Aristoteles
Im Kohl bis an die Füße,
Und dort dreht sich Origenes
Als ein Kapaun am Spieße:
Daneben kräht ein Rezensent,
Und aus den süssen Herrchen brennt
Man dorten Zuckerkandel.

Der richtet feige Memmen zu,
Und brät sie wie die Hasen,
Der kocht ein köstliches Ragout
Aus lauter Schurkennasen:
Der gibt ein paar Tyrannen hier
Mit Menschenblute ein Klystir,
Und macht aus ihnen Plunzen.

Hier bäckt man feines Butterbrod
Aus weichen Menschenseelen,

Statt Krebsen siedet dort sich roth
　　Ein Schock von Kardinälen;
Der macht Gelèe aus Witzlingen,
Und dort hofiert ein Teufelchen
　　Als Bock Diabolini.

Zu diesem Mahl ließ Lucifer
　　Den frommen Helden laden;
Allein Aeneas dankte sehr
　　Für alle diese Gnaden,
Und excusirte sich damit:
　　Er habe seinen Appetit
　　Auf lange Zeit verloren.[35]

(The hero saw the great kitchen of Hell and did not remain unmoved. Many thousand hands were there in motion just so, in order to prepare a grand banquet today for Satan's tasty gluttony.

Here "Father Cook 'em" stood as supreme head chef, with a heart of iron, devising and ordering the dishes. He went about constantly here and there, and as the boss gave orders to the kitchen staff.

Here usurers were boiled soft, there lawyers were larded, and there one saw prebendary paunches frying in large pans; and there the most famous geniuses were ground in a mortar to a costly, strong broth.

Here clerics are turned to salt meat, there princes are fricasseed, there great minds are chopped into small pieces of salami, there flatterers are hung in the smoke and cured, there roast beef is made of coachmen.

Here Aristotle is stuck fast in cabbage down to his feet, and there Origen turns like a capon on the spit; close by a reviewer crows, and from sweet little gentlemen in the fire over there sugar candy is made.

The first one cooks up faint-hearted cowards, and roasts them just like hares, the second one cooks a delicious ragout from nothing but scoundrels' noses; the third one gives a few tyrants an enema with human blood, and makes blood sausage out of them.

Here dainty butter bread is baked from the souls of the effeminate; instead of crabs, a heap of cardinals is boiled red over there. This one makes jelly out of jokers, and there a little devil flatters Diabolini like a ram.

Lucifer had an invitation to this meal extended to the pious hero; Aeneas, however, thanked him very much for all his kindnesses and excused himself, saying that he had lost his appetite for a long time.)

This is all most amusing indeed, but it suggests that by the nineteenth century, the Aeneid is playing a new role in European culture. Many educated people still know the story; otherwise the parody would not seem funny. But many of them no longer take it seriously, as a central source of moral or spiritual guidance.

The impression that Vergil is growing more and more marginalized is confirmed by the last illustration I would like to consider (Figure 12). This picture accompanies a late twentieth-century Polish translation of the Aeneid.[36] Like the one accompanying Perrin's seventeenth-century French translation, it depicts the siege of Troy in Book II, but it does so in a strikingly different way. The French translation invokes the entire ideological apparatus of the ancien régime, and that is serious business—so serious that the effort to illustrate part of it requires two facing pages in that volume. When the same material in the Polish translation is squeezed onto a narrow band at the top of one page, the effect of grandeur is lost. What is more, the approach in the illustration to the Polish translation is fanciful rather than serious, with little stick figures clambering up the side of the horse and the walls of the city. The snakes closing in on Laocoön dwarf the bull behind him, and there is no effort to make any of this appear realistic. There is no reason, of course, that an illustration of the Aeneid should be realistic, but when realism disappears, it takes with it the assumption that art is bound to everyday life in immediate, easily accessible ways. This illustration and the others that go along with it suggest that in our day the Aeneid is not central to the ideals and values of many people. Indeed, Ruth Mortimer confirms this conclusion by noting that most twentieth-century illustrators have turned from the Aeneid to the Eclogues and the Georgics because they have been "interested less in national origins, epic, and the daily life of the gods than in an escape into a supposedly idyllic country life."[37]

The 1502 Strasbourg edition was designed, as its editor notes, to be accessible to a wide range of readers, so that both the educated and the uneducated could find in it a common cultural experience. The Pitt translation and its accompanying illustrations suggest that the poem still mattered, but to far fewer people. The Blumauer parody indicates that by this time the poem was ceasing to matter, and the illustrations to the Polish translation suggest that by the late twentieth century, the Aeneid held an increasingly marginal position in western culture.

## V.

I would not, however, like to close on a pessimistic note, for in fact I am not really pessimistic about the poem and its potential to make an impact on future generations. To be sure, if recent developments in Europe and North America

Cisza zaległa głęboka i wszyscy czekali w napięciu.
Wówczas praojciec Eneasz tak rzekł z wysokiego wezgłowia:

„Niewysłowiony ból rozkazujesz mi wskrzeszać, królowo,
Mówić, jak Troi potężne królestwo runęło żałośnie
Pod ciosami Danaów. Ja sam to nieszczęście widziałem,
Sam bowiem brałem w nim udział niemały. Któż na to wspomnienie
Płacz uśmierzyłby? Nikt, nawet żołnierz srogiego Ulissa,
Ni Myrmidończyk ni Dolop. Lecz oto znika już z niebios
Noc wilgotna i gwiazdy gasnące do snu nawołują.
Skoro wszelako tak pragniesz gorąco usłyszeć o naszych
Przejściach, o mękach Troi ostatnich dowiedzieć się trochę, —
Chociaż boleśnie się myśl przed tym wzdraga i cofa się z lękiem,
Zacznę opowieść.

                    Wodzowie danajscy, znękani bojami,
Kiedy przez tyle lat zawodziły ich losy pod Troją,
Konia, wielkiego jak góra, budują z Pallady natchnienia
Boskiej, a w żebra wprawiają mu deski jodłowe wokoło.
Wieść rozpuszczają, że dar to wotywny przed drogą powrotną.
Za czym przednią drużynę rycerzy tęgich dobrawszy,
Chyłkiem do wnętrza ich wiodą i oto w ciemnej czeluści
Brzucha końskiego zamknięty jest zbrojny huf wojowników.

Z brzegu Troi widoczna jest wyspa słynąca szeroko,
Tenedos, można, zasobna, jak długo Priam królował;
Dzisiaj to tylko zatoka, niepewna przystań dla łodzi.
Owóż tam zaczaiły się wojska na pustym wybrzeżu;
Nam zaś się zdało, że oni już precz odpłynęli do Myken.
Tedy cała się Troja wyzwala z długiej udręki:

47

FIGURE 12 *Aeneid* II. 1 ff. Wergiliusz (*Publius Vergilius Maro*) *Eneida* (London: Polska Fundacja Kulturalna, 1971), p. 47. Princeton University Library.

are any indication, the number of people who will experience the *Aeneid* fully in its original Latin will probably continue to decline. New translations keep appearing, however, and the bimillennium of Vergil's death in 1981–82 generated a surprising amount of interest, not all of it from cloistered academics. And the fact that artists and poets of today continue to turn to Vergil for inspiration suggests that poems like the *Aeneid* should continue to exercise an influence in future generations.

What is more, I would like to encourage us to see some of the theoretical changes in how we study literature and art as opportunities rather than as threats. The certainties promised by positivistic scholarship may be receding ever further into the distance, but the so-called new art history, like the "new historicism" in literary studies, offers us different questions to ask and different ways of seeing the cultural artifacts of the past.[38] If we can agree that "[w]e cannot interpret . . . any historical culture except through the prism of the dominant concepts of our own thought world,"[39] then we can begin asking some questions that older scholarship tended to discourage: How do the artists' fundamental aesthetic and stylistic norms help to determine the ways in which they can see the past? What traces of the artists' own ideologies appear in their renderings of the past? How can assumptions about audience help place the artists' understanding of their source into the culture of their day?

Of course, if artists and scholars of the past cannot view the *Aeneid* objectively, neither can we. Our interpretations are simply the latest in a long chain, beginning with those who first heard the *Aeneid* in ancient Rome and extending through all those artists we have considered here, along with many others. In one sense, this makes the act of interpretation more difficult, for it obligates us to rely more heavily on previous work than did the older paradigm which taught us to understand a poem by experiencing it directly. But by placing our interpretation at the end of the chain, we discover that many others before us saw many things we might miss in the material we love. And this, I believe, more than justifies the additional effort.

# Chapter 10

# NOT-BLANK-VERSE

Surrey's *Aeneid* Translations and

The Prehistory of a Form

STEPHEN MERRIAM FOLEY

BERGSON points out that there are no "negative" conditions in nature. Every situation is positively what it is. For instance, we may say "The ground is not damp." But the corresponding actual conditions in nature are those whereby the ground is dry. We may say that something "is not" in such and such a place. But so far as nature is concerned, what ever is "not" here is positively somewhere else; or, if it does not exist, then other things actually occupy all places where it "is not."

—Kenneth Burke

Blank verse. *Carte blanche.* Let's begin to think about Surrey's *Aeneid*, said to be the first blank verse in English, and the prehistory of blank verse by playing with the name of the form, which according to the OED first appears in Thomas Nash's naughty disparagement (1585) of "the swelling bombast of bragging blank verse." Nash's ironic linking of empty rhetoric and the "blank" verse of early Elizabethan drama depends upon understanding the missing rhyme as a defective theatrical form. And yet if one construes the term neutrally, it says no more than the French *vers sans rime* or *vers non rimés*. If one admires the absence of rhyme, on the other hand, the term "blank verse" celebrates freedom, as does the Italian term that emerged early in the sixteenth century—*versi sciolti*, verses "freed" from the fetters of rhyme, given *carte blanche* to fill in the blank space on the line newly relieved of gothic assonance. Between these conflicting senses falls the rhetorical shadow that follows terms defined by what they are not: *mariage blanc*, shooting blanks, drawing a blank.

With this caution in mind, let us turn to some theoretical and historical problems engaged by some scenes of writing that constitute the prehistory of blank verse. One scene—the point of departure for this chapter—is the translation by Henry Howard, earl of Surrey, of *Aeneid* II and IV (1530s) into a new form, belatedly called the first blank verse in English. Another is the composition by the aristocratic Scots bishop Gavin Douglas of the first full (lowland Scots) translation of the *Aeneid* to circulate in Great Britain (c. 1513), a text legible as "English" in the tradition of "master" Geoffrey Chaucer. Douglas' *Aeneid*, perhaps his finest poem, was one of Surrey's most important sources, as it would be later for Dryden. My interests in these texts—language, form, and translation—intersect the themes that are richly woven through the chapters of this book. Is it possible to translate literary texts across the change of language, form, and culture? If scholarship, as Craig Kallendorf argues in the closing paragraph of Chapter 9, can be shored up against the history of cultural relativism and loss that he illustrates, does not translation have the same recuperative function? If Horace's Greek predecessors were talking back to him, "Why can't I do that to you"? as Joseph Brodsky asks in the epigraph that opens this volume. Here poets and critics, explicitly or implicitly, have been writing about the theory of language and translation. And so, as a philosophical and intermittent gloss on these scenes from early Tudor England and on the other scenes of cultural transmission in this volume, let us consider a key text in the theoretical *lingua franca* of the contemporary academy, Walter Benjamin's "Die Aufgabe des Übersetzers" (The task of the translator), first published as the preface to Benjamin's German translation of Baudelaire's *Tableaux Parisiens* (1927). And, in parting, let us inflect on the blank space of this chapter's final pages the arguments about translation that emerge in Paul de Man's "Conclusions: Walter Benjamin's 'The Task of the Translator' " (where he submits that Jacques Derrida and Benjamin's translators mistranslate "Die Aufgabe") and Derrida's "Des tours de Babel," which one might read as a response to de Man.[1] Like most scenes of translation, then, these inscribe overlapping problems of, on the one hand, identity and plenitude (Surrey's poem *is* the *Aeneid*; Douglas' poem is present in Surrey's; Derrida understands Benjamin; the Word is with God) and, on the other hand, of difference and estrangement (Surrey's poem is *not* the *Aeneid*; Douglas' poem is not present in Surrey's; Derrida mistranslates Benjamin; *Go to, let us go down, and confound their language*). And so the overloading of scenes of translation, or one might say, of translating scenes is deliberate on my part. Let's fill in some blanks.

## Scene of Translation

A scene of translation in the 1530s: at Framingham Castle, the moated stronghold of the Howards in Norfolk, or at Kenninghall, their newly refurbished palace in Suffolk, or perhaps during a trip abroad to France or a brief imprisonment at Windsor—the courtly nobility never stayed anywhere long and found writing a useful contretemps in adversity. Imagine, at one of these locales, the reading materials laid out before Henry Howard, Earl of Surrey, the "proudest boy in England"—heir apparent to Thomas Howard, Duke of Norfolk, Lord Treasurer, hereditary earl martial of England and premier peer of the realm. Imagine the *Aeneid* in the latest Latin redaction with the standard commentaries, either a venerable and pricey manuscript copy or a new continental printed edition, both collector's items in an aristocratic English household dedicated to keeping up with the humanist chanceries, the lawyers, and the French. Beside the Latin *Aeneid* is an equally prized manuscript copy of Gavin Douglas' *Aeneid* in decasyllabic couplets, a vast labor of poetry and scholarship completed by 1513—a year when Douglas found himself in a London exile on suspicion of having taken the "English" side in the aftermath of the battle of Flodden. This English victory, which decimated the Scots nobility and killed their king, was won for Henry VIII by Surrey's grandfather, Thomas Howard, the "Flodden Duke." In addition, imagine open for the perusal of the young earl, on a book-wheel or spread out across a large writing table, one or more of the unrhymed Italian hendecasyllablic Vergilian poems, such as those printed in the *Rime toscane* (1533) of Luigi Alamanni or his earlier (1519) eclogues, a poet in residence at the court of Francis I well known to Wyatt and Surrey, or the translation of Books II and IV of the *Aeneid* composed under the influence of the Medici circle and published as part of a series beginning in 1539.[2]

This is a scene that the labor of scholars from G. F. Nott and F. M. Padelford, Surrey's first two major editors, to more recent and productive contributors like Florence Ridley, Emrys Jones, and O. B. Hardison, allows one to contemplate with some confidence and little hope for further or better information.[3] It is a familiar scene of humanist imitation and emulation as the stylistic ideal of *copia* is defined in theory and reshaped in practice in the overlapping Latin, neo-Latin, and vernacular cultures of the Renaissance. The consummate Vergilian line is both the unattainable model (which the vernacular cannot reproduce linguistically) and the blank in the vernacular culture opened up by that impossibility, a blank that must be inscribed with a new form. And so an aristocratic young man with widely informed taste and the ambition to put himself, and England, onto the new cultural map of human letters emerging in the courts of early sixteenth-century Christendom, finds translating Vergil into a new form to be a cultural opportunity to sharpen the cutting edge of English poetry and to empower for himself, as he wrote of his predecessor Sir Thomas Wyatt, "a hand that taught what might be said in rhyme," or, in this case, without it.[4]

So far, so good. But what causes me to hesitate here is that the narrative as delivered by the scholarship thus far is always at least partially blanked out by the claim that in his *Aeneid* translations Surrey wrote the "first blank verse" in English or—in the words of Thomas Warton, who perhaps first articulated this narrative—that Surrey is England's "first classical poet."[5] In some respects, I should not argue against either of these claims. For a reader whose memory, eyes, and ears are attuned to the blank verse that redounds from the early verse dramas of the 1560s and 70s to our own time, it is impossible *not* to read Surrey's lines as blank verse. To choose but one example, consider these lines from Laocoön's warning in Book II:

> Deem ye the Greeks our enemies to be gone?
> Or any Greekish gifts can you suppose
> Devoid of guile? Is so Ulysses known?
> Either the Greeks are in this timber hid,
> Or this an engine is to annoy our walls,
> To view our towers, and overwhelm our town.
> Here lurks some craft. Good Trojans, give no trust
> Unto this horse, for whatsoever it be,
> I dread the Greeks, yea, when they offer gifts.
>                    (Surrey, II.58–66)

Surrey's line is a flexible one, able to sustain a sense of pattern (as in: To view our towers / and overwhelm our town) and variation (as in: Deem ye the Greeks / our enemies to be gone; or: I dread the Greeks, yea, when they offer gifts). The caesura can be syntactically strong (Devoid of guile? // Is so Ulysses known?) or relatively weak (Or any Greekish gifts // can you suppose). The family resemblance between the prosody of Surrey's translations and the prosody of later blank verse is close enough to warrant the inaugural claim—and indeed it was the claim of national or vernacular priority that Surrey clearly aspired to (why else take on the task taken by the Italians and circulated in France?). In postscript, at least, Surrey's *Aeneid* is blank verse, although at the time no one knew that: the first edition advertises the translation as foreign, "newly drawn in to a strange meter."[6]

I find the larger claim that Surrey is "classical" no less reasonable: his rhetoric of compression, balance, and reserve is one that readers from the eighteenth century on might read as Warton's "justness of thought, correctness of style, and purity of expression."[7] As Emrys Jones, who has perhaps best made the argument for Surrey's classicism, has written: "Surrey's most characteristic verse moves to an assured and regular rhythm which will be familiar to those whose ears are already attuned to Augustan measures. This movement may be termed neo-Latin. It echoes, in thin strains, the rich orchestration of Vergil and of Horace. It shares that Roman concern with quantity and number . . . and reveals itself as part of an intricate balancing system, composed of varied yet predictably recurring patterns. It encourages in the reader a sense of mass and momentum."[8]

Jones' stylistic judgment is acute. But one must also admit that the claim of originality—the first blank verse, the first classical poet—is somehow end-stopped (to borrow a term from prosody) in a patrilineal line. Reconsider the temporal aspect of Jones' claim that Surrey's style is easily available "to those whose ears are *already* attuned to Augustan measures" (italics mine). And if Surrey is so clearly "classical," "neo-Latin," "humanist," or "Renaissance," why do his contemporaries fail fully to congratulate him for it? Why don't they necessarily even find his verse blank? The publication of Surrey's *Aeneid* IV in 1554 and again of *Aeneid* II and IV by the ambitious printer Richard Tottel in 1557 in a text heavily redacted for metrical regularity brought Surrey's *Aeneid* an immediate circulation.[9] Marlowe, for example, read Surrey's *Aeneid* IV in preparing to write his own dramatic blank verse "tragedy," of *Dido, Queen of Carthage*, which survives only in part,[10] and there are lines in the play that clearly echo Surrey. But after this mid-century circulation, Surrey's star falls. Roger Ascham praises Surrey's attempt at unrhymed verse but castigates his blundering "feet of brass."[11] And William Webbe, in looking for the origins of blank verse, found it not in Surrey, but in *Piers Plowman*, of all places.[12] By the time Milton came to defend blank verse and "the known laws of ancient liberty" in his preface to *Paradise Lost*, Surrey wasn't even worth mentioning. The "Renaissance" doesn't always recognize itself in the list of predecessors offered by a posterior line of cultural historiography. One draws something of a blank. Making Surrey's unrhymed line the origin of forms and properties that follow it tends to obscure its relation to the texts that define the scene of its own writing. As Wittgenstein remarks, "It is not possible that there should have been only one occasion on which someone obeyed a rule. . . . To understand a sentence means to understand a language. To understand a language means to be a master of technique."[13] Another way of understanding the blank, then, is to understand it as the "rule" that Surrey is obeying when he appears, on one occasion, to invent a form, or, to inflect Wittgenstein's language another way, to see the "rule" as written in the spaces between the languages he is understanding when he presents himself as the master of a (new) technique.

## LINES OF OPPORTUNITY

In the Italian unrhymed hendecasyllables of translators like Ippolyto and Alamanni, in the rhymed decasyllabic couplets of Douglas, in earlier vernacular *Aeneids* like Mellin de St. Gellais' octosyllabic couplets, in the work of such proponents of unrhymed verse as Trissino and Blaise de Vigénères as well as in the hexameters of Vergil's *Aeneid* itself, Surrey found poems in different languages and representing diverse understandings of prosody. Of these, the most fully theorized and the most prominent in Tudor education was the Latin quantitative meter, in which Tudor school boys were taught to read a rhythm of syntactic stresses imposed over an underlying pattern of long and short syllables forming dactyls or the equivalent.[14] Well known to Surrey through his own practice and the examples of others from Chaucer through the fifteenth century was the ten-syllable English line, with its range of rhythmic opportunities offering up to five stresses of varying strength and susceptible to being understood both as a syllabic system of counted stresses and as a syllabic line with a strong iambic tendency, if not an iambic meter. Well known to Surrey and his courtly readers through their reading of French and Italian poetry are the decasyllabic, hendacasyllabic, and alexandrine lines marked by the placement of line endings, caesuras, and syntactically appropriate stresses. The prosodies available to Surrey, then, were (like English court culture as a whole) multilingual and multicultural—as much the occasion for interlingual exchange as discrete for language codes.

The absence of terminal rhyme in the English decasyllabic or Italian hendec-asyllabic verse shifts the lines of opportunity, giving differing degrees of prom-inence to other prosodic and linguistic elements, to the *constructio* of humanist rhetoric. Such a shift—so simple and yet so radical—opens up space for the echo of Vergil. Of particular importance is the equalizing of line endings and caesurae as the *loci* for syntactic closure or continuation and the enhanced prominence, in the absence of rhyme, of other forms of patterning. Indeed, in a line equalized between line ending and medial break, one could argue that the formal unit becomes the phrase, spread out over varying numbers of hemistiches, com-pressed or extended, its closure or continuation coterminous with the line or hemistich or written over it. And while poets writing in different languages can-not ever be said truly to use the same form, it is easy to see how this phrasal prosody of line and hemistich is a formal opportunity that echoes in another language the Vergilian example. As the accomplished historian of prosody T. V. Brogan has written: "The invention of a wholly new meter is relatively rare; what is not rare, and is vastly more important, is the discovery of what a meter bor-rowed from one language can be made to do in another, based on the particular types of sound clustering (phonological rules), characteristic word shapes (mor-phological patterns), and sentence constructions (syntactic rules) possible in the target language."[15] The formal word order of the sentence may be broken in the interest of aesthetic effect on the whole. In a similar way, Benjamin makes the literalness of the single word prior to the closure of the sentence in translation:

"A real translation is transparent; it does not cover the original, does not block its light, but allows the pure language, as though reinforced by its own medium, to shine upon the original more fully. This may be achieved, above all, by a literal rendering of the syntax which proves words rather than sentences to be the primary element of the translator. For if the sentence is the wall before the language of the original, literalness is the arcade."[16]

Imagine the effect of blanking out the rhymes in Douglas' translation. As an example, let me unrhyme a passage from Douglas, the opening of Book IV:

> By this the Queen, through heavy thoughts beset [unsound]
> In every vein nurses the green wound,
> Smitten so deep with the blind fire of love
> Her troubled mind 'gan from all rest repair. [remove]
> (Douglas, IV.3–6)[17]

Note, for example, how the heavily stressed predicate, "nurses the green wound" achieves terminal prominence. It follows the counterpoint of three half-lines where the inversion of word order and the concentration of prepositional modifiers in rhythmic contrast to one another defer syntactic closure, creating an enhanced opportunity for the resounding cadences of the close.

If the original rhymes are restored, the couplets distract from this heightened sense of composition:

> By this the Queen, through heavy thoughts unsound
> In every vein nurses the green wound,
> Smitten so deep with the blind fire of love
> Her troubled mind 'gan from all rest remove.

The rhyme promotes the degree of stress in both of the terminal words of the couplet—"unsound"/"wound"—and thus diminishes the eerie prominence that the phrase "the green wound" otherwise obtains in terminal unrhymed position. The terminal pause becomes the effect not merely of the sense, but of the obligatory and expected assonance.

Removing the rhyme from the existing decasyllabic line, then, in English—as in French or Italian—provides a formal blank for neoclassical "invention" between the source and the target languages, and I begin by whimsically blanking out Douglas' rhymes instead of examining the relation between Surrey and his Vergilian source in order to acknowledge that it is language rather than content alone that is to be translated. The blank opens up the possibility of something strange in the language of the translator, a blank is to be filled in by what Benjamin calls the "translatability" of the original: "Translation is a form. To comprehend it as form, one must go back to the original, for the laws governing the translation lie within the original, contained in the issue of its translatability. . . . If translation is a form, translation must be a feature of certain works."[18] Suspend in that blank syntactic, etymological, phonological, and morphemic markers that reverberate with those Vergil plays with in his laconic hemistiches, and it is easy to see how Surrey's new form could create an effect that echoes the Vergilian hexameter—at least to a reader whose memory retains the Latin model of what Cardinal Newman called those "pathetic half-lines, giving utterance, which is the voice of Nature herself, to the pain and weariness, yet hope of better things, which is the hope of her children in every time."[19] Or, to quote Benjamin, "Just as the manifestations of life are intimately connected with the phenomenon of life without being of importance to it, a translation issues from the original—not so much from its life as from its afterlife."[20] Recognizing translatability is to acknowledge the constant flux of language, whether original or target, momentarily to circumscribe that flux in the claim of translation, and "to admit," with Benjamin, "that all translation is only a somewhat provisional way of coming to terms with the foreignness of languages."[21]

In Surrey's neoclassical aesthetics, Emrys Jones has commented, "there is an increase in the element of pure verbality: words, phrases, and sentences occupy more attention, they themselves become aesthetic objects."[22] Rather than translating a story, Surrey is suspending one language against another in the interest of aesthetic effect. By reading his Douglas for the echo of Vergil's Latin style, Surrey does not simply classicize Douglas, he hears the classical in it. Consider once again the opening lines of Book IV, which I now quote from Jones' edition:

> But now the wounded Queen, with heavy care,
> Throughout the veins she nourisheth the playe, [wound]
> Surprised with blind flame, and to her mind
> Gan eke resort the prowess of the man,
> And honour of his race: while in her breast
> Imprinted stuck his words and picture's frame.
>                    (Surrey, IV.3–8)

> By this the Queen, through heavy thoughts unsound
> In every vein nurses the green wound,
> Smitten so deep with the blind fire of love
> Her troubled mind 'gan from all rest remove,

Compassing the great prowes of Aenee,
The large worhipful size remembers she
Of his lineage and folks; for aye present
Deep in her breast so was his figure print,
And all his words fixed, that for busy thought,
Not ease her members nor quiet suffer might.
                    (Douglas, IV.3–12)


At regina gravi iamdudum saucia cura
vulnus alit venis et caeco carpitur igni.
multa viri virtus animo multusque recursat
gentis honos; haerent infixi pectore vultus
verbaque, nec placidam membris dat cura quietem.
                    (*Aen*. IV.1–5)

Surrey finds in Douglas a phrasal architecture that echoes the Vergilian line. Noun phrases, prepositional phrases, subjects, and complements are suspended along and across line endings and caesurae, and sense is deferred and gradually completed hemistich by hemistich. His task as a translator was to find a medium that would enhance the interlingual architecture as an element of pure form intersecting with the content of the original at a moment of chance or opportunity. Relieved of the obligation to rhyme, the play of syntax and hemistich can take off. In Benjamin's words: "Just as a tangent touches a circle lightly at but one point—establishing with this touch rather than with this point, the law on which it is to continue, on its straight path to infinity—a translation touches the original lightly and at but one point."[23]


## LINEAR ECHOES

Vergil's first two lines (which resonate with other key lines in the Dido narrative) inscribe a queen pathologically overcome by a love that had taken her unawares:

> At regina gravi iamdudum saucia cura
> vulnus alit venis et caeco carpitur igni.

The power of the lines, beginning with the strong adversative, which establishes the contrast between Dido and Aeneas (between Book III and Book IV), comes from the play of sense and line. The duration and distractedness of Dido's state of mind are reflected in the splitting of modifiers across metrical markers in the first line; the systemic quality of the affliction and the suddenness of its attack mirrored in the alliterative active (*vulnus alit venis*) and passive (*caeco carpitur igni*) verb phrases paired across the caesura of the line. Douglas' first line respects both the duration implied by *iamdudum* in his opening "By this," and the disjointedness of Dido's mind through his deferral of "oppressed" to the end position. Quite flexibly he shifts the suddenness of *caeco . . . igni* to "the green wound," echoing in one epithet the aesthetic effect as well as the sense of the other.

Surrey, operating on an understanding of line and sense that reverberates with Vergil's, captures the unexpectedness with the introduction of a delayed adjectival phrase ("Surprised . . .") in strong initial position:

> But now the wounded Quene, with heavy care,
> Throughout the veins she nourisheth the playe,
> Surprised with blind flame
> 
> (Surrey, IV.3–5)

He tries for the stark depth of *At regina* and (with less success) for the durée of *iamdudum* with his own "But now," the disjointed mind of the queen reflected in the isolation of "with heavy care" from "the wounded Queen" and from the verb phrase that follows.

Such examples are reflective of Surrey's overall practice. Surrey knows how to use line and caesura to echo the most common Vergilian techniques of metrical pointure such as the sudden inflection of a shift in person at the opening of a speech:

> tum sic excepit regia Iuno:
> 'mecum erit iste labor . . .'
> 
> (*Aen.* IV.114–15)

> (Queen Juno then took thus her tale againe:
> "This travail be it mine . . .")
> 
> (Surrey, IV.144–45)

He recognizes the aesthetic importance of stock structural transitions that carry overwhelming pathetic freight, such as the *dixerat* that intervenes between Dido's desperate rhetorical hypothesis of being with child and Aeneas' chilling struggle to contain his conflicted feelings:

'saltem si qua mihi de te suscepta fuisset
ante fugam suboles, si quis mihi parvulus aula
luderat Aeneas, qui te tamen ore referret,
non equidem omnino capta ac deserta viderer.'
    dixerat. ille Iovis monitis immota tenebat
lumina et obnixus curam sub corde premebat.
        (*Aen.* IV.327–32)

("Before thy flight a child had I once borne,
  Or seen a young Aeneas in my court
  Play up and down, that might present thy face,
  All utterly I could not seem forsaken."
    Thus said the queen. He to the god's
advice,
  Unmoved held his eyes, and in his breast
  Repressed his care and strove against his will.)
        (Surrey, IV.424–28)

Similarly, he knows how to use the line to mark the unsettling closure of a speech as the narrative moves in suspense toward its reception, as, for example, Aeneas ends his studied reply to Dido with the powerfully ambiguous half-line *Italiam non sponte sequor:*

ipse deum manifesto in lumine vidi
intrantem muros vocemque his auribus hausi.
desine meque tuis incendere teque querellis;
Italiam non sponte sequor.
        (*Aen.* IV.358–61)

(In bright day light the god myself I saw
Enter these walls, and with these ears him heard.
Leave then to plaint to vex both thee and me.
Against my will to Italy I go.)
        (Surrey, IV.468–71)

He can easily reproduce the effect of rare and powerful authorial interjection:

At regina dolos (quis fallere possit amantem?)
praesensit, motusque excepit prima futuros
omnia tuta timens.
        (*Aen.* IV.296–98)

(Full soon the Queen this crafty slight gan smell,
—Who can deceive a lover in forecast?—
And first foresees these motions for to come,
Yet most assured fearing.)
                    (Surrey, IV.382-85)

And Surrey is also adept at sustained pattern and variation. Consider, for example, how variable construction gives aesthetic movement to series construction, as in the awakening of the hunting party in Book IV following the storm sent by Juno:

Then from the sea, the dawning gan arise.
The sun once up, the chosen youth gan throng
Out at the gates; the hayes [nets] so rarely knit,
The hunting staves with the broad heads of steel,
And of Massile the horsemen forth they break;
Of scenting hounds a kennel huge likewise,
And at the threshold of her chamber door
The Carthage lords did on their queen await;
The trampling steed, with gold and purple trapped,
Chawing the foamy bit there fiercely stood.
Then issued she, awaited with great train,
Clad in a cloak of Tyre embroidered full rich.
Her quiver hung behind her back, her tresses
Knotted in gold, her purple vesture eke
Buttoned with gold.
                    (Surrey, IV.164–78)

The incremental effect of a descriptive rhetoric that builds by the hemistich, the headlong energy of steed and huntsmen, staves in hand, gives pause at the final arrival of the queen, anticipated first at the threshold, as the rhythm of flow and stop slows to admire the golden plaiting of her hair and golden fastening of her purple vestment, alluring borders of body and garment framed in her issue. The effect of Surrey's lines, one might add, is not quite like anything ever heard in English before. Taking the available lines of opportunity, Surrey diverts them to new ends. The new effect conforms to the need to find an English device to create the echo, but in order to "fit," it shifts the lines of opportunity already in place and changes them forever. In this case, just as Warton claimed, Surrey does invent the classical. In Benjamin's words, "Whereas content and language form a certain unity in the original, like a fruit and its skin, the language of the translation envelops its content like a royal robe with ample folds. For it signifies a more exalted language than its own and thus remains unsuited to its content, overpowering and alien."²⁴

Given such a battery of stylistic echo and extension, one might well conclude that understanding the prosodies available to Surrey's imagination in terms of an aesthetics of *copia*, of plurality, and polyphony is perhaps more fruitful than merely displaying their differences. The complex intersection of any of these prosodies with patterns of syntax and sense means that they open up ever-changing lines of poetic opportunity. Each of the prosodies is not simply a metrical grid of so many ictuses in this position or that but a changing flow of syllabic patterns, with shifting relationships of phrases and clauses. Such creative ways of apprehending units of composition change from line to line, from poet to poet, and within the oeuvre of a single author, across languages, and throughout the history of form. The "rules" that Surrey was following, one might argue, were more like aesthetic blanks to be filled in between literatures and language systems than mere protocols of versification.

The most useful metrical theory, as Roman Jakobson suggests, finds the origins of verse types in the properties of the language itself. As Donald Wesling and others have argued,²⁵ there is a systematic homology between language and meter, sentence and line, phrase and hemistich, word and foot, syllable and position. Or, to put a Renaissance inflection on metrical theory, the practice of prosody between languages becomes a material instance of *copia*. To write a sonnet in English or a Horatian lyric or a Vergilian line is not merely to translate a poem but, through form, to put cultures in dialogue. Or, to put the *copia* of the Vergilian line in the frame of translation theory as well prosodic theory, consider the words of Benjamin (and his translator): "The task of the translator consists in finding the particular intention toward the target language which produces in that language the echo of the original. This is a feature of translation that basically differentiates it from the poet's work, because the intention of the latter is never directed toward the language as such, at its totality, but is aimed solely at specific linguistic contextual aspects. Unlike a work of literature, translation finds itself not in the center of the language forest but on the outside facing the wooded ridge; it calls into it without entering, aiming at that single spot where the echo is able to give, in its own language, the reverberation of the work in the alien one."²⁶

In the language forest of English, the romance languages, and Latin and Greek, the space of the unrhymed line is one such blank to aim at. As the echoes of English language translations of Vergil resonate from Surrey to John Dryden and to Robert Fitzgerald, C. Day Lewis, and Allen Mandelbaum,²⁷ the blank that is filled by rhyme or emptied of it continues to be at play. For Dryden, translating

Vergil in the decades following the publication of *Paradise Lost*, the invention of the heroic couplet becomes a means of canceling the echo of the Miltonic line. His preferred term for blank verse is *prose mesurée;* among his many sources is Douglas, whom he turns to *for the rhyme.*[28] For Lewis and Fitzgerald the unrhymed line is a modernist erasure of Dryden's couplets and the tedious stanzaic forms of the Victorian and Edwardian translators. And for Allen Mandelbaum, the irregular alliteration and off-rhyme likewise slows the forward motion of modernist blank verse to the pace of Vergilian reflectiveness:

> I sing of arms and of a man: his fate
> had made him fugitive; he was the first
> to journey from the coasts of Troy as far
> as Italy and the Lavinian shores.
>
> (Mandelbaum, I.1–4)

### DOUGLAS AND THE *TRANSLATIO STUDII*

The plot thickens when the longer story of Douglas' work and the full text of his *Aeneid* are added to the mixture. As the best commentators on the problem have recognized, Douglas as well as Surrey is a Renaissance poet, whose humanist textual practices reflect the integrity of the Latin. We have seen the use Surrey made of Douglas in his own ambitious humanist project. But what did he decline to use in Douglas? And so another scene of translation: this time one spaced out over time and geography, between the place of Vergil and the *Aeneid* in the late empire and in the world of the church fathers through his shifting reception in the European literatures from Bede to Dante.

Douglas was working from one of the best available editions of Vergil, the 1501 Paris edition prepared by Badius Ascensius (Joost Bade). And Douglas assigns himself the task of rescuing the text of Vergil from those who have abused it, from the learned Laurentius Valla to poor William Caxton, and even his beloved English master Geoffrey Chaucer. Yet his protest imitates the form of the very manuscript tradition it protests. The ongoing identification in Douglas' extratextual matter of the author/translator and his spiritual journey as a writer with Aeneas' journey are surely of a piece with the manuscript Vergilianism of the late Middle Ages. As Christopher Baswell comments in the "coda" to his *Virgil in Medieval England:*

> Despite his claim to an austere textual purity, further, Douglas makes elaborate and canny use of the late-medieval book of Virgil, with its hierarchical

system of accessus, vitae, verse summaries, and commentaries. Upon that system Douglas models his own apparatus of vernacular Scots summaries, prologues, afterwords, and prose marginalia. This codicological super-structure, neatly separated from the central Virgilian text, becomes the area for Douglas' own voice, his readerly preoccupations, and his poetic am-bitions. Indeed, the justly famed Prologues are virtual conspectus of late-medieval vernacular forms, and make up an almost competitive dialogue with the varieties of Virgilian style that Douglas resisters, often dazzlingly well, in the translation itself . . . Douglas thus uses the inherited frame-work of the Virgilian book at once to acknowledge, contest, and yet (quite literally) marginalize contending traditions.[29]

And so Douglas' writing table, as he passes from book to book, from prologue to prologue, becomes the locus of dispute (*flyting* is the Scots genre through which he makes vernacular and humanist currency of this longstanding scholastic practice) with the Vergil of his predecessors—John of Salisbury, Augustine, Ser-vius, the medieval commentators, as well as Dante, Petrarch, Boccaccio, Landino, and Badius Ascensius.

If the translation is intended to bring the reader the text of the *Aeneid* "broad and plaine," his prologues present a narrative of the castigating textual scholar and embellishing poet as knight-author, whose *Aeneid* will thereby be something superior as a whole to the sense-by-sense translation he has written. The prologue to the descent of Book VI, as Lois Ebin comments,

> makes more explicit . . . the power of poetry to go beyond the original sentence of an author and produce new meaning for later audiences. As he ventures, like Aeneas, into the unknown—a realm where past, present, and future meet—he symbolically parts company with Virgil. In an association that apparently is original with Douglas, the narrator turns from Aeneas' "Sibilla Cumane" to another sibyl, Mary, . . . to distinguish the course he will follow as a Christian poet.[30]

Douglas provides the familiar case for justifying poetry as a source of truth opened up under the garments of fiction. In pledging to retain the text of his poet, the translator moves beyond the lines he preserves, delivering the "sen-tence" in order to allow the reader, like Douglas himself, to move beyond it, through the medium of a "knightly style."

Douglas' theory of translation remains what Karlheinz Stierle has identified as vertical. Just as Douglas' "knightly style" tends to shift the heroic scene to the present, translating *miles* as knight, his apparatus traces a *translatio studii* as the pagan veil of the original text is lifted to reveal, to successive Christian readers, larger and clearer allegorical understanding.[31] One way of understanding Surrey's use of Douglas' text, then, is to read the inherited allegory, like the rhymes, as a blank. Surrey found in Douglas a vigorous decasyllabic line and an available poetic diction with a good family resemblance to Chaucer as well as to Vergil— forms rather than stories or allegories. Once the *translatio studii* is a blank, the appropriation of Vergil and Douglas becomes another field: the historical differ- ence between Surrey and Vergil or Surrey and Douglas or Surrey and Chaucer is not to be displaced, overcome, moved: difference is the given of such translation. It is at this historical moment, Stierle comments, that in French and Italian "to translate" becomes *traduire/tradurre* and *la translation / la translatione* remain re- served for physical removal alone. Vergil's text, Douglas' couplets, Surrey's own translation are a field of likeness and difference suspended in *copia*, creating for this poet as he self-consciously inscribes an inaugural scene an instant interlin- gual and transhistorical canonicity of style. There are always spaces between the lines of such *copia*. The relationship between the texts is, in Stierle's formulation, horizontal: they echo one another without cancellation. Benjamin's metaphor of the broken vessel or amphora of translation may be emblematic: "Fragments of a vessel that are to be glued together must match one another. . . . In the same way a translation, instead of imitating the sense of the original, must lovingly and in detail incorporate the original's way of meaning, thus making both the original and the translation recognizable as fragments of a greater language, just as fragments are part of a vessel. For this very reason translation must in large measure refrain from wanting to communicate something, from rendering the sense."[32]

## TRANSLATING SCENES

My quotations from Benjamin are intended to introduce an anachronous element to the argument of this chapter, as is appropriate for any story of translation, which is by definition a violation of time and place. As such a violation, trans- lation, which Benjamin places midway between poetry and theory, has a theo- retical dimension that poetry does not. Like philosophy, translation makes a proposition "to be / or not to be a translation of the *Aeneid*." I wish to insert this discussion of translation between the lines of the continued parable of "The Task of the Translator," making theory explicitly a space to explore those paradoxes of proposition and cancellation that I have woven through the trope of the blank. The blank, I have suggested, is what is left out (the rhyme, the allegory, the meter of the other language, the text to be translated) and it is also those elements that fill in the blank and thus change the target language through translation. In translation theory as in prosodic theory, the relation between original and translation or between the metrical set and the actual line can lapse, if insufficiently contemplated as elements of language itself, into a yearning to escape from such contradictory conditions or into regret at being trapped within them. If a meter (*metron*, Greek "rule") is not really a rule (Latin *regula*, rule), what is it? If a translation is not the original, what is it? What kind of presence does an original text or a metrical norm have in a poem? Are they *not* there? What does "of" mean in the phrase "a translation *of* the Aeneid" or "in" in the phrase "a poem *in* blank verse"? Isn't the blank verse rather "in" the poem? Isn't Surrey's *Aeneid* rather "the *Aeneid of* a translation"? Benjamin is surely right to insist, both in his explicit claims and in his metaphorical exercises (the forest, the circle, the arcade, the broken vessel), upon the necessary relation of translation and philosophy. "The philosopher's task consists in comprehending all of natural life through the more encompassing life of history."[33]

The philosopher's task is thus likewise secondary and recuperative. Like the philosopher, the translator contemplates the truth in the moving time of language, capturing it as the mental stillness between the movement of tongues in translation: "If there is such a thing as the language of truth, a tensionless and even silent depository of the ultimate secrets for which all thought strives, then this language of truth is—the true language. And this very language, in whose devination and description lies the only perfection for which a philosopher can hope, is concealed in concentrated fashion in translations. There is no muse of philosophy, nor is there one of translation." These arts have no muse precisely because their tasks are parabolic intersections of the past rather than words simply invoked or projected into the pure future of fiction. They may have no muses, Benjamin later comments, but there is a nostalgic *ingenium* (he does not translate the term) in them: "But despite the claim of sentimental artists, these two are not philistines. For there exists a philosophical genius, whose most proper characteristic is the nostalgia for that language which manifests itself in translation."[34] The theory of translation and the theory of language are the same.

The best theories of translation are fragments, lodged, like translations themselves, on borders. And if they are not fragments, quotation quickly breaks them down. For the twentieth century, the tropes of Benjamin's essay have echoed anew the fragmentary *loci* of a translation theory that never quite gels in the centuries of discourse that record it. Between the traditional poles of fidelity and freedom in Benjamin's playful and powerful text resonate Horace's *nec verbum verbo*, the story of Babel, the Johannine beginning of the Word, Jerome's mystery of the *ordo verborum*, the seventy-two authors and seventy-two days of composition of the single text of the Septuagint, the killing letter and the living spirit, the moment of *tikkun* in kabala. Benjamin's own tropes—the refusal of the reader, the echo in the forest of language, the folds of the royal robe, the intersection of the circle and the line, the broken vessel—establish in the ambient propositional form of his essay a performative countertext, creating a series of echoing parables that demand to be translated again and again against one another, as the possible meanings shift in changing context. Translation as topic becomes a vehicle for pure metaphor, the one term an etymological translation of the other. Benjamin's "few pages," Willis Barnstone comments,[35] "have taken on the quality of Scripture, for they are profound, intuitive, elusively obscure, and at the same time illuminating." Benjamin's essay becomes his own ideal of translation: "to some degree, all great texts contain their translation between the lines; this is true above all of sacred writings. The interlinear version of the Scriptures is the prototype or ideal of all translation."[36]

In the presence of such Scripture, scholars of fourfold interpretation will not find it surprising that it is the "most literal" of questions which motivates the arch scholiast Paul de Man's commentary on "The Task of the Translator," an essay that is an echo even in its textual history, the text having been reconstructed from notes and a tape recording of de Man's last Messenger (messenger?) lecture at Cornell:

> We now then ask the simplest, the most naive, the most literal of possible questions in relation to Benjamin's text, and we will not get beyond that: what does Benjamin say? What does he say, in the most immediate sense possible? It seems absurd to ask a question that is so simple, that seems to be so unnecessary, because we can certainly admit that among literate people we would at least have some minimal agreement about what is being said here, allowing us then to embroider upon this statement, to take positions, discuss, interpret, and so on. But it seems that, in the case of this text, this is very difficult to establish. Even the translators, who had to read it closely to some extent, certainly don't seem to have the slightest idea what Benjamin is saying; so much so that when Benjamin says certain things rather simply in one way—for example he says that something is *not*—the translators, who at least know German well enough to know the difference between something *is* and something is *not*—don't see it![37]

De Man proceeds, following the example of Carol Jacobs,[38] quite "literally" to catalogue a series of mistranslations by Harry Zohn and Maurice de Gandillac,

Benjamin's English and French translators: "translatable" becomes *intraduisable;* "unlike" becomes *n'est pas sans ressemblance.* But apart from the corrections (to which he will add his own deconstructive pseudo-corrections), de Man's protests are a coy invitation to open up the traditional questions of translation theory: form and content (*what* does Benjamin *say?*); literalness or closeness (the most literal of questions, very close to the text); intention and reception (minimal agreement about what is being said). It seems "absurd," de Man mockingly comments, to ask such a question. Thus asking the question quite neatly moves from *seems* to *is* in de Man's arch-commentary and delivers the absurd, the equation of what *is* and what *is not* in the space of the translation, favoring the "is not."[39]

The balance of de Man's "Conclusions" gravitates, with due consideration of the consequences, toward a privative ethics, a systematic equation of necessary mistranslation, absence, and death against the Benjaminian tableau of pure language, echo, and the afterlife of form. The "task" (*Die Aufgabe*) of the translator becomes that which he has "given up": "If you enter the Tour de France and you give up—'*er hat aufgegeben,*' he doesn't continue in the race anymore." The "birth pangs" which translation evokes in allowing for the afterlife of an original are to de Man translated "by 'death pangs' as much as by 'birth pangs' and the stress is perhaps more on death than on life." Benjamin's *überleben* becomes: "to live beyond your own death in a sense. The translation belongs not to the life of the original, the original is already dead, but the translation belongs to the afterlife of the original, thus affirming and confirming the death of the original."[40]

De Man's revision of the translation of the metaphor of the broken vessel, again heavily derivative of Carol Jacobs, is the climactic castigation of the essay. He claims to see the lasting fragmentation rather than seamless totality of the vessel:

> All you have to do, to see that, is translate correctly, instead of translating like Zohn—who made this difficult passage very clear—but who in the process of making it clear made it say something completely different. Zohn said, "fragments of a vessel that are to be glued together must match one another in the smallest detail." Benjamin said, translated by Carol Jacobs word by word: "fragments of a vessel, in order to be *articulated* together"— which is much better than *glued* together, which has a totally irrelevant concreteness—"must *follow* one another in the smallest detail"—which is not at all the same as *match* one another. What is already present in the difference is that we have *folgen,* not *gleichen,* not to match.[41]

What I must stress again is that in "correcting," de Man self-consciously and purposively delivers himself back into the rhetoric of literalism. Correcting the bad translation, Jacobs translates "word for word," so that "closeness" and "clarity" become opposing terms, clarity the result of the freedom to be wrong. In looking for the word best to translate *folgen*, "to follow" rather than "to match," de Man is looking for the word that matches. The gesture is performative. The essay is a challenge. The contested ground is not translation but the theology of the Word, which de Man declines to listen to. And the person challenged is none other than Jacques Derrida.

Once again, the gesture is performative: an overheard lesson in the Paris seminar of M. Derrida, the grammatologist, lies at the center of de Man's "Conclusions." Note how much "saying" and "hearing" ("so I am told") falls into de Man's diction in this essay, correcting errors in written translations—a teasing whisper that challenges the priority of the letter. This fleeting moment of de Man's essay turns upon Derrida's overheard reliance on Maurice de Gandillac's French mistranslation. But this mistranslation, corrected at such great length in the development of the essay, appears here to be merely one side of a reversible image. Philosophical or critical commentary is displaced into "comedy":

> What adds some comedy to this particular instance is that Jacques Derrida was doing a seminar with this particular text in Paris, using the French— Derrida's German is pretty good, but he prefers to use the French, and when you are a philosopher in France you take Gandillac more or less seriously. So Derrida was basing part of his reading on the "intraduisable," on the untranslatability, until someone in his seminar (so I'm told) pointed out to him that the correct word was "translatable." I'm sure Derrida could explain that it was the same—and I mean that in a positive sense, it is the same, but still it is not the same without some additional explanation."[42]

The scene is, of course, a comedy of the philosophical absurd: fallacious by reason of contradiction. Having insisted with staged naïveté upon the absolute difference between what is and what is not, de Man now posits ("in a positive sense") that "it is the same." Or at least it will be the same, if a philosopher can explain it, the philosopher's supplement offering the sole warrant of the translator's fidelity. And what exactly is "it"?

De Man's lecture notes diverge from the tape recording, William Jewett, the transcriber, comments, "only on the last sheet, where de Man wrote: 'Im Amfang was das Wort und das Wort war bei Gott / Dasselbe war bei Gott / ohne Dasselbe' (the last two words lined out) in the beginning of Luther's translation of St.

John's gospel, which Benjamin quotes in Greek and to which de Man made reference in the question session following the Cornell lecture."[43] Derrida's reply puts the canceled Word back in the text. "Des tours de Babel," an essay published in French as an appendix to a volume containing its English translation (with a French title), is a tour-de-force rereading of Benjamin's "Die Aufgabe" that understands translation and language as inseparable functions. The essay also continues the cabalistic trajectory of "The Task," finding in the confusion of multiple tongues after Babel a point of untotalized unity, a sacred *pas de sens*, the *pas* being both a "step" forward and the negation (which Joseph Graham, the English translator of the essay, ably renders as "skip").

The problem of faith is written in the letters of the problem of fidelity. Like de Man's lecture, "Des tours de Babel" is a resounding rehearsal of Benjamin's "Die Aufgabe" in which the echo of redemption, duty, and survival drowns out de Man's rhetoric of mere cancellation and death. The scene is set by the naming of Babel, a "singular example, at once archetypical and allegorical," which "could serve as an introduction to all the so-called theoretical problems of translation." Babel is not only the untranslatable proper name of a city and a common noun for confusion—both the "pouring together" of tongues and the confusion of the builders over the incomplete tower—but, etymologically the name of "God the father."[44] If the Semites sought monolingual imperialism, God the father proclaims his name and:

> ruptures the rational transparency but interrupts also the . . . linguistic imperialism. He destines them to translation, he subjects them to a law of translation both necessary and impossible; in a stroke with his translatable-untranslatable name he delivers a universal reason (it will no longer be subject to the rule of a particular nation), but he simultaneously limits its universality: forbidden transparency, impossible univocity. Translation becomes law, duty, and debt, but the debt one can no longer discharge.[45]

"Die Aufgabe des Übersetzers" is to Derrida, then, from its first word, "the commitment, the duty, the responsibility"[46] that the translator must render and thus reach a reconciliation. The commitment of the translator is the duty of survivor and the responsibility for ensuring the survival—living on, living beyond of the original. Like seeds of living organisms, the words of translation allow the growth and maturity of the original by transforming themselves repeatedly in mutation.[47] The metaphor of the seed joins the metaphor of marriage. The relation between the original and the translation is one of difference: "A translation weds the original when the two adjoined fragments, which are as different as possible, complete each other to form a greater language, in the course of the afterlife which changes them both. . . . This at least is my interpretation—my translation, my 'task of the translator.' It is what I have called the contract of translation: hymen or contract of marriage with the promise of inventing a child, the seeding of which will give rise to history and growth."⁴⁸ Translation is necessarily incomplete, but it allows in the image of the adjoining fragments a vision of the infinite.

As Graham writes,⁴⁹ in explaining why he has not translated the title, "Des tours de Babel could be translated 'Of the towers of Babel,' 'From the towers of Babel,' 'About the towers of Babel.' And 'tours' can mean 'towers, tricks, turns, or tropes. . . . ' Thus 'Of the tropes,' 'From the tropes,' unsw. Des and tours together are a homonym with detour—'Detours from Babel.' And, following Derrida, Babel is also the name of God the Father—'Of the towers of God,' 'Away from the towers of God,' 'About God's tricks,' 'About God's tropes,' 'God's detours.' " An image of the necessary incompleteness of translation, yes, but here we see also in the "letters" of language the pure language of the sacred. Reconciliation is only promised. "But a promise is not nothing." A new literalism emerges. "There is only letter, and it is the truth of pure language, the truth as pure language. . . . This law . . . grants a liberty to literality. In the same event, the letter ceases to oppress insofar as it is no longer the exterior body or corset of meaning. The letter also translates itself of itself, and it is in this self-relation of the sacred body that the task of the translator find itself engaged." Derrida's last lines are thus literally a quotation of Benjamin's last lines (in translation): "The interlinear version of the sacred text is the model or ideal of all translation."⁵⁰

I decline here fully to retrace the trajectory of Derrida's "tours," but let me take the reconciliation of sacred faith and fidelity in translation as a pretext to return in closing to the Aeneid. Servius' commentary⁵¹ on the fidus . . . Achates of Aeneid I.188 draws a distinction between fidus (dependable, trustworthy) and fidelis (faithful). The gloss has often been extended to the famous dictum of Horace's Ars Poetica: nec verbum verbo curabis reddere fides / interpres (133–34).⁵² The morphological play of verbum verbo, the replacement of one word with a nonidentical declension of itself, is a verbal icon of the exact copy that Horace declines, and the deferral of the subject fidus interpres, set ironically in broken line position, evokes the full force of Servius' distinction. Such a translator is merely dependable, like a dog or a slave, or comfortable and familiar, like a favorite slipper, "a dependable old word-trader." The faith of the believers is different: this faith is a form of knowledge, the substance of things hoped for, the evidence of things unseen. In obeying sacred law, in being fidelis rather than fidus, Derrida has observed, literalism obtains a liberty.

Can we flip the question here and ask what kind of faith Surrey's blanking out of the typological Aeneas suggests? One answer would be that it takes a man out of the sacramental order and delivers him to the scrutiny of a consciousness aware, above all, of *salvatio fide sola*. While Vergil can take Dante or Douglas by the hand only so far, while their *Aeneids* are veiled in eschatological clarity, the *Aeneid* of Surrey is bare: the judgment lies open. The faithfulness of the translation leaves the reader in the blank spaces of doubt and hope. *tantaene animis caelestibus irae? sum pius Aeneas.*

# Chapter 11

# VERGIL READING HOMER

## A CONVERSATION BETWEEN
## ROBERT FAGLES AND SARAH SPENCE

Just at the moment when Robert Fagles was first turning his attention from Homer to Vergil and starting to think about translating the *Aeneid*, he and I sat down and discussed the Latin epic and some issues of its translation.

SARAH SPENCE (S): Let me ask you about translation in general, and about your relationship with Homer in particular. How would you characterize your relationship to him? Are you an aggressive reader of the texts you translate or a reverential one?

ROBERT FAGLES (F): Oh, both at once, I think. I'm partly on my knees with reverence and partly keeping my dukes up too, trying to lay a glove on the great master. That sort of thing. It's both affiliation and combat, a warm hug and a submission hold, love and kinds of envy too, and of course I'm hopelessly outmanned. What I feel these days, however, having spent some twenty years with Homer, is bereft. I remember Robert Fitzgerald gave a reading of his *Iliad* at Princeton, when he was nearing the end of his fine translation. I drove him back to Newark to catch a plane the next day and asked a fatuous question on the way: "It's an awfully long poem, isn't it, Robert?" And he replied, putting me in my place, "Yes, Bob, but I wake up every morning with Homer as my companion. That's the privilege." Well, I've experienced that too, for many years, and it's a great privilege, and to give it over now is very hard.

S: Do you feel as if you have breathed Homer's air?

F: I feel as if I *ought* to breathe his air, *try* to breathe his air, respiring with him line by line if possible.

S: Do you also find that you've had to destroy him?

F: Perhaps, but I really think it's less deconstructive than that. I think it's more . . . if you're doing your job well, it's more constructive, restorative, or it ought to be. I'm often asked, "What were the inadequacies of Translator X or Y or Z that led you to do your own translation?" It's not a question of their abilities at all—or mine, for that matter. Each of us has dealt with Homer the best way that he can, and each can offer the reader something in the bargain. It's a question of the capacity of Homer to sustain himself in the face of his translators—he's the great survivor!—and more, to invigorate us, and our writing too, if we're lucky.

S: What about Vergil as a translator of Homer? Joseph Brodsky has said "Homer was Vergil's only audience." Would you agree with that?

F: Homer's the one who would have understood it best.

S: Do you think Vergil was a good translator?

F: Matchless. The model for all translators, thanks to Vergil's courage. I'm not convinced that the anxiety of influence should apply to each and every writer. Take Vergil, Shakespeare, and Milton—they may suffer less from an anxiety of influence than they exult in the act of emulation. They feel the challenge to overcome, rather than the fear of being overcome by, the greater master. That's what lights the fires.

S: Do you think the *Aeneid*, Books II and III in particular, are in some way a taking on of Homer?

F: Certainly.

S: Isn't Book III a bad *Odyssey*, an *Odyssey* without a goal?

F: Yes, though the way it drifts about in quest of the receding city has its meaning too. But Book II is a more than satisfactory *Iliad*.

S: Very violent.

F: Very violent. Memorable because of its violence. That's where the emulative strife occurs between Vergil and Homer. "Let me do you one better," says Vergil to Homer. Almost, "Let me show you how it's done. In my language and in my era and with my sensibility." Two great poets engaged in a tug-of-war.

S: Some have argued that the violation of Priam's palace in Book II is to be seen as a rape. Do you think it's also a rape of Homer?

F: A rape of Homer? I think it's more a violent service performed for Homer. The second book of the *Aeneid* is where the *Iliad* necessarily ends. This is what the Homeric fragments of the fall of Troy—say, in the eighth book of the *Odyssey*— really lead to.

S: So it's a sort of transaction between the living and the dead, the present and the past.

F: Absolutely. Just as much as it is between Anchises and Aeneas in the sixth book of the *Aeneid*. That kind of commerce.

S: Perhaps that is the reason that I have terrible problems separating the poet from the poem, Vergil from Aeneas.

F: That can refer to the relationship between Homer and Odysseus as well, especially in Homer's simile for his hero's stringing of the bow—"like an expert singer skilled at lyre and song—/ who strains a string to a new peg with ease, / making the pliant sheep-gut fast at either end"—then plucking the string to get the pitch just right. In some sense Odysseus is turning Homer's art into a form of action. In a sense, too, Homer is conferring his art on Odysseus. He's saying "Here, here's the harp, come play it. And play me a new song, too." And so he does, a song that rids his kingdom of its discords and strikes up a note of harmony at last. It's a terrific moment in the *Odyssey*. And I think it's a paradigm for the relationship between the Maker and the Made. There's a healthy kind of rivalry between them. Adam Parry and Richard Martin point to it in the case of the *Iliad*, particularly in the language of Achilles. There's a bracing tension between the hero and his creator. Each asks the other, "Can I outdo your language, your intensities, your achievements?"

S: Do you see it with Aeneas and Vergil?

F: I'm not sure I can answer that. But I'm haunted by a remark of Adam Parry that may bear on the relationship between the poet and his subject. (It's a passage I turned to a week ago, thinking it might come up when I spoke with you today.) Adam writes:

> Aeneas arrives in Carthage and sees the busy construction of the city.
>
> > O fortunate you, whose walls already rise!
> > he cries out.
> > O fortunati, quorum iam moenia surgunt!
>
> The line is memorable, too memorable perhaps for spontaneity. What Vergil has done is to turn to peculiar account what is at once the weakness and the glory of much of Latin verse: its monumentality, and its concomitant lack of dramatic illusion.[1]

I have to come to grips with Adam's observation, if I can. If there is, in fact, a good deal more monumentality than dramatic illusion in Vergil, then I'm not the one to translate the *Aeneid*. Not after twenty years with Homer and his dramatic powers, and after many years with Greek tragedy as well. As a writer (if you can speak of a translator as a writer, and I hope you can), I need the challenge of performance, drama, the speaking voice in motion. But I'm not at all sure that it's *not* in Vergil, too. He recited his own work, after all, and effectively, what's more. That should count for something.

S: Aeneas is certainly very static and much of the poem is very chiseled, but Juno represents a dynamic force. And I think that if you are going to approach the poem, through translation or interpretation, that's the angle to take.

F: And Dido too, very dramatic, I would say. In fact—though this might play into Adam's notion of Vergil's artifice rather than his spontaneity—some of the grand operatic arias in the *Aeneid*, Dido's first among them, may offer me the kind of work I like to do.

S: And those arias are terrifically powerful.

F: But there's no power that can match the silence of Dido in the Underworld.

S: No, there's no way to win. There silence is more powerful than words, emotion stronger than logic. I think, I really do, that Vergil is given a great disservice if you look at him only in terms of Stoic reason and logic. That's why I think this Homeric angle is so pertinent.

F: So do I. It's one of the things that would draw me to Vergil. He's obviously writing in the service of, and in homage to, Homer at the same time that he's trying to outdo him. I think it's the most total act of assimilation of one poet by another that we have, unless we should include Dante's assimilation of Vergil and Joyce's of the *Odyssey*.

S: Let's turn to specific instances of Homeric influence on the *Aeneid*. In what way do you see the two halves of the *Aeneid*—Books I–VI and Books VII–XII—as Homeric?

F: I think the Homeric aspect of the *Aeneid* is wonderfully complex. To begin with, as many remind us, the received wisdom about the poem—that it's an *Odyssey* of wanderings and an *Iliad* of wars—needs to be reworked a good deal. Not only because there's battle or *Iliad* aplenty in the Odyssean first half of the poem, but there's *Odyssey* aplenty in the Iliadic second half as well. So many objectives there—destroying suitors, securing a wife, and battling home—have a distinctly Odyssean flavor. So I think there's an intriguing mix and merger, with different kinds of Homeric emphases, as we move from the first to the second half of Vergil's poem.

S: Do you think that we are supposed to read the start of the opening line, *arma virumque*, as some sort of formula?

F: As a return to Homeric formula, you mean?

S: Or as sort of a program for reading the poem.

F: Yes, it is a sort of program for reading the poem, and I think that Michael Putnam and others have been very illuminating on the subject.

S: Do you see this opening as flouting epic convention? There is an invocation of the Muse but it's delayed. There is the Homeric project in the first two words but there's also the *cano* at the end of that first half-line.

F: Well, what shall I say? There's a great historicization of the epic convention in the Aeneid. The Iliad invokes a single event in the tenth and final year of the Trojan War. The Odyssey . . . why does the invocation stress the crew's devouring the cattle of the sun? How does it serve to introduce Odysseus? As a contrast to the hero, perhaps: the crew's atasthalia, their recklessness, underscores his steadiness of purpose, his resolve. But some believe—though I'm not one of them—the contrast could be more explicit in Homer's invocation. Vergil's invocation—once he gets to his Muse, that is—could hardly be more explicit about his subject: the gods' wills, the gods' wrath, their relationship not only to Aeneas but to human history as well. Questions which are scarcely answered even at the end of the Aeneid.

S: So why use a lyric verb, a verb that for Vergil is associated with the pastoral?

F: Perhaps it's Vergil's way of adopting Homer's aeide in the Iliad. In the Odyssey it's rather hard to say what ennepe, Mousa means. I translate it as "sing, [Muse,]" though that's something of a stretch, I suppose, but the verb means more than simply "tell" to me. At any rate, Vergil hardly has a corner on a singing Muse. Clearly Homer has a share in her as well, and some would say an even greater share than Vergil. Remember what Pope said? "Homer makes us Hearers, and Virgil leaves us Readers."

S: Vergil's first verb introduces the subject, the invocation of the Muse really introduces Juno. It certainly starts a sort of split vision.

F: That's true, between a kind of historical abstraction on the one hand and the poet's particular, performing Muse on the other. And that's a problem that runs throughout the Aeneid. How does Vergil bring his individual voice into harmony with the enormous, global dilemmas he wants to narrate? Homer had songs to sing, a repertory right at hand, which he was free to adapt in his own sweet way. Vergil has history to formulate at the same time that he works that history into a specific cadence and a song.

S: What does he think about Augustus? I mean, is it the same, complex balance?

F: Yes, Aeneas is Aeneas, of course, yet he's also a prefiguration of Augustus. Many suggest that Aeneas killing Turnus is tantamount to Caesar defeating Antony and Cleopatra at Actium, though that equation may lift Aeneas too bodily from the fabric of his poem. At any rate, there's a continuity between the mythical and the historical leaders, a continuum of prehistory and Vergil's present.

S: Is this layering of Aeneas' character only historic and mythic?

F: No, it's textual too. One of the almost insurmountable problems in translating the Aeneid is that the poem encloses—as if in an echo chamber—not only history but Homer in the process. Those Homeric echoes . . . I'd like to try my hand at them, but Vergil's also echoing himself, as Bernard Knox often reminds me in conversation. And I wonder if any translator can do those internal echoes justice as well as so many commentators have done in their Vergilian criticism? How much of that can be conveyed in an English translation, I just don't know, but it's clearly very important for the whole effect. And the whole effect will depend on the Homeric echoes too. One of the most intriguing aspects of Vergil is the way he can give a single figure a multiple Homeric valence. I find it fascinating.

S: Such as?

F: Well, Aeneas as Achilles on the march, Aeneas as a successful Hector, Aeneas as Odysseus who secures a homeland. Aeneas is like many Homeric figures simultaneously or in turn. The larger the Vergilian character, in fact, the more Homeric facets that character attracts, and the more important the very *sequence* of the Homeric roles that he or she will play.

S: And the more confusing.

F: The more . . . yes, confusing. There are ramifications of this feature of the *Aeneid* that make my head swim. It's hard to keep the multiple Homeric effects in suspension, but there they are, parts of the poem's richness, germinating in individual Vergilian figures, reincarnated in those figures. An intriguing technique, and I think it should affect the way one translates Vergil too, but I can't define it for myself—not yet.

S: It certainly is a destabilizing technique in its effect on the reader. You have to work constantly.

F: You do, indeed. We've said that the first half of the poem is not simply an *Odyssey* of wandering, the second half not simply an *Iliad* of wars. In Homeric terms the *Aeneid* is much more interesting, more intricate, more arresting than that.

S: Do the female characters function in the same way? How do they relate to the women in, let's say, the *Odyssey*, I guess? The connection to Helen in the *Iliad* is clearer. . . .

F: More important than the Helen connection, I think, is the Penelope connection. I was drawn to the *Odyssey*, as many others have been, perhaps primarily by the women in the poem and their relationship to the men. I don't think there's any part of the *Odyssey* that I labored over, or cherish more, than the slow, gradual steps that lead to the reunion of Odysseus and Penelope. Garry Wills said it handsomely when he described their reunion in the twenty-third book as "the greatest picture in all literature of a mature love demanded and bestowed on both sides equally." I don't know of anything like that in the *Iliad* or the *Aeneid*. I don't mean that Aeneas is incapable of such emotions, but he never gets the chance to exercise them fully.

S: What about Dido?

F: Dido is a kind of Nausicaa.

S: She is Nausicaa.

F: She's also someone who, in the face of Roman destiny, would "calypso" the hero: hide him, conceal him for years. And she has some of Circe's ambivalence too, impeding the hero and then (against Dido's wishes, of course) serving to speed him on his way. And she's a potential Penelope, but she's never given the chance to play the loyal, longstanding partner of Aeneas. It's Richard Jenkyns' point, and others' too, that Dido is virtually every female figure in the *Odyssey*.

S: Let's talk more about the connection between Dido and Penelope. How do you think Vergil was playing with Penelope in his depiction of Dido?

F: In terms of Dido's steadfastness, I suppose. One of the most moving parts of the scene in the Underworld, as some suggest—beyond the analogy between Dido and Ajax—is her return to Sychaeus in the shadows. There's an abiding fidelity about the way she reclaims her first husband, in the place where time stands still.

S: Is it a fidelity comparable to Aeneas' loyalty to Pallas?

F: I don't find that farfetched at all.

S: Do you think we are supposed to think of Italy as female—Italy is referred to as the "ancient mother," you know.

F: Of course. The alma mater, and Rome in the offing as the ultimate female symbol, the great vessel of the people. Something I don't think that Vergil ever makes explicit but I think it's there. Subliminally, perhaps. Do you feel it?

S: I do, actually. I think that Italy is very much the lover who keeps eluding his grasp. She's like Venus in Book I, who taunts him even though she's his mother.

F: It's very moving. . . . And I'm thinking of Creusa too, Vergil's first adaptation of the Homeric encounter with the dead in the twenty-third *Iliad* and the eleventh *Odyssey*—and the inability of the living to embrace the dead.

S: Which I think is the great metaphor for much of what he is trying to do: embracing the past and failing to capture it.

F: Absolutely, all of those receding, evanescent things. It's obviously a poem of great nostalgia, sorrow, and loss, and that makes Robert Graves' attack on the *Aeneid* as official propaganda open to question, and makes Adam Parry's "The Two Voices of Vergil's *Aeneid*" all the more revealing.

S: At least two. What I am puzzled about these days is how these forces interact and shift.

F: Me too . . . and I think the balance of what Eliot would call "the profit and loss" is very hard to determine in the *Aeneid*. It's one of the overriding challenges of the poem; it challenges every reader, every critic, every translator.

S: It's very hard to figure out. The absence of Penelope is probably important too. Not only are there allusions, there are also negative allusions. People who are expected, the stage is even set for them, but they don't appear.

F: And, as I've said, perhaps too often, I think it's a problem translators face, and so do critics and readers as well. But the translator, as Maynard Mack might put it, has to live along the (Latin) line like Pope's spider and try to spin it into English. You've got to find a way to sound out those two voices, even to bring them together into one.

S: We have discussed circularity and linearity in Homer earlier and I wonder if you see any of that in Vergil.

F: I do, more and more. Thanks to Michael Putnam, and K. W. Gransden, and others.

S: Putnam argues for the circularity of the epic, although even he in his more recent essays has acknowledged a grand thrust forward at the end of the poem. I have never really pinned him down on this, but I am curious how this works exactly.

F: I'd be curious too, especially since I think he believes, as most others believe, that it's a poem that lives for the future as much as for "ancient history" and the present. So in the *Aeneid* all frames of time are being coalesced.

S: But do you think there is movement? Putnam's early and most publicized stance asserts that there is no change from the opening to the end. Juno recurs. . . .

F: I think there's a lot of recurrence, and a lot of circularity, but I don't think the circularity is imprisoning. And I like to think as well (this is something I've harped on, I suppose, in teaching and talking with others) that there is such a thing as an Odyssean motion, and it shapes the *Iliad* as well as the *Odyssey* itself. Though it may sound paradoxical, both poems move along a line at the same time that they circle back upon themselves. In other words, I don't see a contradiction between linearity and circularity in the epic.

S: The way I sometimes talk about it is in terms of a spiral.

F: A spiral may be more accurate.

S: That there is movement, but that you are always coming back over the same turf in almost a neurotic way.

F: Neurotic perhaps, compulsive, yet constructive too. I sense it most in the

*Odyssey*, I think. There's a fine circularity in the hero's return to the island he left some twenty years before, and especially in his reembrace of Penelope in Book XXIII—described by "the marvelous simile," as the Victorians called it, the simile of the shipwrecked sailor and the struggle back to land, for man and woman both. At the same time, Odysseus is driven by a linear thrust as well, and, as I'd suggest, both motions cooperate. Returning, driving forward, both at once.

S: But that's more Odyssean than Iliadic.

F: Perhaps, though many—Bernard Knox in the lead—have pointed to the circularity of the *Iliad*, suggesting that the poem ends as it began: on the eve of battle. And though some will disagree, I know, I don't see any change of heart in Achilles. Rather a momentary pause in his forward thrust. Even in his brief reconciliation with Priam, he leaves his tent—to accept the ransom and release Hector's body—like a lion on the pounce, and some of his warnings to Priam are really very harsh. There are only eleven days set aside for Hector's funeral, and then on the twelfth you know exactly what will happen: the fighting will resume, and Achilles will die, thrusting forward, we may assume, and blazing out in battle any day.

S: So there's not much change. How about in Aeneas? Do you see him changing at the end?

F: I think that Putnam's formulation is very good. It's less that the character of Aeneas changes than that the circumstances surrounding him become more complex. That may be the best way of putting it. And it's welcome news to me, because I had always contrasted primary and secondary epic in terms of how they characterize their heroes. If the heroes of primary epic are basically unchanging—they gather up their many features, displaying facet after facet as their situation grows and swirls around them—then I'd thought that a hero of secondary epic like Aeneas is undergoing, rather self-consciously, in a self-limiting way, the Education of a Prince. That's a dubious polarization, far too simple. And, as I say, I like Michael's poise between the changes that Aeneas may undergo and the increasing complexities of history that settle in around him with a vengeance. In short, our perspective on history changes more than our perspective on Vergil's hero. He becomes a Homeric hero, in his own way.

S: He's very much Achilles.

F: Very much Achilles.

S: And not our favorite Achilles, either.

F: Speak for yourself, friend. You're speaking about a man I love. My favorite Achilles, I would say.

S: The Aeneas killing Turnus is your favorite Achilles?

F: No, the Achilles who would be *motivated* to kill Turnus. My favorite Achilles, in terms of Vergil, would be the one who is passionately loyal to the dead, to Pallas. And of course it's impossible to separate the two Achilles. Achilles kills Hector because Hector killed Patroclus—it's a chain reaction, mixing love and hate to reach a flash point, and Vergil gives us its analogue in the *Aeneid*.

S: But does it have to be that way? Does Aeneas have to react violently out of his loyalty to Pallas? I think the loyalty to Pallas is the key issue at the end.

F: I think so too. And I think it's Vergil's telling adaptation of "the wrath theme" in the *Iliad*. I think he did a service to the *Iliad* on the one hand and to the necessities of Roman history on the other. Aeneas doesn't hesitate and stop. He hesitates, all right, but will not stop. Cannot stop.

S: So both are positive?

F: I think that both are affirmations of a kind. But please bear in mind the obvious: that I'm not a professional Vergilian, just an amateur at the start of a Vergilian adventure. Though I do have some Homeric reflexes.

S: So what about the wrath of Aeneas at the end of the poem?

F: I think Aeneas' wrath is reminiscent of Achilles' wrath. It's reminiscent of Odysseus' wrath too, for Odysseus has an Achilles in him when he needs it; he conducts the largest single slaughter in either Homeric poem. But Aeneas' wrath is quite distinct as well. It's yoked to the dynamics of history in a way that can't be said of Odysseus and his violence. As C. S. Lewis put it, ironically—he had rather little taste for primary epic—"There is no pretence, indeed no possibility of pretending, that the world, or even Greece, would have been much altered if Odysseus had never got home at all." The historical world perhaps, but the world of our imaginations would have been infinitely poorer.

S: Does the *Oresteia* figure in?

F: Let's talk about the *Oresteia*. The trilogy is prey to a lot of oversimplification. Some tend to dilute the end of the *Oresteia*, watering it down into a new era of the Eumenides—"a kinder, gentler world." But the ending is more complex, more compelling than that. The more the Eumenides (who are also the *Semnai Theai* and the Furies—they wear three hats) call down their blessings on Athens, the more Athena reminds them of their necessary severity in the future. All our infractions remain; it's just that now we can refer them to a higher court, thanks to the *Oresteia* and to Athens, the city of Athena. In other words, there's a balance struck between the Eumenides and the Furies. They're still and forever the Erinyes—Aeschylus never lets us forget that, any more than he lets us forget that we will always have our failings, our brutalities, our crimes. I think at the end of the *Aeneid* there is a similar effect, a similar, hard reconciliation between *furor* and . . . should we think of Aeneas' hesitation as an instance of *clementia*? Surely it's a very ambiguous, wrenching moment for the hero, and the reader too. I can't believe, any more than many others believe, that when Aeneas kills Turnus he's personifying the Roman ideal of Civilization which Anchises advances in "the dream center of the sixth book" (Arthur Hanson's phrase). Aeneas has become subject to, even as he exemplifies, a crueler, more unforgiving set of historical pressures by the end of the twelfth book.

S: Do you feel the presence there of the end of the *Oresteia*?

F: The paradox of the ending of the *Oresteia*, yes, the tension between a civilized ideal and a hard assessment of the facts. *Parcere subiectis* . . . a very noble ideal, and Aeneas' hesitation suggests that it more than crosses his mind. But it's just not possible to practice at his moment in time, if it ever will be.

S: What about the end of the *Aeneid* and the end of the *Odyssey*?

F: There's a memorable open-ended spirit about the *Odyssey*'s future, its *Nachleben*. Odysseus' final journey, the founding of the inland worship to Poseidon is still to come. I think the *Odyssey* and the *Aeneid* are both poems that stop but never really end. Nor do I think the *Iliad* reaches closure either, though some may feel that the poem ends on a note of calm, rational humanity in Achilles' tent. I think that's highly debatable.

S: It doesn't end focused on Achilles.

F: No, it doesn't seem to.

S: I mean, if it were really to end, to stop, it would have to bring the attention of the audience back to Achilles.

F: Yes, but of course it ends with an image of Hector, dead and buried, and Hector's death prefigures at least two other deaths—the imminent death of Achilles and the eventual death of Troy—and the latter, in fact, will be the work of one Odysseus.

S: That's true.

F: And of Epeus, who built the horse. *Iliad*, *Odyssey*, *Oresteia*, *Aeneid*: they're all about *dike*, *dike* in the pagan world, Greek or Roman, a world of rough justice, at least as their most formative epic poems would describe it.

S: It has to be.

F: It has to be. It doesn't mean there can't, in the long run, be some glimmer of redemptive justice too, but it's going to be, first and foremost, a painful sort of justice.

S: It's a justice that blurs our vision rather than clarifying it. The clean lines that are drawn at the beginning—maybe this is what Parry is referring to, that monumental sense—become so blurred by the end. And, as you point out, the characters, too, become increasingly complex as the poem progresses. Like

Aeneas. Maybe one way to see his action at the end is in terms of the blurring of the lines of his character.

F: Yes, you can't stake all on any single set of values. You live in the fear and the joy of both cities on Achilles' shield—the city at war and the city at peace—and the shield shows them forged and waiting side by side. There's always a sense of multiplicity, of indeterminacy, irresolution. You remember the words that Ruskin puts in Homer's mouth in *Modern Painters?* "These are the facts of the thing. I see nothing else than these. Make what you will of them."

S: Right, and that's why it is so impossible to sort out.

F: And really rather modern, or potentially so, at any rate.

Chapter 12

# LACRIMAE RERUM
## The Influence of Vergil on Poets and Scholars

I invited a series of poets and scholars (none trained primarily or exclusively as a classicist) to write briefly about Vergil's significance or influence on them as a means of mapping the ancient poet's legacy in the nonclassical, literary world today. I then pieced these meditations together into the "virtual roundtable" which follows.

KARL KIRCHWEY:
There is a stretch of Interstate 91 approaching the capital city of Connecticut which my grandmother always referred to as the "Hartford Spaghetti," so bewildering, tortuous, and layered are the whorls of its entrance and exit ramps. During one academic year I commuted regularly by car between New York and western Massachusetts to teach, a drive of three hours which was ideal for listening to long audiotapes of epic poetry. Thus I found myself approaching this tangled concrete skein one winter afternoon, with the sun setting in a rack of livid cloud, just at the moment early in Vergil's poem when Aeneas, fleeing Troy, realizes that he has lost his wife Creusa along the way. His father, his son Iulus, his household gods, all he has carried safe to the rallying point outside the ruined city; but he must retrace his steps, made fearful, now, of the marauding Greeks by love of the one for whom he searches. At last Creusa's ghost appears to him, and says:

> "What's to be gained by giving way to grief
> So madly, my sweet husband? Nothing here
> Has come to pass except as heaven willed.
> You may not take Creusa with you now."
> (Fitzgerald, II.1007–10)

The translation is Robert Fitzgerald's; the reading was by an English actor, quite good. And for a moment, as I listened, I was as lost in the tangle of the Hartford Spaghetti as Aeneas was in those burning city streets which had to cost him his wife. And I felt the huge weariness of the hero as he was told, with a wisdom surpassing human understanding, that he would build his life over again and found a new race in a new land, just as his son Iulus would be known, in this new land, as Ascanius. This prophecy, the inexorability of the exchange of what one loves best for what fate will have one do, seemed so authentically to mix bitterness and rapture, my own vision blurred for a while as the lights came on outside Hartford and I continued home.

J. D. McCLATCHY:

Nearly four decades ago, when I first read Vergil (I was a college freshman and part of a small group selected to be that year's "Virgilian Academy," which would devote a year to the *Aeneid* and then, with an unmarked copy of the Oxford edition as our only companion, be publicly examined on our understanding of the poem by no less a master than Bernard Knox), I thought him an exotic, stiff with gold and purple (in Robert's Lowell's phrase), fire-crested plumage and blood-clotted spear. The hero never emerged from the scenery—or was it the grammar? Years later, a novice teacher myself, explaining the poem's panorama but unconvinced of the truisms I'd outline on the blackboard, I insisted on the prerequisites of duty, the steep cost of both repressed passion and ruthless empire. This was as likely as not an echo of what I was at the same time complaining about to my psychiatrist. Both the poem and my life I saw then as an immense marble staircase with a narrow red runner rising toward an empty sky.

Nowadays, I am at last old enough to read the poem without the burden either of being deaf to its emotional appeal or of having to carry it on my shoulders from some burning classroom, and it seems an altogether different work, at once smaller in scope and larger in resonance. Two strains have come to dominate. First, I watch it all—voyage or contest or battle, camp or palace—through a scrim, the *sfumato* effect of sadness. The sadness is neither grief nor weariness. It is psychological perspective and moral tone. Vergil wrote the consummate elegy of aftermath. Second—and in this he resembles no writer more than Proust— the *Aeneid* is a poem about memory, its intolerable system of weights and releases, the screech owl beating against the shield. Memory is fury and muse, and drives the poem's plot and characters. The poet's use of prophecy—"hindsight as foresight" in Auden's scolding phrase—is his shuttle. No earlier poem, and few later, pleated time so seamlessly. The past can force a civilization, or turn a heart inside out. In either case, only suffering is finally of use. Like his master Lucretius, Vergil saw love and war—Venus the mother of Aeneas, and Mars the father of

Romulus—as the ancestors of Rome, as they are of memory itself, which both restores and festers. Just so is peace, whether in the lonely hearts of all the poem's heroes or in the realm of the *Pax Augusta*, an aftermath distilled from sadness and memory, if only sadness enshrined and memories projected.

And the style of it all? On the swags of syntactical and narrative brocade, the emotional pattern is stitched with a simple and subtle clarity. The half-light against which the poet's images flicker the more briefly and brilliantly dims until Dante and seems, after Leopardi and Montale, to be characteristically Italian. English's more garish and insistent maneuvers miss the cloudy lining of silvered words—though Robert Fitzgerald captures more than any translator has, or probably could. The poem's symphonic organization, its harmonies and modulations, its swelling set-pieces and tender gestures, together define the lyrical epic. Pallas on his pyre, his head wrapped in Dido's gold-woven cloth, the trophies of war piled over the naked youth, and Aeneas' tight-lipped farewell . . . it is at such passages that the lines blur. Rarely has a public moment been rendered so intimately, nor the private so eloquently modeled into monumental sculpture.

KENNETH HAYNES:

Montaigne found that Venus was more beautiful in the *Aeneid* than she is *toute nue, et vive, et haletante.*[1] He was discussing the scene in Book VIII when she arouses Vulcan. What did he see in Vergil's language? *Niveis hinc atque hinc diva lacertis / cunctantem amplexu molli fovet* (VIII.387–88):[2] this is supposed to be sexier than a living, panting Venus? I wonder who has thought so besides Montaigne. Aren't we more likely to respond (like a character in a story by Guy Davenport) with exasperation at the "blurred, depilated generalization"?[3]

C. S. Lewis suggests that it is our fault if we miss the sensuous vitality of Vergil. He thinks that "classroom classicality" has come between us and Vergil, arguing that Gavin Douglas does greater justice to the vivid and sensuous elements of the poem than Dryden does.[4] After all, *rosea cervice refulsit* must be closer to "Hir nek schane lyke onto the roys of May" (Douglas) than to "she turned and made appear / Her Neck refulgent" (Dryden). It is we, like Dryden, who import "refulgent" when we read "refulsit," who hear the Latin as Latinate.[5]

Still, I have my doubts. Rosy necks, ambrosial hair, and snowy arms are stylized, not sensuous, descriptions. *Sterto*, which was good enough for Lucretius,[6] is not good enough for Vergil, and Servius approves the periphrasis: *toto proflabat pectore somnum.*[7] In this avoidance of the everyday, Vergil is unlike Douglas but like Dryden, who intensifies such classicizing, for example by refusing to translate the "village words" in the *Aeneid*, like *mollis amaracus.*[8] Dryden, that is, extends something already present in the *Aeneid*, the exclusion of much of the life of the body. Classicizing has begun to replace the classical; ordinary things have been excised, not transfigured.

The world of the *Georgics* is different, in part because the genre does not require the same elevated diction. The third book is (among other things) a meditation on what it means to have a body, to be a piece of meat, and to suffer the fate of a piece of meat. There is no evasion in the line of Vergil that Montaigne quotes next: *quo rapiat sitiens venerem interiusque recondat.*[9] The humiliating impotence of age is not euphemized, least of all in Dryden's translation, in which he expands Vergil's description with all the crude force he is capable of. The old stallion, burdened with disease and slow with age, still "languishes and labours in his Love"[10] but "Dribling he drudges, and defrauds the Womb."[11] Homeliness has its own power and rhetoric. The *Aeneid* is the greater poem; it is one of the greatest poems; but it is less perfect than this, "the best Poem of the best Poet."[12]

PAUL ALPERS:

When people speak of reading Vergil or recalling something "in Vergil," they usually mean the *Aeneid*, as "Milton" usually means *Paradise Lost*. That is no doubt as it should be. We can now see that the astonishing range and power of the first six books of the *Aeneid* are matched, in the second half of the poem, by the sterner human conflicts and the more stringent ironies with which Vergil, for centuries regarded as the authorizer of Western imperialism, reveals the costs of empire, in a way that our own age perhaps can uniquely value. But it would be a shame if the *Georgics* and the *Eclogues* were no longer known to those who feel one should know "Homer" and "Vergil," just as one knows "Dickens" and "Proust." The *Georgics*, though certainly the greater work, are perhaps more endangered. The oddness of their project means that their subsequent influence has been comparatively narrow, hence not felt to be significantly present in many vernacular poems we value; their complex poetry survives translation less well than the poetry of the *Aeneid*, which is narrative and dramatic, and the consciously more exiguous style of the *Eclogues*. It is the latter, I hope, that will continue to live as a founding example, in Western literature, of poetry that can both enact and reflect on the claims and dilemmas of its felt powers. It is amazing how much Vergil engaged by his fiction of herdsmen as representative human beings and of the poet as the one who represents them (in both senses). As their immense progeny in European literature shows, much of what matters most in our thinking about poetry is in these ten bucolics: the individual poet's dependence, both welcomed and resisted, on predecessors and contemporaries; the possibility that expressing powerful emotions is inherently a coming to terms with them; the way utterance, in isolation or in social ceremonies, can deal with separation and loss; the degree to which those with social power determine the way the rest of us live and express ourselves.

PAUL A. CANTOR:

As a Shakespeare scholar, I am fascinated by the way Vergil's *Aeneid* anticipates Shakespeare's Roman plays, especially *Antony and Cleopatra*. This claim may strike classical scholars as odd. After all, the *Aeneid* celebrates the reign of Augustus Caesar, whereas Shakespeare gives a pallid and largely negative portrait of the young Octavius (before he became Emperor), and seems to prefer his great rival, Mark Antony. Indeed I would initially go further in contrasting Shakespeare and Vergil. As I have argued in my book *Shakespeare's Rome: Republic and Empire*, Shakespeare on the whole preferred the Roman Republic to the Empire. In *Coriolanus* he portrays the early Republic as an austere, disciplined community, dedicated to martial virtue, embodying all the heroic qualities that eventually enabled the Romans to conquer the Mediterranean world. By contrast, in *Antony and Cleopatra*, Shakespeare portrays the nascent world of Imperial Rome as corrupt and decadent, with all the old Roman virtues fast dissolving and dying out. On the surface, then, Shakespeare's vision of Roman history would seem to be the opposite of Vergil's. And yet I detect an undercurrent of skepticism about Imperial Rome in the *Aeneid*, despite all Vergil's efforts to present Augustus' one-man rule as the culmination of Roman history. On Aeneas' shield in Book VIII, Vergil presents Mark Antony as in effect Augustus' evil twin. In surrendering to Cleopatra's Egyptian charms, Antony has allowed himself to be orientalized, becoming effeminate and whoring after foreign, inhuman, and bestial gods. This is roughly Shakespeare's view of Antony, only he emphasizes the positive, liberating aspects of Antony's openness to non-Roman influences. Moreover, Vergil seems to believe that Augustus was able to contain the threat to Roman discipline created by Antony's decadence, while Shakespeare treats Antony as the representative man of the Imperial Era and hence a harbinger of the rapid decline of the Empire into excess (Shakespeare's main source, Plutarch, reminds us that Nero was descended from Antony). But in the end, I am not sure that Vergil differs completely from Shakespeare on this issue. As the court poet of Augustus, he had to put the best face on Caesar's triumph over Antony at Actium, but there are hints throughout the *Aeneid* that Vergil understood the forces working to corrupt Imperial Rome. Much like Shakespeare, he portrays the poverty and simplicity of Rome in its early days, and links these qualities to the discipline that made

Rome great. He hints at several points that idleness is the great threat to Roman virtue, but idleness is precisely what Augustus' *Pax Romana* was to make possible for Romans. And the great myth of the *Aeneid* is that Rome's heritage was Trojan. Faced with an overwhelming anxiety of influence with respect to Greek culture, Vergil invented the idea that Roman culture could be traced back to Troy and not to Athens. But Troy was in the East, and ever since the appearance of the effeminate Nastes in Book II of the *Iliad*, Troy has been orientalized in the Western imagination. Vergil implies that the orientalization of Mark Antony may have been part of a larger movement, and thus may not be as easily containable as Augustus hoped. The corruption of Rome by its eastern conquests may be the hidden theme of the *Aeneid*. If so, then *Antony and Cleopatra* and the *Aeneid* are not that far apart. Perhaps Vergil actually influenced Shakespeare's understanding of Rome, or perhaps this is a case of Shakespeare's understanding of Rome helping us to detect a subversive countercurrent beneath the surface celebration of Augustan Rome in the *Aeneid*.

I may seem to leave Shakespeare wavering between a positive and a negative portrait of Antony. Let me clarify my position: Shakespeare on the whole prefers the Roman Republic to the Empire, but within the Imperial context, he prefers Antony to Octavius. As the Roman regime changes and begins to close down the possibilities for heroism, the man who is open to non-Roman influences and seeks to transcend the limits of the regime becomes more attractive than the man who simply accepts those limits and his unheroic role as essentially an administrator of the imperial system.

GLENN MOST:

The most familiar part of Vergil's legacy to Western culture is exquisitely literary in character, and comprises not only certain unforgettable characters (like Dido, whose fictitious sufferings moved Augustine to tears that made him forget his own real sins) and a specific constellation of literary genres which he invented or definitively formulated (bucolic, georgic, national epic) but also an ideal of poetic style precisely attuning syntactic ambiguity and semantic richness, and a deeply moving capacity for being deeply moved himself by figures of his own invention. But beyond this purely literary dimension, Vergil is also the European poet in whom, for the first time, we discover a new and epoch-making sense of historical time. Vergil is fascinated by people who feel lost in history, who are being propelled by forces they cannot understand towards a future from which they cannot escape, figures who can be truly animated not by the abstraction of their future and the confusion of their present, but only by an implacable love for the past—for a past which may perhaps not even ever have existed in reality but is now in any case irrevocably lost in all but memory. It is above all to the discrepancies, the tensions, the subtle strains of historical time that Vergil most movingly gives voice. His very first published poem, the first *Eclogue*, deploys a poignantly beautiful dream of flight into unhistorical bucolic ease in order to render all the harsher by contrast the brute historical realities of the Roman civil wars, and balances in the wistful *dialogue des sourds* of one character who can only mourn the past happiness he has now lost and another one who is trapped within the present happiness he has now achieved two mutually uncomprehending versions of a present thoroughly dominated by the past. So, too, his didactic poem in praise of agriculture, the *Georgics*, envisions an Italy which displays not only all the timeless bounty of nature but also every historical scar of human cruelty, so that the poem turns aside over and over from its optimistic, technical, Hesiodic program to regret the loss of the pristine, natural innocence which will inevitably fall victim to the very same agricultural progress for which it calls so insistently.

But it is above all in his historical epic, the *Aeneid*, that Vergil explores the paradoxes and constraints of historical action. Characteristically, Vergil seems to have discovered that the only way to persuade his reluctant hero to embark upon a voyage of imperial conquest and the foundation of new cities was by persuading him that he was really thereby returning to the ultimate source of the home he almost died in rather than leave. In Book V of that epic, the funeral games which Aeneas organizes in honor, not of his companion (as Achilles did for Patroclus), but of his father (once again, the dominion of the past), are interrupted by a dreadful calamity: the Trojan women, frightened by all they have experienced and misled by an inimical divinity, set fire to the boats upon which they and their men have escaped Troy together and have now, after seemingly interminable voyages, almost reached their promised goal, Italy. Their error is disastrous, culpable, and at the same time understandable and even historically necessary— indeed, by saying that they were trapped "between a wretched love for the land that they could see and the kingdom calling to them with the voice of destiny" (*miserum inter amorem / praesentis terrae fatisque vocantia regna*) (Aen. V.655–56), Vergil makes it clear that the maze of error within which they are wandering is not different from Aeneas', from Dido's, and from his own. Like the Angelus Novus that Walter Benjamin adapted from Paul Klee, it is only by looking backward that Vergil, too, can bring himself to go forward—from the *Eclogues* to the *Georgics* to the *Aeneid*, in a paradigmatic poetic career moving ever higher to genres which become ever greater in literary ambition yet at the same time ever more hopelessly compromised politically. Moving backward towards the future, Vergil passes through Europe's history, and passes through us; saluting him, we recognize ourselves.

MARGARET ANNE DOODY:

One of the few advantages of growing older is a growing ability to appreciate Vergil's long narrative's complex sadness, a sadness far exceeding—though never transcending—the story of Dido which so vividly represents the personal pain that goes into political construction, expediency, and evasion. We can paradoxically enjoy the fulfillment of a story of complex melancholy by following the *Aeneid*'s pattern of repetition, which becomes more and more emotive as the reader increasingly (if reluctantly) gains patience in this journey of life we are bound upon.

Repetition is almost a trope of Vergil's epic, and a key to it. Repetition is a subject of discussion and complaint within the narrative. Look at the words of a minor character, in Book V, during a storm at sea, with high waves and heavily pouring rain:

> effusis imbribus atra
> tempestas sine more furit tonitruque tremescunt
> ardua terrarum et campi; ruit aethere toto
> turbidus imber aqua densisque nigerrimus Austris. (V.693–96)

Or rather, we should say, *yet another* storm, echoing the famous storm at sea (caused by Aeolus at Juno's behest) described in Book I, the scene in which we initially meet Aeneas (I.84–92). Now, in Book V here is an echo, a repetition of that scene—and the reader is likely to pick it up only to have the fact of repetition immediately made explicit within the epic itself by Nautes, who thus addresses Aeneas: "Oh goddess-born, let us follow wherever the fates drag us back and forth" ('*nate dea, quo fata trahunt retrahuntque sequamur*') (V.709). But we can hear underneath this an alternative statement: "You may be the son of a goddess but all we do is get dragged back and forth, tracing and retracing our steps, and doing the same things over and over." In that first line of Nautes' brief speech, it is the *re* in *retrahuntque* that does the business. No wonder this skilled sailor wants to suggest a way out: let the women, children, and old ones off the boats— let them at least live somewhere. This is the first real colonization, the dropping off of those who cannot stand any more of the perfectionist repetition of the core colonizers, the retracing, the redoing.

This brief speech and the action that follows (including Anchises' ghostly counsel, as well as the founding of Acesta) remind us that colonialism in action is the result of both a love of repetition and a fear of it. Colonizers go elsewhere—Plymouth or Nova Scotia or Latium—with the purpose of creating a restored order, a repetition of "back home"—but in some way perfected. The search for perfection, however, is likely to lead to what feels like idle iteration in the search itself, a circularity that looks less pious than unmotivated. The process is suspended between death and life—the old city or country is dead as far as the wanderers are concerned, even if it has not been overthrown as fully as Troy. The new place is yet to be born. Meanwhile they are just journeying, as the woman Beroë (or Iris as Beroë) complains earlier in Book V,

> cum freta, cum terras omnis, tot inhospita saxa
> sideraque emensae ferimur, dum per mare magnum
> Italium sequimur fugientem et voluimur undis (V.627–629)

(we fare forth (or are borne away) through so many straits, all kinds of lands, such inhospitable rocks and hostile stars while delusively through the great sea we chase an ever-fleeing Italy, and are tossed on the waves)

Aeneas and his companions are living in the crack, on the cusp between times and worlds. They sustain repeated action without effect—only the same old thing over and over, going round and round in the waves. This is a good nowhere situation in which to go crazy. Repetition, which itself on occasion supplies some sort of comforting prophylactic against disaster, can be ironically catastrophic in its nature. Repetition itself is often craziness, representing a delusive state.

The problems and complexities arising from such eddies, such vortices of perfectionism and failure circling in repetitious energies, are the cause of Vergil's problems in completing his epic, and the stimulus to some of his best effects. In searching to create "another Troy" Aeneas is searching for the impossible. Rome is really ultimately *another* place, it has a future history, whereas all Troy has is a past. But Vergil's epic, like its Trojan characters, can seem driven to repeat the war and the scene of defeat, as if the epic itself had a kind of obsession with that primal defeat of Priam's city—a point of firstness, a high mark of failure too important to be let go. . . .

The glory, jest, and riddle of the colonial moment must lie in its multipartite and stubborn—and often brutal—efforts to create a future from a past. This creation, a bruised and fantastic creation, necessitates hypotheses about solidity and permanence which can be countered by the very terms and images in which such hypotheses most naturally express themselves. Vergilian sadness arises from the destruction and self-destruction which seem so inevitably to be the psyche's stubborn response to pain and loss. Destruction and self-destruction when described require repetition. As Dante knew in managing and imagining his *Inferno*, how else save through repetition can either physical or spiritual pain make itself known? Vergil—partly against his own apparent design—leaves us wondering: do the love of Rome and lust for the future constitute a splendid and repetitive delusion? Prophecy can only be given by shades to those who, by the time we read about them, are already themselves shades; we see them, these always-already shady characters, as they are about to go and repeat the past.

# Notes

## CHAPTER 1. IMAGINARY ROMANS

1. The translations of Florus are by Edward Seymour Forster in the Loeb Edition (1929; 3rd separate edition, 1984).

2. For the context of Mussolini's maps, see Roger Eatwell, *Fascism: A History* (New York, 1995), pp. 35, 48, 59, 66, 73–74, 85, 96, 111, and Romke Visser, "Fascist Doctrine and the Cult of Romanita," *Journal of Contemporary History* 27 (1992): 5–22. For the place of cartography in the process of constructing images of national identities, see Benedict Anderson, *Imagined Communities: Reflections on the Origin and Spread of Nationalism* (London, 1983), pp. 164–178. Missing from my collage was Varro's charming map, *Rerum Rusticarum*, 1.2.1–8. For Campania as *uberrimus ager* and *horreum populi Romani*, see Livy, 7.31 and 38.

3. For the dynamics of *fortuna/virtus* in Florus, see Luigi Bessone, "Floro: un retore storico et poeta," *Aufstieg und Niedergang der römischen Welt* 34.1 (Berlin, 1993): 115–117.

4. Sir Ronald Syme, *The Roman Revolution* (Oxford, 1939), pp. 86–87. The chapter in which M. Cary treats of these conflicts is titled, properly to my mind, "The Italian Wars, 91–83 B.C." (London 1935, 1954), pp. 316–30; see also H. H. Scullard, who hesitates between "the Italian or Social War" and conflates "it" with civil war in his *From the Gracchi to Nero: A History of Rome 133 B.C. to 68 A.D.* (London, 1959, 5th ed. 1982), pp. 64–68, 77–78. See also the recent, authoritative versions by Emilio Gabba, *Cambridge Ancient History IX* (1994), "Rome and Italy: The Social War," pp. 104–28; Michael Crawford, *The Roman Republic* (Cambridge, MA, 2nd ed., 1992), "The World Turned Upside Down," pp. 138–53; Emma Dench, *From Barbarians to New Men: Greek, Roman, and Modern Perspectives of Peoples of the Central Apennines* (Oxford, 1995).

   The history of the Italian Wars of the first century BCE (that is, the way that history is represented) is in the process of being revised: see Fergus Millar, "The Last Century of the Republic: Whose History?" *Journal of Roman Studies* 85 (1995): 236–43. See also Michael Crawford, "Italy and Rome," *Journal of Roman Studies* 71 (1981): 154–60, and "Italy and Rome from Sulla to Augustus," *Cambridge Ancient History X* (1996), pp. 414–33. T. J. Cornell, *The Beginnings of Rome: Italy and Rome from the Bronze Age to the Punic Wars (c. 1000–264 BC)* (London, 1995), pp. 364–68, offers interesting arguments for considering the Romanization of Italy as being essentially complete by the middle of the third century BCE, but he ignores defections to Hannibal and also the later Italian Wars, which merit the very brief mention in his *Atlas of the Roman World* (with John Matthews) (New York, 1982), pp. 62–63. Crucial to the study of the Italian Wars are E. T. Salmon's *Samnium and the Samnites* (Cambridge, England, 1967) and *The Making of Roman Italy* (Ithaca, 1982); see also Arthur Keaveny, *Rome and the Unification of Italy* (London and Sydney, 1986), pp. 117–61, and especially pp. 197–206, and Jean-Michel David, *The Roman*

*Conquest of Italy* (Oxford, 1997), pp. 140–56. Sympathetic ancient versions of the Italian Wars that should not be ignored: Velleius Paterculus, 2.15–17 and 27 (with its sketch of the death of the Samnite leader, Pontius Telesinus; see Salmon, 1967, p. 386) and Diodorus Siculus 32.2.

5. The missing agenda is neatly designed by Millar, pp. 237–38, note 4.

6. For problems with the poem's divine machinery, see my "Dismal Decorations: Dryden's Machines in the *Aeneid*," *The Two Worlds of the Poet: New Perspectives on Vergil*, ed. Robert Wilhelm and Howard Jones (Detroit, 1993), pp. 443–47, and "Dis Aliter Visum: Self-Narration and Theodicy in Aeneid 2," in *Reading Vergil's Aeneid*, ed. Christine Perkell (Norman, 1999).

7. For the moods and structures of Book IV, see my "Final Exit: Propertius 4.11," *Classical Closure*, ed. D. Roberts, F. M. Dunn, and D. Fowler (Princeton, 1997), pp. 177–79. See also the excellent discussion of Propertian hybridity by Catherine Edwards, *Writing Rome: Textual Approaches to the City* (Cambridge, England, 1996), pp. 55–57. For Cicero's adroit yet not quite persuasive elision of an Italian Roman's "two fatherlands," see *De legibus* 2.5. No less sanguine in his readings of the perfection of Vergil's Cisalpine hybridities ("an amalgam of sentiment which is a fusion of the past and the countryside and Italy, the name and experience of his nation," p. 125) is Richard Jenkyns, *Virgil's Experience: Nature and History: Times, Names and Places* (Oxford, 1999): see pp. 92–99 for his elegant discussion of Cicero's "two fatherlands"; Vergil's own (tensionless) "blend of Roman and Italian patriotism" (note the silent elision, p. 97) and "the sense of national unity-in-diversity" that he captures (p. 127) are discussed on pages 97–127. For Livy's breathtaking elision of all Italians united in an imaginary war with Alexander the Great ("and let civil wars be silent"), see IX.19.15.

8. The translations are by G. P. Goold in his Loeb Edition (1990).

9. The perspective on the *Aeneid*'s cultural materialism that I argue for here, "the actual means and condition of [its] production" (Raymond Williams, *Writing in Society*, London, 1984, p. 210), includes within it recognition of a Vergilian or Augustan nostalgia for a primal Italian innocence, here filtered through a powerful postcolonial lens; but that complex nostalgia is further complicated in this perspective by a countervailing desire for the success of modernity and naturalized Romanitas (call it the "wanting to have one's cake and eat it too" dilemma, which is part of the thematic repertoire of post-colonial nationalism). The quality of this nostalgia for archaic purity found its classic evocation in Adam Parry's incomparable essay, "The Two Voices of Virgil's *Aeneid*" (1963), reprinted in *Virgil, A Collection of Critical Essays*, ed. Steele Commager (Englewood Cliffs, NJ, 1966), pp. 108–11; for Parry's connection with the equally important essay by R. A. Brooks, "Discolor Aura, Reflections on the Golden Bough" (1953), also reprinted in the Commager collection, see his note on p. 121. In an appendix to Nicholas Horsfall's *A Companion to the Study of Virgil* (Leiden, 1995), pp. 313–14, Wendell Clausen explains his relationship (or lack thereof) with "the Harvard School" and discusses the revisions of his 1949 lecture, "An Interpretation of the Aeneid," the last of which appeared the year after Michael Putnam's *The Poetry of the Aeneid*, in the Commager volume, the revi-

sion of an earlier revision, *Harvard Studies in Classical Philology* 68 (1964). William Nethercut suggested to me *viva voce* that the shaping spirit behind the powerful readings offered by Brooks, Parry, and Michael Putnam may have been Cedric Whitman; see Nethercut's "Invasion in the *Aeneid*," *Greece and Rome* 15 (1968): 82–83, for adumbrations of the "Harvard" perspective in the 30s and 40s. For what the Harvard perspective was reacting against, see my review of Theodore Ziolkowski's *Virgil and the Moderns*, in *Comparative Literature Studies* 33.1 (1996): 136–40. The pristine inculpabilities of Vergil's Latium are deftly dismantled by Richard F. Moorten, "The Innocence of Italy in Vergil's *Aeneid*," *American Journal of Philology* 110 (1989): 105–30, but he then goes on to play prosecuting attorney in the continuing trial of Turnus, the chief purpose of which is to vindicate Aeneas (interesting recent examples of the genre: P. Hardie's edition of Book IX, Cambridge, 1994, pp. 71, 98–100, 221, 229, 231, 243; the equation "bad king" = *tyrannos* = Turnus, which James J. O'Hara neatly dissolves, *True Names: Vergil and the Alexandrian Tradition of Etymological Wordplay*, Ann Arbor, MI, 1996, pp. 185–86). One way to stop the trial is to focus on the uniform conflictedness of the poem, of the poem and the pressure its Italian/Roman indeterminacies put on it: see Charles F. Saylor, "The Magnificent Fifteen: Vergil's Catalogues of the Latin and Etruscan Forces," *Classical Philology* 69 (1974): 249–57, and James J. O'Hara, "They Might Be Giants: Inconsistency and Indeterminacy in Vergil's War in Italy," *Colby Quarterly* 30 (1994): 206–32.

10. For the nature and dynamics of such a shift toward polyglossia, see M. M. Bakhtin, *The Dialogic Imagination: Four Essays*, trans. C. Emerson and M. Holquist (Austin, TX, 1981), pp. 45, 61–68.

11. For Ausonia, see C. J. Fordyce, *Aeneidos Libri VII–VIII*, 65. It is a daredevil virtuosity that uses Ausonia and Hesperia as metonyms for Italy (or rather, Latium) at VII.537 and 542, respectively: the first designates the land's archaic innocence as embodied in Galaesus and the second denotes the wasteland Allecto abandons when her job is done—this in a space of six verses! It would probably be worthwhile to make a careful analysis of the handling of these metonymies (Italy, Hesperia, Ausonia, Latium) for the ironies and patterns of indeterminacies they might reveal (see, for example, VII.601, *mos erat Hesperio in Latio*), but for my present purposes it seems of some significance that in the book most crucial to this theme (the hero's arrival in Latium) "Ausonia" is mentioned slightly more frequently than is "Italy" (eight occurrences versus seven), whereas in other books "Italy" surpasses "Ausonia": in Book III, fourteen to seven; in Book XII, eleven to six. "Hesperia" appears four times in Book VII (as against five times in Book III), but after that it all but disappears from the second half of the poem. ("Latium" appears fifteen times in Book VII, twelve times in Book XII.) Metonymic indeterminacy in constant motion keeps post-colonial anxieties at the boiling point: see VIII.329–32 (*"posuit nomen, Itali diximus; amisit verum vetus nomen"*; see also O'Hara (note 9 above), pp. 88–91, 126–27, 208).

12. See Dench, *From Barbarians* (note 4 above), pp. 122, 213–15.

13. See Salmon (*Roman Italy*), p. 144, note 4.

14. For the heterogeneity of Cisalpina, see Nicholas Purcell, "The Creation of Provin-

cial Landscape: The Roman Impact on Cisalpine Gaul," *The Early Roman Empire in the West,* ed. Thomas Blagg and Martin Millett (Oxford, 1990), p. 11. For the intriguing fantasy that Vergil's mother was a Samnite, see Salmon (1967), p. 388. Strange (yet not so strange) to see that "the mythical state of Padania in northern Italy" is, under the leadership of Umberto Bossi, seeking its independence (*The New York Times,* August 23, 1996, "Secession for Northern Italy Goes Forward, Symbolically").

15. Small but reasonable hopes for humankind's eventually extricating itself from such illusions are offered by E. J. Hobsbawm, *Nations and Nationalism Since 1780: Programme, Myth, Reality* (Cambridge, England, 1992), pp. 187–92. For the structure of the illusion, here centered on "the descent from distinguished migrants," see Victor Turner, *From Ritual to Theatre: The Human Seriousness of Play* (New York, 1982), pp. 67–68.

## CHAPTER 3. PASTORAL VALUE IN VERGIL

1. Joseph Brodsky, "On Grief and Reason," *On Grief and Reason: Essays* (New York, 1995), p. 234.

2. Harry Berger, "The Origins of Bucolic Representation: Disenchantment and Revision in Theocritus' Seventh *Idyll, Classical Antiquity* 3 (1984): 7.

3. Bruno Snell, *The Discovery of the Mind: The Greek Origins of European Thought,* trans. T. G. Rosenmeyer (New York, 1960). See Paul Alpers, *What Is Pastoral?* (Chicago, IL, 1997), pp. 8–44, for an exhaustive and thoughtful study of the history of the reception of pastoral. See also Alpers, "Schiller and the Modern Idea of Pastoral," in *Cabinet of the Muses: Essays on Classical and Comparative Literature in Honor of Thomas G. Rosenmeyer,* eds. Mark Griffith and Donald J. Mastronarde (Atlanta, GA, 1990), pp. 319–33.

4. E.g., David M. Halperin, *Before Pastoral: Theocritus and the Ancient Tradition of Bucolic Poetry* (New Haven, CT, 1983), p. 65: "Pastoral achieves significance by oppositions, by the set of contrasts, expressed or implied, which the values embodied in its world create with other ways of life. The most traditional contrast is between the little world of natural simplicity and the great world of civilization, power, statecraft, ordered society, established codes of behavior, and artifice in general."

5. Michael C. J. Putnam, *Virgil's Pastoral Art: Studies in the Eclogues* (Princeton, NJ, 1970); A. J. Boyle, *The Chaonian Dove: Studies in the Eclogues, Georgics, and Aeneid of Vergil* (Leiden, 1986).

6. This does not mean that "weak" pastoral may not be "complex," "ironic," "critical," and "tensional," according to Berger (1984), p. 3. Cf. Leo Marx, *The Machine in the Garden: Technology and the Pastoral Ideal in America* (Oxford, 1964/1981): "In one way or another, if only by virtue of the unmistakable sophistication with which they are composed, these works manage to qualify, or call into question, or bring irony to bear against the illusion of harmony in a green pasture" (p. 25). From Alpers' (1990) summary of Schiller's reflections on pastoral come the terms "nostalgic" and "satirical." Marx terms the distinction "popular" and "sentimental" versus "imaginative" and "complex" (pp. 3–33).

7. Berger (1984): "Such pastoral constructs within itself an image of its generic traditions in order to criticize them and, in the process, performs a critique on the limits of its own enterprise even as it ironically displays its delight in the activity it criticizes" (p. 2).

8. Alpers (1997), pp. 35–36.

9. Even the first-person speaker is an impersonation. Berger (1984) notes that the construction of the first person speaker varies with the genre: "the epic ego, the epinician ego, the lyric ego, the elegiac ego. The literary ego is a fictive construction that models attitudes inherent in these conventions" (p. 13).

10. This is true from, e.g., Servius to Annabel Patterson, *Pastoral and Ideology: Virgil to Valéry* (Berkeley, CA, 1987).

11. Cf. Patterson on the "dialectical structure" that Vergil "bequeathed to us" (p. 6).

12. The relevant passages from *Eclogues* I and X are cited below; that from *Eclogue* II follows. It is spoken by Corydon, as he imagines a future moment with Alexis, the object of his passion:

> huc ades, o formose puer: tibi lilia plenis
> ecce ferunt Nymphae calathis; tibi candida Nais,
> pallentis violas et summa papavera carpens,
> narcissum et florem iungit bene olentis anethi;
> tum casia atque aliis intexens suavibus herbis
> mollia luteola pingit vaccinia calta.
> (Ec. II.45–50)

(Come hither, beautiful youth. See, for you the nymphs bring baskets filled with lilies. For you the fair naiad, plucking pale violets and the heads of poppies, joins narcissus with the blossom of sweet-smelling fennel. Then, interweaving casia and other sweet herbs, she paints the delicate hyacinth with yellow marigold.)

13. I have presented a similar reading of this poem in "On *Eclogue* 1.79–83," *Transactions of the American Philological Association* 120 (1990):171–81.

14. Translations of the *Eclogues* are from Putnam (1970), with some small modifications.

15. Cf. Marx (1964/1981): "The echo, a recurrent device in pastoral, is another metaphor of reciprocity" (p. 23).

16. Paul Alpers, *The Singer of the Eclogues: A Study in Virgilian Pastoral* (Berkeley, CA, 1979), p. 84.

17. See, e.g., Robert Coleman, ed., *Vergil: Eclogues* (Cambridge, 1977), ad loc.

18. J. G. Wright, "Virgil's Pastoral Programme: Theocritus, Callimachus, and *Eclogue* I." *Pacific Coast Philological Society* 209 (1983): 112, for "pastoral tag"; Alpers (1979) "breakthrough to the sublime for the whole poem" (p. 71).

19. I have discussed this poem in "The 'Dying Gallus' and the Design of *Eclogue* 10," *Classical Philology* 91 (1996): 128–40. I take the term "Eclogue poet" from E. W.

Leach, *Vergil's Eclogues: Landscapes of Experience* (Ithaca, 1974), who summarizes the construction of the Eclogue poet: he is interested in the new Roman poetry, in literary theory, does not make political utterances, is more sophisticated than his speakers (pp. 246–47, 261–62).

20. Ross, *Backgrounds to Augustan Poetry* (Cambridge, 1975), p. 106.

21. Servius tells us that "All this is taken from Gallus," although he does not specify precisely what verses he means, nor does he provide the referenced verses from Gallus. Much scholarly discussion, therefore, aims at reconstruction of the lost work of Gallus, based largely on this poem of Vergil's and on other possible allusions to Gallus in Ovid, Tibullus, and Propertius. Necessarily, much of this scholarly argument is circular, arguing conclusions from its own hypotheses. Nevertheless, it does seem plausible that, at the very least, *omnia vincit amor* derives from a poem written by Gallus, since it fits elegiac pentameter so resonantly. Other phrases and possibly the themes of Gallus' utterances in this eclogue are also taken from Gallus' poetry. For readers of this poem, however, the challenge is to read the utterances of the textual Gallus as constructed here.

22. Max Pohlenz, "Das Schlussgedicht der *Bucolica*," *Kleine Schriften* II (Hildesheim, 1930, 1965), p. 112, and G. B. Conte, "Il genere e suoi confini:Interpretazione dell'*Egloga* Decima di Virgilio," in *Studi di poesia latina in onore di Antonio Traglia* (Rome, 1979), pp. 401–2 and note 36, have both seen this possibility.

23. Boyle (1975), p. 33, Ross (1975), p. 106.

24. I have discussed the Aristaeus epyllion in *The Poet's Truth: A Study of the Poet in Virgil's Georgics* (Berkeley, CA, 1989), pp. 70–85, and the farmer/poet opposition, pp. 27–46. William Batstone "Virgilian Didaxis: Value and Meaning in the Georgics" in *The Cambridge Companion to Virgil*, ed. Charles Martindale (Cambridge, 1997), pp. 125–44, works to undermine the clarity of oppositions between these figures: "In formal and substantive matters the poem fragments as it unifies the reader's perspective and creates a simultaneous sense of continuity, discontinuity, and interdependence" (p. 129).

25. David O. Ross, *Virgil's Elements: Physics and Poetry in the Georgics* (Princeton, NJ, 1987), thinks that Orpheus represents "scientific poetry"; his failure to bring back Eurydice therefore suggests the failure of knowledge (pp. 226–27); G. B. Conte, *The Rhetoric of Imitation: Genre and Poetic Memory in Virgil and Other Latin Poets* (Ithaca and London, 1986), pp. 130–40, thinks Orpheus represents only love poetry that is impotent in the world of power.

26. A recent positive reading of the *bougonia* is T. N. Habinek, "Sacrifice, Society, and Vergil's Ox-Born Bees" in *Cabinet of the Muses: Essays on Classical and Comparative Literature in Honor of Thomas G. Rosenmeyer*, eds. Mark Griffith and Donald J. Mastronarde (Atlanta, GA, 1990), pp. 209–23, who interprets it as constructive within the symbolic language of Roman religious practice, a renewal of "right relations between humans, gods, and beasts" (p. 213). Richard Thomas, "The 'Sacrifice' at the End of the *Georgics*, Aristaeus, and Vergilian Closure," *Classical Philology* 86 (1991): 211–18, has substantive criticisms of this reading, particularly on the grounds that Habinek extracts the passage from its context in the poem and reads it instead

within another sign system, i.e., that of Roman sacrificial ritual, wherein even so it fits only imperfectly.

27. Cf. Marx: "Most important is the sense of the machine as a sudden shocking intruder upon a fantasy of idyllic satisfaction. It is invariably associated with crude, masculine aggressiveness in contrast with tender, feminine, and submissive attitudes traditionally attached to the landscape" (p. 29).

28. E.g., David Quint, *Epic and Empire: Politics and Generic Form from Virgil to Milton* (Princeton, NJ, 1993), pp. 3–41.

29. Aelius Donatus' *Life* of Vergil (fourth century CE) tells us that Vergil became famous with the publication of the *Eclogues*—sufficiently famous to be recognized on the street in Rome, on which occasions he would take refuge in the nearest house.

### CHAPTER 4. ARISTAEUS, ORPHEUS, AND THE *GEORGICS*

I am grateful to Glenn Most for once again clothing my thoughts in the decency of English and for discussing these interpretative problems with me without renouncing his customary obstinacy. The chapter has greatly benefited from the suggestions of Mario Labate, Giuliano Ranucci, Michael D. Reeve, and Gianpiero Rosati.

This interpretative essay was sent to the editor of the present volume several years ago. Some time afterward, a book appeared by Llewelyn Morgan entitled *Patterns of Redemption in Virgil's 'Georgics.'* Unfortunately, I was no longer able to take account of this book in my own discussion; despite the learning and richness of its analyses and the interesting research perspectives its author proposes, a rapid first reading of it made clear to me that it does not interfere with the line of argument and the interpretative substance of my own critical discourse. I wish to congratulate the author for having written a book from which I would have been happy to be able to profit in these pages of mine.

1. "The Fourth *Georgic*, Virgil and Rome," in J. Griffin, *Latin Poets and Roman Life* (London, 1985), pp. 163–82 (an improved version of an article which had appeared in *Greece and Rome* 26 [1979]). One can find here a practically complete list of the principal studies on the epyllion.

2. Some scholars have resolutely taken this path: cf. in particular C. P. Segal, "Orpheus and the Fourth *Georgic*: Vergil on Nature and Civilisation," *American Journal of Philology* 87 (1966): 307–25 (*Orpheus: The Myth of the Poet*, Baltimore/London, 1989, pp. 36–53); A. Parry, "The Idea of Art in Virgil's *Georgics*," *Arethusa* 5 (1972): 35–52; M. C. J. Putnam, *Virgil's Poem of the Earth. Studies in the Georgics* (Princeton, 1979), pp. 270ff.; G. B. Miles, *Virgil's Georgics. A New Interpretation* (Berkeley and Los Angeles/London, 1980), pp. 257ff.

3. A striking example is provided by L. P. Wilkinson, *The Georgics of Virgil* (Cambridge, 1969), pp. 108–20, who, with a truistic minimalism, concludes: "To sum up, I believe that Virgil would have thought an *aition* for 'Bugonia' a suitable ending for a book, Aristaeus a suitable hero for this *aition*, and epyllion a suitable form for it" (p. 120). In an appendix (pp. 325–26), Wilkinson discusses earlier contributions from his point of view.

4. So A. La Penna, "Introduzione" to *Virgilio: Georgiche* (Milan, 1983), p. 101. This whole interpretation is in fact a good example of paraphrastic criticism. It recounts the story of Aristaeus and Orpheus; the quantity of information does not increase, but here and there a tender note of commentary is added to testify to the critic's admiration.

5. Cf. G. B. Conte, *The Rhetoric of Imitation. Genre and Poetic Memory in Virgil and Other Latin Poets*, ed. C. Segal (Ithaca/London, 1986), pp. 100–129.

6. Cf. Griffin, *Latin Poets*, pp. 180ff. The supporters of Servius' notice sometimes use arguments of doubtful value. For example, they try to trace out a large number of narrative incoherences in the mythic story, without considering that many presumed irregularities can be explained perfectly well in terms of the "Alexandrian" narrative technique adopted by Vergil (asymmetrical narration, nonuniform narrative time, erudite oscillation between mythological and geographical variants). Or else they try to demonstrate, on the basis of (admittedly real) similarities with certain passages in the *Aeneid*, that the Aristaeus epyllion was composed during work on the new poem, with hasty reuse of expressions already coined for episodes of the *Aeneid*. These are highly uncertain arguments, upon which a critical judgment cannot be based. But considerations of another sort preclude our dismissing as false the report of a revision.

Above all, no one has yet explained who could have invented *ex nihilo*, and why, a notice of this sort. It may be added that, even if the search for cases of narrative incoherence has turned out to be fruitless, there nonetheless exists an evident textual problem—of an unparalleled gravity in the manuscript tradition of the *Georgic*— in the brief passage which serves as an introduction to the theme of *bugonia* and to the etiological narrative: lines 290–93 are transmitted in a different order in each of the three most important manuscripts, and it has long since been noticed that these verses discuss Egypt, Gallus' province. At this point some scholars have tried to excogitate an intermediate solution, supposing, for example, that a brief mention of Gallus was hastily deleted and that the text still bears a trace of an imperfect readjustment. But this explanation, which does have some points in its favor, ends up forgetting the exact statement of Servius, our source, who speaks not of a deletion and a brief revision but of a massive substitution. A final *non liquet* leaves, as always, a sense of disappointment, but it should not preclude an attentive and objective evaluation of the Aristaeus epyllion, which remains the only secure terrain for critical analysis.

An excellent discussion of the problems connected with Servius' notice and of the many solutions that have been proposed for this question can be found in H. D. Jocelyn, "Servius and the 'Second Edition' of the *Georgics*," in *Atti del Convegno mondiale scientifico di studi su Virgilio (Napoli 19–24 settembre 1977)* (Milan, 1981), pp. 431–48, but I believe that his position is too extreme. I find very interesting and plausible the recent suggestion of M. L. Delvigo, "Ambiguità dell'*emendatio*: edizioni, riedizioni, edizioni postume," in *Formative Stages of Classical Traditions: Latin Texts from Antiquity to the Renaissance. Conference held at Erice, 16–22 October 1993*, ed. O. Pecere and M. D. Reeve (Spoleto, 1995), pp. 14–30. See also note 32 below.

7. I neglect here, as insufficiently methodical, attempts to connect the contents of the

"substituted" epyllion allegorically with Gallus' historical vicissitudes (I mean the suggestion that the epyllion refers in code to Cornelius Gallus, the governer of Egypt, rather than to the founder of the new love poetry): e.g., R. Coleman, "Gallus, the Bucolics, and the Ending of the Fourth Georgic," in American Journal of Philology 83 (1962): 55–71.

8. K. Gaiser, Platone come scrittore filosofico. Saggi sull'ermeneutica dei dialoghi platonici (Naples, 1984), pp. 125–50, is fundamental; G. Arrighetti, "Platone fra mito, poesia e storia," Studi Classici e Orientali 41 (1991): 1–22, is also important. Both Gaiser and Arrighetti well discuss the function of the myth in the body of Platonic dialogues, but they also succeed in explaining persuasively the aversion Plato displays for the poets' myths, which he often rejects as false. See also L. Brisson, Platon: Les mots et les mythes (Paris, 1982).

9. Cf. Gaiser, Platone come scrittore filosofico, p. 134.

10. So F. Stok in the excellent introduction to his Cicerone: Il sogno di Scipione (Venice, 1993), p. 29.

11. F. Klingner, Virgil (Zürich/Stuttgart, 1967), pp. 326–63, in particular pp. 359–63.

12. La Penna, Virgilio: Georgiche, p. 100.

13. B. Otis, Virgil: A Study in Civilized Poetry (Oxford, 1963), pp. 190–214; K.-H. Pridik, Virgils Georgica: Strukturanalytische Interpretationen (Diss. Tübingen 1971), pp. 220ff. L. P. Wilkinson, op. cit., pp. 327–28, is by and large useless. The best analysis among those which consider the episode in the tradition of the "new" Alexandrian epyllion is given by A. Perutelli, "L'episodio di Aristeo nelle Georgiche: struttura e tecnica narrativa," in Materiali e Discussioni 4 (1980): 59–76. On the technique of the "framed narrative" there are acute observations in G. Rosati, "Il racconto dentro il racconto: Funzioni metanarrativa nelle Metamorfosi di Ovidio," Materiali e contributi per la storia della narrative greco-latina (Perugia, 1981), pp. 297ff.

14. Cf. especially Parry, "Idea"; cf. also Putnam, Virgil's Poem, p. 314, note 61: "Aristaeus . . . absorbs, we presume, the lesson of Orpheus."

15. At least since the magisterial analysis by E. Norden, "Orpheus und Eurydike," Sitzungsberichte der Preussischen Akademie der Wissenschaften 12 (1934): 626–83, it has been an established fact that as a whole the epyllion is one of Vergil's most original creations. The sources do not connect Aristaeus with the bugonia or with Proteus, and there is even less trace of any relation whatsoever between Aristaeus and Orpheus before Vergil. So, too, the story of the death of Eurydice, bitten by a snake while she tries to escape from Aristaeus, seems to be an original invention on the part of the Latin poet.

16. Cf. J. March, "The Creative Poet: Studies on the Treatment of Myths in Greek Poetry," Bulletin of the Institute of Classical Studies of the University of London, Suppl. 49 (London, 1987).

17. Cf. G. W. Most, The Measures of Praise: Structure and Function in Pindar's Second Pythian and Seventh Nemean Odes (Göttingen, 1985), and G. Arrighetti, Poeti, eruditi e biografi: Momenti della riflessione dei Greci sulla letteratura (Pisa, 1987), pp. 76–97. And naturally I am omitting the version of the myth in Euripides' Andromache.

18. W. Jaeger, *Paideia: The Ideals of Greek Culture*, trans. Gilbert Highet, 3 vols. (Oxford, 1944/1977), vol. 3, pp. 172–73.

19. Already the mythological tradition made Aristaeus the cultural hero of the agricultural world: cf. P. Chuvin, ed., *Nonnos de Panopolis: Les Dionysiaques, Chants III-V* (Paris, 1976), pp. 91ff.

20. Cf. R. F. Thomas, ed., *Virgil: Georgics* (Cambridge, 1988), I.68 and 71. The procedure of periphrastic *grîphos*, which makes the reader curious and alert, is notoriously praised by Horace at *Ars* 143–44: *ex fumo dare lucem / cogitat, ut speciosa dehinc miracula promat.*

21. Cf. my article "Aristeo," in *Enciclopedia Virgiliana*, vol. I (Rome, 1984), pp. 319–22.

22. These are strong signs of free poetic elaboration, which have misled some interpreters into analyzing and appreciating the form of the expression in Vergil's discourse more than the structuring of the content, and hence into neglecting the correspondences between the two parts of the epyllion which are set in contrast with one another. Some critics had already gotten lost because of the impressionistic mode of reading that guided them. Thus La Penna goes so far as to assert: "Aristeo [ . . . ] non è particolarmente attivo e industrioso perchè possa servire da modello etico in nessun senso: nell'epillio di Aristeo a Virgilio interessavano il viaggio fiabesco nel mondo sotterraneo delle acque e il ricantamento con gusto alessandrino del mito di Proteo" (La Penna, op. cit., p. 101).

23. Cf. *Aen.* IX.45 *praecepta facessunt;* IV.295 *iussa facessunt.* Cf. A. Biotti, ed., *Virgilio: Georgiche libro IV* (Bologna, 1994), p. 412.

24. Moreover, the fact that in lines 548–53 many of the expressions that describe Aristaeus' miraculous actions are repeated from the instructions dictated by Cyrene (537–47) has a precedent in Homer, *Od.* X.517–25 and XI.25–33 (the ritual prescriptions imparted by Circe to Odysseus for evoking the souls of the dead): cf. Biotti, *Virgilio: Georgiche libro IV*, p. 412. When Aristaeus exactly repeats the religious ritual as it has been prescribed to him, he is fully exercizing his farmer's *pietas*; still unaware of the miracle, he will be rewarded for his obedience and discipline.

25. R. F. Thomas notes in his comment on these verses: "words crucial to the poem, and indicating one of the main connections between Orpheus and the participants of the agricultural *Georgics*; Orpheus, paradigm for the man who controls not only nature, but even the powers of the Underworld, finds his own *labor* destroyed by a momentary lapse—a lapse caused by *amor*, one of the very forces of nature which destroyed man's work in Book III. Cf. I.325–26 (of the storm): *sata laeta boumque labores / diluit;* III.525: *quid labor aut benefacta iuvant"?*

26. *Illa: 'quis et me' inquit 'miseram e te perdidit, Orpheu, / quis tantus furor?':* (494–95) in presenting love as a ruinous folly, Vergil's language resorts to elegiac accents. Cf. Prop. II.28a.7: *hoc perdit miseras, hoc perdidit ante puellas.*

27. See G. B. Conte, *The Rhetoric of Imitation*, pp. 100–129. Cf. Prop. I.18.27–29; I.20.13–14; cf. also A. Barchiesi, ed., *Virgilio:Georgiche* (Milan, 1980), pp. 130–31.

28. The date of composition of Horace's ode can be placed with some probability in 27 BCE. There is an excellent treatment of the problem in Nisbet-Hubbard, *A Com-*

*mentary on Horace: Odes Book II* (Oxford, 1978), pp. 137–38; but see also pp. 135 and 145, where Horace's relation with the verses of Cinna's *Zmyrna* (fragment 6 Morel) is well discussed.

29. See G. B. Conte, *Genres and Readers* (Baltimore/London, 1994), pp. 37–43.

30. Important in this connection is the comparison with *Geo.* II.207–11, where the farmer exercizes his dominion upon nature by deforesting the land to free it from sloth and assign it to productivity; but the didactic poet views this violent action from the perspective of the birds that lived in the trees that are being cut down when they see their nest sacrificed to the farmer's hard necessities: *unde iratus silvam devexit arator | et nemora evertit multos ignava per annos, | antiquasque domos avium cum stirpibus imis | eruit; illae altum nidis petiere relictis.* The protagonist of the *Georgics*—the patient, tenacious *agricola*, able to crown his toil with success—is also a character not free of shadows, and he, too, requires victims.

31. See the excellent article by G. Rosati, "Sabinus, the *Heroides* and the Poet-Nightingale: Some Observations on the Authenticity of the *Epistula Sapphus*," *Classical Quarterly* 46 (1996): esp. 214–15, who offers a full discussion and a rich bibliography (noteworthy is the comparison with Callimachus' epigram [*Anthologia Palatina* 7.80 corresponds to 2 Pfeiffer] in memory of his friend Heraclitus, an elegiac poet).

32. Perhaps we may even understand Servius' notice about Gallus in this light. Glenn Most suggests to me that if, in Vergil's lifetime, the Aristaeus epyllion was read in just this way, as a refusal to write poetry like Gallus' and as a counterpart to the end of the *Bucolics* (cf. note 27 above), it might have been said that the end of the *Georgics* was "really" about Gallus. At some later point, readers might have wondered why then he is not mentioned by name, and the story could have been invented that an earlier version mentioning him had been suppressed. Thilo P. *Vergili Maronis Carmina* (Lipsiae, 1886), p. xxiv (cf. M. L. Delvigo Ambiguità," pp. 24 and 27) and R. G. Nisbet in *Journal of Roman Studies* 77 (1987): 189 had already put forward a similar suggestion.

33. See the fine discussion in J. Griffin, op. cit., pp. 174–80, with a good reconstruction of the ideological-cultural ambience which provides a background for the specific ideology of Vergil's poem and for the literary symbols which express it. Especially attractive is the correct way in which he studies the so-called Augustan ideology not as an immediate and brutal reflection of the regime's politics and propaganda, but as a coherent discourse to which intellectuals (poets and writers in general) give expression. It is hard to believe that some interpreters of the literary texts of the period speak of "Augustan ideology" and neglect the autonomous creativity of the great men of letters, who themselves were the creators of that ideology and not just its mouthpieces—interpreters, perhaps, but original ones.

## CHAPTER 6. MORTAL FATHER, DIVINE MOTHER

1. My article, "The Aeneid as Drama of Election," *Transactions of the American Philological Association* 116 (1986): 305–34, contains a fuller demonstration of the view of the

*Aeneid* as a drama of acceptance of eventual divinity validated by Venus' embrace. It also contains a fairly extensive bibliography of relevant issues.

## CHAPTER 7. VERGIL'S *AENEID*

1. Further suggested reading on the conclusion of the *Aeneid*: R. Heinze, *Virgil's Epic Technique*, trans. H. and D. Harvey and F. Robertson (Berkeley, 1993), pp. 176–80; V. Pöschl, *The Art of Vergil*, trans. G. Seligson (Michigan, 1962), pp. 109–38; B. Otis, *Virgil: A Study in Civilized Poetry* (Oxford, 1964), pp. 379–82; M. C. J. Putnam, *The Poetry of the Aeneid* (Ithaca, NY, 1988), pp. 151–201; W. R. Johnson, *Darkness Visible* (Berkeley, CA, 1976), pp. 114–34; S. Farron, "The Abruptness of the End of the *Aeneid*," *Acta Classica* 25 (1982): 136–41; P. Hardie, "Closure in Latin Epic," in *Classical Closure*, ed. D. Roberts, F. Dunn, and D. Fowler (Princeton, NJ, 1997), pp. 139–62, especially pp. 142–51.

## CHAPTER 9. THE *AENEID* TRANSFORMED

I thank Steve Ferguson, curator of rare books at Princeton University Library, and his staff for making available to me the material on which this chapter is based, and Richard J. Golsan and Christoph Konrad for their help in refining the translations (translations are my own unless indicated otherwise). An earlier version of this chapter was presented at the University of Bristol and the University of Texas at Austin.

The epigraph is from Charles Martindale, *Redeeming the Text: Latin Poetry and the Hermeneutics of Reception*, Roman Literature and Its Contexts (Cambridge, England, 1993), p. 10. Although I see some things a little differently from Martindale, the chapter that follows is indebted to this book at every turn.

1. The historical development of modern philological principles can be followed in Rudolf Pfeiffer, *History of Classical Scholarship 1300–1850* (Oxford, 1976); and in the essays collected in Anthony Grafton, *Defenders of the Text: The Traditions of Scholarship in an Age of Science, 1400–1800* (Cambridge, MA, 1991), with bibliography.

2. The ideas sketched out here may be pursued at greater length in the works of reader-response critics and theorists of *Rezeptionsaesthetik*, especially Wolfgang Iser, *The Act of Reading: A Theory of Aesthetic Response* (Baltimore, 1978); and Hans Robert Jauss, *Toward an Aesthetic of Reception*, trans. Timothy Bahti with an introduction by Paul de Man (Minneapolis, 1982). Two efforts by classicists to bring some of the issues raised here to bear on our understanding of the *Aeneid* may be found in Karl Galinsky, "Reading Vergil's *Aeneid* in Modern Times," in *Classical and Modern Interactions: Postmodern Architecture, Multiculturalism, Decline, and Other Issues* (Austin, TX, 1992), pp. 74–92; and Craig Kallendorf, "Philology, the Reader, and the *Nachleben* of Classical Texts," *Modern Philology* 92 (1994): 137–56.

3. Recent work on the *fortuna* of Vergil is summarized in Alexander G. McKay's "Vergilian Bibliography," published annually in *Vergilius*. Work prior to 1990 is analyzed in Craig Kallendorf, "Recent Trends in the Study of Vergilian Influences," in *Vergil*, ed. Craig Kallendorf, The Classical Heritage, 2 (New York, 1993), pp. 1–20, reprinted from *Vergilius* 36 (1990): 82–98.

4. General surveys may be found in the catalogue of an exhibition held at Rome's Biblioteca Nazionale Centrale, 24 September–24 November 1981, *Virgilio nell'arte e nella cultura europea*, ed. Marcello Fagiolo (Rome, 1981); Alexander G. McKay, "Vergil Translated into European Art," *Proceedings and Transactions of the Royal Society of Canada* ser. 4, 20 (1982): 339–56, reprinted in Kallendorf, *Vergil*, pp. 345–64; and Nigel Llewellyn, "Virgil and the Visual Arts," in *Virgil and His Influence*, ed. Charles Martindale (Bristol, 1984), pp. 128–40.

5. The most helpful essays that consider two or more sets of illustrations are Erich Odermann, "Vergil und der Kupferstich," *Buch und Schrift* 5 (1931): 13–25; Ruth Mortimer, "Vergil in the Rosenwald Collection," and Eleanor Winsor Leach, "Illustration as Intepretation in Brant's and Dryden's Editions of Vergil," in *The Early Illustrated Book: Essays in Honor of Lessing J. Rowenwald*, ed. Sandra Hindman (Washington, DC, 1982), pp. 175–210 and 211–30, respectively; Ruth Mortimer, "Vergil in the Light of the Sixteenth Century: Selected Illustrations," in *Vergil at 2000: Commemorative Essays on the Poet and His Influence*, ed. John D. Bernard (New York, 1986), pp. 159–84; and Alexander G. McKay, "Book Illustrations of Vergil's *Aeneid* A.D. 400–1980," *The Augustan Age* 6 (1987): 227–37, with illustrations following p. 269. The essay which comes closest to what I am trying to do here is Werner Suerbaum, "*Aeneis picturis narrata—Aeneis versibus picta*: Semiotische Überlegungen zu Vergil-Illustrationen oder Visuelles Erzählen: Buchillustrationen zu Vergils *Aeneis*," *Studi italiani di filologia classica* ser. 3, vol. 10 (1992): 271–334, but I am approaching the Vergilian material from a different theoretical perspective. Some of the French and Italian illustrations in this chapter are also mentioned in Bernadette Pasquier, *Virgile illustré de la Renaissanceà nos jours en France et en Italie* (Paris, 1992), which came to my attention after this chapter was in press. In my title, I have borrowed a phrase from the title of Leach's essay.

6. Formed by the nephew of the financier J. P. Morgan, this is one of the finest Vergil collections in the world; it contains four copies of the 1501 Aldine edition, for example, which notwithstanding its fame as the first book printed in italic type, happens to be very rare. A short-title checklist of books in the collection, which was prepared by Shirley H. Weber in 1956, is available from the library, either as a photocopy of the original typescript or on computer disk, but this checklist is brief, out of date, and occasionally inaccurate. I am currently preparing a full catalogue of this collection. I have tried to concentrate on the lesser-known illustrated books, with the exception of the Brant-Grüninger edition.

7. Charles Martindale, *Redeeming the Text*, p. 9.

8. Much worthwhile information about this process may still be found in Roberto Weiss, *The Renaissance Discovery of Classical Antiquity* (Oxford, 1973).

9. *Publii Virgilii Maronis opera* (Strasbourg, 1502), shelf mark: VRG 2945 1502 4q c.2. (In transcriptions from early printed editions, I have modernized capitalization and the usage of u/v and i/j, but I have retained the vagaries of the original orthography.) As the most famous illustrated edition of Vergil, this book has been written about a good deal; in addition to the essays cited in note 5, a basic bibliography would include T. K. Rabb, "Sebastian Brant and the First Illustrated Edition of

Vergil," *Princeton University Library Chronicle* 21 (1960): 187–99; Martine Gorrichon, "Sebastien Brant et l'illustration des oeuvres de Virgile d'après l'édition strasbourgeoise de 1502," in *Acta Conventus Neo-Latini Amstelodamensis*, Proceedings of the Second International Congress of Neo-Latin Studies, Amsterdam 19–24 August 1973, ed. P. Tuynman, G. C. Kuiper, and E. Kessler (Munich, 1979), pp. 440–52; Bernd Schneider, " 'Virgilius pictus'—Sebastian Brants illustrierte Vergilausgabe und ihre Nachwirkung: Ein Beitrag zur Vergilrezeption im deutschen Humanismus," *Wolfenbütteler Beiträge: Aus den Schätzen der Herzog August Bibliothek* 6 (1983): 202–62; and Annabel Patterson, *Pastoral and Ideology: Virgil to Valéry* (Berkeley, CA, 1987), pp. 92–106. One hundred thirty-six woodcuts from this edition are reproduced in *Vergil. Aeneis*, trans. Johannes Götte, ed. Manfred Lemmer (Leipzig, 1979).

10. Mortimer, "Vergil in the Light of the Sixteenth Century," p. 174.

11. *L'opere di Vergilio. Cioè la Buccolica, Georgica, & Eneida. Nuovamente da diversi eccellentissimi auttori tradotte in versi sciolti* . . . (Venice, 1586), shelf mark: VRG 2945 2586.

12. The Cleyn engravings, which originally accompanied the translation of John Ogilby, are discussed by Leach, "Illustration as Interpretation," pp. 175–210; and Patterson, *Pastoral and Ideology*, pp. 169–85. The relationship between Dryden's translation and the Ogilby-Cleyn volume may be pursued in L. Proudfoot, *Dryden's Aeneid and Its Seventeenth Century Predecessors* (Manchester, 1960); and Reuben Brower, "Visual and Verbal Translation of Myth: Neptune in Vergil, Rubens, Dryden," *Daedalus* 101 (1972): 155–82.

13. *The Works of Vergil:* . . . *Translated into English Verse, by Mr. Dryden, in Three Volumes* . . . (London, 1716), shelf mark: VRG 2945 2716 v. 1–3. Some of the engravings in these volumes were executed by Vander Gucht, others by du Guernier, and a third group by an unknown engraver.

14. *Picturae antiquissimi Virgiliani codicis Bibliothecae Vaticanae a Petro Sancte Bartoli aere incisae* . . . (Rome, 1780–82), shelf mark: VRG 2945 351. The history of these engravings is difficult to unravel. An initial group of 55 plates was published in 1677 under the direction of Petro San Bartoli and reprinted in 1725; additional material was added to the 1741 edition, which was reprinted in 1782, but the plates were used in other editions as well, and the 124 plates in the edition I consulted were designed and engraved by a group of artists. Information about the publishing history of these engravings may be found in Jacques-Charles Brunet, *Manuel du libraire et de l'amateur de livres* . . . , 5th ed. (Paris, 1864), vol. 5, pt. 2, col. 1291; and Odermann, "Vergil und der Kupferstich," p. 18.

15. The importance of these manuscripts has long been recognized; recent facsimile editions and basic scholarly works include Erwin Rosenthal, *The Illuminations of the Vergilius Romanus (Cod. Vat. Lat. 3867): A Stylistic and Iconographic Analysis* (Zürich, 1972); Kurt Weitzman, *Late Antique and Early Christian Book Illumination* (New York, 1977), pp. 32–39, 52–59; D. H. Wright, *Vergilius Vaticanus*, Codices e Vaticanis selecti, 40 (Graz, 1980); Thomas B. Stevenson, *Miniature Decoration in the Vatican Vergil: A Study in Late Antique Iconography* (Tübingen, 1983); and David Wright, "From Copy to Facsimile: A Millennium of Studying the Vatican Vergil," *British Library Journal* 17 (1991): 12–35.

16. Odermann, "Vergil und der Kupferstich," p. 18.

17. F. Haskell and N. Penny, *Taste and the Antique: The Lure of Classical Sculpture, 1500–1900* (New Haven, CT, 1981), pp. 243–47.

18. *The Works of Vergil, Translated into English Verse by Mr. Dryden. . . . A New Edition, Revised and Corrected by John Carey, LL.D. . . .* (London, 1803), shelf mark: VRG 2945 2803 v. 1–3.

19. *Leneide de Virgile fidellement traduitte en vers heroiques avec le latin a costé, . . . par M. P. Perrin . . .* (Paris, 1664), shelf mark: VRG 2945 311 164 2 v. 1–2.

20. Ibid., ff. 3r-v.

21. A richly documented account of this process may be found in Marie Tanner, *The Last Descendant of Aeneas: The Hapsburgs and the Mythic Image of the Emperor* (New Haven, CT, 1993).

22. *Virgile en France, ou la nouvelle Énéide, poëme héroï-comique en style franco-gothique, . . . par Le Plat du Temple . . .* (Brussels: Weissenbruch, 1807–8), shelf mark: VRG 2945 311 307 v. 1–2. Information on Leplat may be found in the article by Ed. van Even in *Biographie nationale, publiée par L'Académie Royale des Sciences, des Lettres et des Beaux-Arts de Belgique* (Brussels, 1890–91), vol. 11, cols. 884–86.

23. *Virgile en France,* 1:176.

24. Ibid., 1:188.

25. Ibid., 1:76.

26. Ed. van Even, "Victor-Alexandre-Chrètien Leplat," vol. 11, cols. 885–86.

27. This point is taken up in Richard Waswo, *From Virgil to Vietnam: The Founding Legend of Western Civilization* (Hanover and London, 1997).

28. The first copy at Princeton contains extensive marginal and interlinear notes by a series of early readers; the second copy contains occasional notes in at least two sixteenth-century hands, presumably left by monks in the Augustinian monastery in Bruges, where the book remained until the monastery was closed in 1822.

29. *Publii Virgilii Maronis opera,* Part 2, f. 33v. The first four lines are quoted by Patterson, *Pastoral and Ideology,* pp. 104–5, whose translation I have used here.

30. Further discussion of which social classes provided readers for the *Aeneid* in the Renaissance may be found in my *Virgil and the Myth of Venice: Books and Readers in the Italian Renaissance* (Oxford, 1999), pp. 140–204.

31. *The Works of Vergil, in Latin and English. . . . The Aeneid Translated by the Rev. Mr. Christopher Pitt, the Eclogues and Georgics, with Notes on the Whole, by the Rev. Mr. Joseph Warton . . .* (London, 1753), shelf mark: VRG 2945 1753 3 v. 1–4.

32. William Whitehead, "Observations on the Shield of Aeneas," in *The Works of Vergil . . . ,* 3:457–58.

33. Ibid., 3:477–78.

34. *Virgils Aeneis travestiert von A. Blumauer in neuen Gesängen mit 36 Skizzen von Franz Seitz . . .* (Leipzig, 1841), shelf mark: VRG 2945 59 12. The travesty of Leplat, discussed above, was inspired in part by Blumauer (Ed. van Even, "Victor-Alexandre-Chrètien Leplat," vol. 11, col. 885).

35. *Virgils Aeneis*, pp. 184–86.

36. *Wergiliusz (Publius Vergilius Maro) Eneida* . . . (London, 1971), shelf mark: VRG 2945 311 Pol 971.

37. Ruth Mortimer, "Vergil in the Rosenwald Collection," p. 221.

38. Among recent works taking up these issues, several strike me as especially interesting: David Carrier, *Principles of Art History Writing* (University Park, PA, 1991); and Vernon Hyde Minor, *Art History's History* (Englewood Cliffs, NJ, 1994), and *Critical Theory of Art History* (Englewood Cliffs, NJ, 1994).

39. Norman F. Cantor, *Inventing the Middle Ages: The Lives, Works, and Ideas of the Great Medievalists of the Twentieth Century* (New York, 1991), p. 37.

## CHAPTER 10. SURREY'S *AENEID* TRANSLATIONS

1. Walter Benjamin, "Die Aufgabe des Übersetzers," in *Gessamelte Schriften* IV.I (Frankfort, 1972), 7–21; quoted from the translation of Harry Zohn in *Selected Writings* I (Cambridge, MA, 1996), 253–63. De Man's essay first appeared in *Yale French Studies* 69 (1985), 25–46, and is reprinted in *The Resistance to Theory* (Minneapolis, 1986). Derrida's essay first appeared in Joseph Graham's *Difference in Translation* (Ithaca, 1985), 165–248, with a translation by Graham.

2. On Alamanni, see Henri Hauvette, *Un exilé florentinà la cour de France au XVIe siècle: Luigi Alamanni* (Paris, 1903), 335–48. The first six books of the Italian translation were published in 1540 as *I sei primi libri del Eneide di Vergilio* (Venice, 1540). Book II was translated by Cardinal Ippolito di Medici; Book IV by Bartolomeo Piccolomini.

3. George Frederick Nott, *The Works of Henry Howard, Earl of Surrey, and of Sir Thomas Wyatt the Elder* (London, 1815); Frederick M. Padelford, *The Poems of Henry Howard, Earl of Surrey*, revised editon (Seattle, WA, 1928); Florence Ridley, *The Aeneid of Henry Howard, Earl of Surrey* (Berkeley, CA, 1963); Emrys Jones, *Henry Howard, Earl of Surrey: Poems* (Oxford, 1964); O. B. Hardison, *Prosody and Purpose in the English Renaissance* (Baltimore, MD, 1989). Hardison provides an able summary of the previous scholarship. See also Herbert Hartman's transcription and facsimile of the 1554 edition by the printer John Day and the editor William Owen, *The Fourth Boke of Virgil* (Purchase, NY, 1933). In the interest of clarity, I have modernized or translated all quotations of Surrey's Aeneid II, which are taken from Jones.

4. Jones, *Surrey: Poems*, no. 27, line 13.

5. Thomas Warton, *The History of English Poetry* vols. I–II (London, 1774), p. 27.

6. Hartman, *Fourth Boke*, title page of facsimile.

7. Warton, *History*, p. 27.

8. Jones, *Surrey*, p. xiii.

9. For the editing of the Tottel text, see Henry B. Lathrop, *Translations of the Classics into English from Caxton to Chapman, 1477–1620* (Madison, WI, 1933), 100.

10. For Marlowe's use of Surrey, see Hardison, 41–44.

11. *The Scholemaster*, in *English Works of Roger Ascham*, ed. W. A. Wright (Edinburgh, 1904).

12. See Hardison, 39–40.

13. *The Wittgenstein Reader*, 98.

14. See Derek Attridge, *Well-Weighed Syllables* (London, 1974), for the best examination of meter in the schools.

15. "Meter," Alex Preminger and T. V. F. Brogan, co-editors; Frank J. Warnke, O. B. Hardison, Jr., and Earl Miner, associate editors, *The New Princeton Encyclopedia of Poetry and Poetics* (Princeton, NJ, 1993).

16. Benjamin, *Selected Writings*, p. 260.

17. David F. S. Caldwell, ed., *Vergil's Aeneid Translated in Scots verse by Gavin Douglas* (Edinburgh, 1950–64).

18. Benjamin, *Selected Writings*, p. 260.

19. John Henry Newman, *Grammar of Assent* (New York, 1947), p. 60.

20. Benjamin, *Selected Writings*, p. 254.

21. Benjamin, *Selected Writings*, p. 257.

22. Jones, *Surrey: Poems*, p. xvii.

23. Benjamin, *Selected Poems*, p. 261.

24. Benjamin, *Selected Poems*, p. 258.

25. Roman Jakobson, *Poetry of Grammar and Grammar of Poetry, Selected Writings*, vol. III (s-Gravenhage, 1962–80); Donald Wesling, *Grammetric and Reading* (Ann Arbor, MI, 1996).

26. Benjamin, *Selected Poems*, p. 258.

27. Robert Fitzgerald, *Aeneid* (New York, 1983); C. D. Lewis, *Aeneid* (London, 1956); Allen Mandelbaum, *Aeneid* (New York, 1971).

28. William Frost and Vinton Dearing, eds., *The Works of John Dryden*, vol. VI (Berkeley, CA, 1987), 864–65.

29. Christopher Baswell, *Virgil in Medieval England: Figuring the 'Aeneid' from the Twelfth Century to Chaucer* (Cambridge, 1995), p. 276.

30. *Illuminator, Makar, Vates : Visions of Poetry in the Fifteenth Century* (Lincoln, NE, 1988).

31. "Translatio Studii and Renaissance Culture: from Horizontal to Vertical Translation," in Stanford Budick and Wolgang Iser, eds. *The Translatability of Cultures* (Stanford, CA, 1996), 55–67.

32. Benjamin, *Selected Writings*, p. 260.

33. Benjamin, *Selected Writings*, p. 259.

34. Ibid.

35. Willis Barnstone, *The Poetics of Translation: History, Theory, Practice* (New Haven, CT, 1993), 240.

36. Benjamin, *Selected Writings*, p. 263.

37. Paul De Man, " 'Conclusions': Walter Benjamin's 'The Task of the Translator' Messenger Lecture," Cornell University, March 4, 1983, p. 32. See the introductory note for the origins of the text in the Messenger Lecture.

38. *Telling Time: Levi-Strauss, Ford, Lessing, Benjamin, de Man, Wordsworth, Rilke* (Baltimore, MD, 1993).

39. De Man, " 'Conclusions,' " p. 40.

40. De Man, " 'Conclusions,' " pp. 33, 38.

41. De Man, " 'Conclusions,' " p. 43.

42. De Man, " 'Conclusions,' " pp. 32–33.

43. De Man, " 'Conclusions,' " p. 25.

44. Jacques Derrida, "Des Tours de Babel," p. 174.

45. Ibid.

46. Jacques Derrida, "Des Tours de Babel," p. 175.

47. Jacques Derrida, "Des Tours de Babel," p. 178.

48. Jacques Derrida, "Des Tours de Babel," p. 191.

49. Jacques Derrida, "Des Tours de Babel," p. 204–6.

50. Benjamin, *Selected Writings*, p. 263.

51. *Servii Grammatici Commentarii*, ed. G. Thilo (Hildesheim, 1887).

52. *Horace on Poetry*, ed. C. E. Brink (Cambridge, 1971).

## Chapter 11. Vergil Reading Homer

1. Adam Parry, "The Two Voices of Virgil's *Aeneid*," Arion II.4 (1963): 66–80; rpt. *Virgil*, ed. Steele Commager (Englewood Cliffs, NJ, 1966), p. 118.

## Chapter 12. *Lacrimae Rerum*

1. Montaigne: "Sur des Vers de Virgile." "Panting" overtranslates *haletante*. Richard Jenkyns describes the embrace of Venus and Vulcan as lush and voluptuous. I can't agree; his phrase about Vergil's "evocation of an impalpable, evanescent femininity" is perhaps a better description (in *Virgil's Experience*, New York, 1999).

2. "With snowy arms the goddess caresses him, on this side and that, lingering in her soft embrace" (*Aen.* VIII.387–88).

3. Guy Davenport: "On Some Lines of Virgil," *Eclogues* (San Francisco, CA, 1981).

4. C. S. Lewis: *English Literature in the Sixteenth Century, Excluding Drama* (Oxford, 1954).

5. *Aeneid* I.402.

6. *sterto* in Lucretius: "to snore" (III.1048). It was also good enough for Milton, *Epitaphium Damonis* 54.

7. "He blew forth sleep from his whole breast" (*Aen.* IX.326).

8. *mollis amaracus*: "soft marjoram" (*Aen.* I.693).

9. "Athirst she may seize love and take it deeply" (*Georgics* III.137).

10. Dryden, *Georgics* III.156 (cf. Vergil, *Georgics* III.97–100).

11. Dryden, *Georgics* III.158 (cf. Vergil, *Georgics* III.97–100).

12. Dryden, Dedication, *Georgics*.

# CONTRIBUTORS

PAUL ALPERS is Class of 1942 Professor of English Emeritus at the University of California, Berkeley. He is the author of books on Spenser's *Faerie Queen* and Vergil's *Eclogues*, and, most recently, of *What Is Pastoral?* (Chicago, IL, 1996).

HELEN H. BACON is Professor Emeritus of Classics at Barnard College of Columbia University. She has published *Barbarians in Greek Tragedy* (New Haven, CT, 1961) and, in collaboration with the poet Anthony Hecht, a translation of Aeschylus' *Seven Against Thebes* (Oxford, 1973: nominated for a National Book Award); also articles on Vergil, Plato, Greek tragedy, and Classical influences on Robert Frost.

At JOSEPH BRODSKY'S memorial service in 1996 a group of the world's best living poets honored the Russian émigré with readings in Russian and English of some of the best elegies—by Brodsky, by Frost, by Mandelstam, by Akhmatova, just to name a few. The service ended with a tape recording of Brodsky himself reading; the Nobel Laureate's voice continues to resonate through the publication and republication of his award-winning essays, poems, and translations.

PAUL A. CANTOR is professor of English at the University of Virginia. He is the author of *Shakespeare's Rome* (Ithaca, 1976), *Creature and Creator: Myth-making and English Romanticism* (Cambridge, 1984), and the *Hamlet* volume in Cambridge's Landmarks of World Literature series (Cambridge, 1989), and a collection of essays on popular culture, *Gilligan Unbound* (Rowman & Littlefield, 2001).

GIAN BIAGIO CONTE is professor of Latin literature in the Department of Classical Philology at the Università di Pisa. Books of his which have been translated into English include: *The Rhetoric of Imitation: Genre and Poetic Memory in Virgil and Other Latin Poets* (Baltimore, MD, 1994); *Genres and Readers* (Ithaca, NY, 1986); *Latin Literature: A History* (Baltimore, MD, 1994); and *The Hidden Author: An Interpretation of Petronius' Satyricon* (Sather Classical Lectures, vol. LX, Berkeley, CA, 1996). He is editor of the Classical journal *Materiali e Discussioni per l'analisi dei testi classici* (MD).

MARGARET ANNE DOODY is John and Barbara Glynn Family Professor of Literature at Notre Dame University. From 1992 to 1999 she was director of the comparative literature program at Vanderbilt University. Her interest in Classical literature is reflected in a number of her works, particularly *The True Story of the Novel* (New Brunswick, 1996) and the mystery story *Aristotle Detective* (New York, 1978).

ROBERT FAGLES is the Arthur W. Marks '19 Professor of Comparative Literature at Princeton University. The recipient of the PEN/Ralph Manheim Medal for Translation in 1997 and an Academy Award in Literature from the American Academy of Arts and Letters in 1996, Fagles was elected to membership in the American Academy of Arts and Sciences and the American Philosophical Society. His translation of Homer's *Odyssey* (New York, 1996) was recently published by Viking Penguin; his translation of Homer's *Iliad* won the 1991 Harold Morton Landon Translation Award by the Academy of American Poets (New York, 1990) and is published in Penguin Classics.

STEPHEN M. FOLEY teaches in the Department of English and Comparative Literature at Brown University. He has published books on Thomas More and Thomas Wyatt and writes articles on Renaissance literature and literary theory.

KENNETH HAYNES teaches in the Department of Classical Studies and in the Editorial Institute at Boston University.

W. R. JOHNSON is emeritus professor of Classics and comparative literature at University of Chicago. He has given the Martin Lectures (on Lucan) at Oberlin and the Townsend Lectures (on Horace) at Cornell. Among his books are *Darkness Visible: A Study of Vergil's* Aeneid (Berkeley, CA, 1976), *Horace and the Dialectics of Freedom* (Ithaca, NY, 1993), and *Lucretius and the Modern World* (London, 2000).

CRAIG KALLENDORF is professor of English and Classics at Texas A&M University. In addition to several bibliographies on Renaissance topics, he is the author of *In Praise of Aeneas: Virgil and Epideictic Rhetoric in the Early Italian Renaissance* (Hanover, 1989), and *Virgil and the Myth of Venice: Books and Readers in the Italian Renaissance* (Oxford, 1999).

KARL KIRCHWEY is creative writing and senior lecturer of the arts at Bryn Mawr College. From 1987 to 2000 he was director of the Unterberg Poetry Center of the 92nd Street YM-YWHA in New York City. His third book of poems, *The Engrafted Word* (New York), was published in 1998.

J. D. MCCLATCHY'S recent books are *Ten Commandments* (New York, 1998), a collection of poems, and *Twenty Questions* (New York, 1998), a collection of essays.

GLENN W. MOST studied comparative literature and Classics in the United States, England, and Germany, and is currently professor of ancient Greek at the University of Heidelberg and professor in the Committee on Social Thought at the University of Chicago. He has published widely on ancient and modern literature and philosophy, on the history of Classical scholarship and of the Classical tradition, and on literary theory. He is currently completing books on the figure of Doubting Thomas and on Nietzsche and nineteenth-century German Classical scholarship.

CHRISTINE PERKELL has taught at Dartmouth College and is currently an associate professor of Classics at Emory University. She has published a number of articles on the poems of Vergil, is the author of *The Poet's Truth: A Study of the Poet in Vergil's Georgics* (Berkeley, CA, 1989), and is editor of and contributor to *Reading Vergil's Aeneid: An Interpretive Guide* (Oklahoma, 1999).

MICHAEL C. J. PUTNAM is W. Duncan MacMillan II Professor of Classics and professor of comparative literature at Brown University. He is the author of eight books devoted to Latin poetry, of which the latest, *Virgil's Epic Designs: Ekphrasis in the Aeneid*, was published by Yale University Press (New Haven, CT, 1998). He is a fellow of the American Academy of Arts and Sciences and member of the American Philosophical Society as well as trustee of the American Academy in Rome and the American Philological Association.

SARAH SPENCE is professor of Classics at University of Georgia. She has published two books, *Rhetorics of Reason and Desire* (Ithaca, NY, 1988) and *Texts of the Self in the Twelfth Century* (Cambridge, England, 1996), and a translation of the French *chansons* of medieval poet Charles d'Orléans (New York, 1986). She is editor of *Literary Imagination*, the journal of the Association of Literary Scholars and Critics.

MARK STRAND teaches at the Committee on Social Thought at University of Chicago. He is the author of ten books of poems, the latest of which, *A Blizzard of One*, was published by Alfred Knopf (1998). He won the Bollingen Prize in poetry in 1993 and the Pulitzer Prize in poetry in 1999. He is a MacArthur Fellow and was Poet Laureate of the United States in 1990–91.

ROSANNA WARREN is the Emma MacLachlan Metcalf Professor in the Humanities at Boston University. She teaches in the University Professors Program and the Department of English. She is the author of one chapbook of poems (*Snow Day*, 1981) and two volumes of poems, *Each Leaf Shines Separate* (New York, 1984) and *Stained Glass* (New York, 1993). She edited and contributed to *The Art of Translation: Voices from the Field* (Boston, 1989), and with Stephen Scully she translated Euripides' *Suppliant Women* (Oxford, 1995).